Talking Minds

Talking Minds: The Study of Language in Cognitive Science

edited by

Thomas G. Bever, John M. Carroll, and Lance A. Miller

The MIT Press
Cambridge, Massachusetts
London, England

PUBLISHER'S NOTE

This format is intended to reduce the cost of publishing certain works in book form and to shorten the gap between editorial preparation and final publication. Detailed editing and composition have been avoided by photographing the text of this book directly from the editors' prepared copy.

This book was printed and bound in the United States of America.

Library of Congress Cataloging in Publication Data
Main entry under title:

Talking minds.

    Bibliography: p.
    Includes index.
    1. Psycholinguistics. 2. Verbal behavior.
3. Cognition. I. Bever, Thomas G. II. Carroll, John M., 1950-
III. Miller, Lance A.
BF455.T28 1984   401'.9   83–22277
ISBN 0-262-02181-1

47,833

CONTENTS

CONTRIBUTORS

Thomas G. Bever
Psychology Department, Columbia University, New York, NY

Lawrence Birnbaum
Computer Science Department, Yale University, New Haven, CT

John M. Carroll
Computer Science Department, IBM Thomas J. Watson Research Center, Yorktown Heights, NY

Charles Fillmore
Linguistics Department, University of California, Berkeley, CA

Ray Jackendoff
Linguistics Department, Brandeis University, Waltham, MA

Jerrold J. Katz
Ph.D. Program in Linguistics, CUNY Graduate Center, New York, NY

Walter Kintsch
Psychology Department, University of Colorado, Boulder, CO

Mitchell P. Marcus
Linguistics and Speech Analysis Department, AT&T Bell Laboratories, Murray Hill, NJ

Lance A. Miller
Computer Science Department, IBM Thomas J. Watson Research Center, Yorktown Heights, NY

Charles E. Osgood
Psychology Department, University of Illinois, Champaign-Urbana, IL

David Premack
Psychology Department, University of Pennsylvania, Philadelphia, PA

Roger Schank
Computer Science Department, Yale University, New Haven, CT

ACKNOWLEDGMENTS

The papers collected in this volume were originally presented in a series of Distinguished Lectures on Language at the IBM Thomas J. Watson Research Center in 1979-80. In addition to the contributors to this volume, the following individuals participated in that series of lectures:

Richard Boyd (Cornell University)
Gilbert Harman (Princeton University)
David McNeil (University of Chicago)
Marvin Minsky (Massachusetts Institute of Technology)
Paul Postal (IBM Thomas J. Watson Research Center)
Zenon Pylyshyn (University of Western Ontario)
Harris Savin (Thompson Pennsylvania),
Joseph Weizenbaum (Massachusetts Institute of Technology).

We thank each of them for sharpening and deepening the lectures, and in so doing, the papers collected herein.

We thank William Brewer for editorial consultation, and Cay Dietrich and Tom Way for assistance in the preparation of this volume.

Talking Minds

INTRODUCTION

This volume contains chapters by a number of distinguished linguists, psychologists, and computer scientists. In the past several decades, new approaches to the description of language and thought have appeared in each of the disciplines these authors represent. In the winter of 1979-80, we invited the authors to discuss their own work in the light of three questions:

▶ To what extent can a theory of language behavior be developed without a theory of linguistic structure?

▶ To what extent can there be a linguistic theory without a general theory of cognitive functioning?

▶ To what extent can there be a cognitive theory without a theory of language behavior?

These questions focus on three fundamental issues in the philosophical and methodological bases of modern research on language and mind:

▶ the relation between language behavior and linguistic structure;

▶ the relation between linguistic structures and cognitive processes; and

▶ the relation between cognitive processes and language behavior.

In dealing with these questions, each chapter often works from assumptions that have crystallized during the past several centuries, without making those assumptions explicit. It is useful to understand how each article attempts to meet or avoid the basic issues. To this end, we review six basic questions about the scientific study of behavior, each with two extremely different traditional answers.

1. How Do Human Beings Acquire Knowledge?

This question comes down to the matter of what the newborn child is prepared to learn from the world. One of the earliest positions on this question is that of Plato, who suggested that when we seem to be learning essential forms we are actually awakening built-in memories. This claim that knowledge is innate contrasts with the more recent position that all empirical and formal knowledge derives from objects and experiences available to the child in the world around it. In recent years the conflict between empiricism and nativism has stirred up much controversy, especially in relation to claims about the innateness of linguistic structure.

At first blush, the debate seems puzzling. After all, it is trivially true that a child is innately equipped to learn to do everything that it learns to do. In that sense, we must accept nativism. We must also accept the fact that the environment informs us in crucial ways. At issue are the specific details of the relationship between the environment and the individual. The empiricist argues that the child learns only what there is to learn – that is, what can be learned by induction over objective experience. The nativist argues that the child forms a representation of what is innate, to a large extent regardless of what he is exposed to. The standard nativist argument for language, as presented by Chomsky and others, takes the following form:

- Language has property P.
- Property P cannot be acquired by any known mechanism of learning.
- Therefore, P is innate.
- Therefore, language is innate.

The strength of this nativist syllogism depends on the extent to which P is unique to language, the extent to which it is explicitly represented in the child's experience, and the speed with which the child learns it. These are empirical matters, which will undoubtedly take a long time to resolve. Some current evidence, however, weakens the empirical force of each premise in this syllogism. Many linguistic universals are at least logically derivable from independently motivated cognitive processes and systems. Recent linguistic research has demonstrated that the abstract properties of sentences are directly represented in their apparent structure, and thus has reduced the puzzle of how those abstract properties might be discovered. And careful studies of language acquisition have shown that children may take as much as ten years to master certain universal properties of language.

The complexity of P would seem to be an important feature of the nativist syllogism. The more complex it is, the more plausible the claim that no learning theory adequately accounts for its acquisition. This depends on a particular definition of *learning* as "learning by induction" – that is, by examination of the environment, without any prior structure or hypothesis. Here it is useful to distinguish between two kinds of potentially innate hypotheses: "linguamental" and "modality-specific." An innate structure that is intrinsic to all human mental activity, or one that is a compound of such structures, is linguamental. An innate structure that applies only to a particular kind of mental activity, such as language, is modality-specific. Clearly, since all mental activity involves linguamental universals, language is innate. If those universals themselves can combine to generate structural hypotheses adequate for linguistic structure, then language can be innate without being based on corresponding modality-specific innate structure. The more complex and cognitively unique a linguistic property is, the greater the burden on any theory of linguamental universals – and the more likely it seems that the property results from a modality-specific universal limited to language.

This leads us to formulate a notion of "learning/c," which we propose as a label for the process of acquiring structures by combining basic linguamental structures. This stands in contrast to the usual notion of "learning by induction." If induction fails in general, it fails to account for the acquisition of language in particular. The argument that language is innate is moot, since the acquisition of learning clearly – and by definition. of learning/c – involves learning/c, which in turn recruits innate structures. The interest of the current claim that language is innate depends on the extent to which one invokes modality-specific innate structures that cannot be accounted for by the mechanisms of learning/c. In arguing for this, the linguistic nativist has taken the high ground by appearing to lump together "learning by induction" with learning/c, thus placing the linguamental nativist on the defensive. By contrast, the linguamental nativist could construct the following syllogism:

- Language has property P.
- P cannot be transmitted by any known genetic mechanism.
- Therefore P is learned/c.
- Therefore language is learned/c.

As with the nativist argument, the strength of this argument depends on the complexity of P. If P is complex, the burden on genetic theory is high. The linguamental syllogism provides an alternative to the linguistic syllogism without committing us to mindless induction. It also clarifies how the issue of nativism can become empirical.

To decide between these views, we require the deepest possible understanding of language in human beings. For the linguistic nativist, the goal is to determine adequate mechanisms of genetic transmission. For the linguamental nativist, the goal is to determine mechanisms of coordination of linguamental processes that can account for their ability to represent language.

The struggle between the general and the specific nativist is not a hopeless philosophical debate. Current empirical investigations can be expected to clarify the claims and lead to a resolution. Why, then, has the issue generated so much controversy? Part of the reason is its relation to behaviorist restrictions on what count as possible data for a psychological theory.

2. What Can a Psychological Theory Explain?

The science of the mind grew out of efforts to deal with problems in three older disciplines: physics, medicine, and philosophy. In nineteenth-century physics, the problem of the human observer and his relation to the material world became an unavoidable concern of astronomers and physicists. In medicine, it became impossible to explain insanity without referring to mental processes as well as to physiological mechanisms. And philosophy had long set the goal of determining the sources of knowledge. In attempting to deal with problems originally raised in the context of physics and medicine, the new science of psychology seemed to offer an experimental method for studying mental processes, rather than the traditional a priori basis.

Wilhelm Wundt developed several different kinds of experimental psychology. He and his students explored objective methods – such as the measurement of reaction times – and applied them widely. In the study of higher mental processes, they relied most strongly on the use of introspection, itself a methodological inheritor of Cartesian rationalism. The presumption was that internal cognitive states could be directly perceived, once one was adequately trained in self-analysis. This method was ultimately abandoned for several reasons, including its inapplicability to animal behavior and its variability from person to person and from time to time. Clearly, many aspects of our state of mind influence what we perceive it to be. Either a theory of introspection itself must be available, or introspective evidence must be outlawed. The latter alternative was the most salient.

There was a more general reason why psychology, unlike other sciences, required an a priori fiat on the method of choosing relevant data. Because many of the relevant inadequacies of its parent sciences were directly related to the problem of conscious observation, psychology could not avoid confronting that problem in order to establish a firm foundation for itself. The solution was the doctrine of behaviorism, the position that only observable or potentially observable facts may bear on a theory of behavior. At first this doctrine would seem unexceptionable, since one would certainly not want to require that a theory explain only facts that are in principle unobservable. However, strict behaviorism excludes phenomena of obvious psychological importance, such as percepts, beliefs, intentions, and consciousness. This led to the corresponding doctrine of associationism, which limits behavioral operations to one apparently simple kind.

3. What Are Possible Psychological Operations?

It has long been taken for granted that a basic theoretical problem in describing behavior is to specify the relation linking separate psychological units. A change in behavior as a function of experience can be interpreted as the new appearance of a contiguity between hitherto unrelated events. When constructing a theory that accounts for the existence of observable contiguous behaviors in relation only to observable aspects of the environment, one still has a choice of how rich an internal theory of the organism to ascribe. The simplest possible relation between two units specifies only that they are "associated," without ascribing any internal structure to the relation; this position characterizes associationism. On the alternative position, relationalism, relations are wide-ranging, including "precede," "cause," "is greater than," or "sense," "know," and "represent."

Simplicity would seem to dictate that the first step in the description of every phenomenon should be to posit only associations. More elaborate relations would then be described as compounds of associations. The difficulty is that since an association imputes absolutely no structure to the relation between units, no amount of simple combination of them can yield more complex relations: any number of zeros sums (or multiplies) to zero. The theoretical cost of maintaining associationism may be a proliferation of different kinds of rules of combination, or of distinct units that can be combined in only one way.

Many psychologists believe, nevertheless, that some yet unknown laws of combination, which perhaps apply only when very large numbers of associations are at issue, will provide enough descriptive power. There is a separate reason to hold out for this possibility, namely that associations would seem to be understandable in behaviorist and empiricist terms. The naïve child (and the correspondingly naïve theoretical psychologist) can observe that separate units become related in time, so that one regularly occurs with another. He cannot, however, distinguish between associations that differ only internally. Accordingly, if the only association is that of unanalyzed contiguity, the behaviorist and empiricist paradigms can proceed untroubled. There is a further reason to restrict mental relations to association, namely that association can be understood in direct mechanistic terms. This brings us to the next question.

4. What Is Necessary for a Scientific Explanation?

A scientific theory is not accepted as complete until it reaches the status of an explanation. But what qualifies as a true explanation as distinguished from an orderly description? One frequent answer has been based in reductionism: an explanation reduces a phenomenon to a different level of description, with postulated units to which known principles apply. The molecular theory of matter, the atomic theory of the molecule, and the subatomic theory of the atom stand as touchstones for such scientific explanations. Reductionism does not require that a phenomenon be explained only by description of events at a *lower* level. Astrology is as much a reductionist theory as molecular chemistry: it ascribes aspects of our everyday behavior to correspondence laws that interpret the physical relations between planets.

Reductionism sets strong constraints on the form of descriptions of behavior: any postulated behavioral mechanisms must be reducible to a correspondence with some physical description. This constraint binds the practicing psychologist to state his theories in the terms that can be most easily understood mechanistically; hence it applies a further pressure towards the mechanistically transparent formulations of associationism and behaviorism.

It is not clear that the simple kind of reductionism we have just presented has ever worked for any but isolated phenomena. A complete description at any given level, even in physics, seems usually to have required the invocation of laws not previously known at other levels, as well as special rules on how one level of description corresponds to another. Nor is it clear that human behavior is the same sort of phenomenon as that described in the physical sciences. Certain behavioral phenomena do not seem satisfactorily explained by any conceivable reduction. The reductionist description of ethical, emotional, and mathematical relations might seem adequate but irrelevant. Such phenomena seem best characterized by "functional" descriptions, explaining the properties of an entity by reference to functional relations between that entity and others at the same level of description.

Many phenomena are behavioral but obviously require functional explanation. Consider the concept of "it" in a child's game of tag. Suppose we attempted to explain what "it" is by reference to the behaviors we observe in actual games of tag. No description is adequate. We cannot refer to the child who seems to be running after the other children, since certain children enjoy being "it" so much that once they get tagged they refuse to chase anybody else.

Conversely, we cannot describe "it" as the child from whom all other children run, because the same perverse child who enjoys being "it" will refuse to run away from the incumbent. To see how to deal with this problem, we must turn to the rules for the game of tag.

1. Decide to play a game of tag.
2. Everybody shouts, "Not it."
3. The child who is judged to have shouted "Not it" last is "it."
4. "It" tags another child, who thereupon becomes "it."
5. Repeat (4) until extrinsic circumstances halt the game.

Under these rules, it is not necessary for anybody to run away from anybody else. Children could stand in a big circle and produce a peristaltic cyclic wave of tagging behavior. They would properly be said to be playing a game of tag, although not one that would be much fun.

The point is that many children know the rules of the game, regardless of its physical instantiation. "It" is defined functionally – not in terms of the behavior of anybody in the game but in terms of the states specified by the rules.

A functionalist psychology is liberated from any mechanistic constraints on possible theories. At first this may seem unwise, since all the behavior we see is in fact produced by physical entities. But cognitive psychology can be viewed as the study of the states that underlie behavior as well as the behavior itself. The analogy of L'homme Mâchine provides a useful perspective. As has been known for centuries, human-like behavior can be produced by machines that probably do not have human physical states. The current growth of computational devices brings us closer to machines capable of assuming states that may turn out to be those of human beings. Clearly a computer program could represent the game of tag, and computer-driven bugs could play it. We would then define the bug that is "it" in terms of the stage of the game that had been played through. But the physical manifestation of that stage could differ according to the particular hardware configuration, time-sharing contingencies, and so on. We must define "it" in terms of the stage in the program itself, not in terms of any particular physical manifestation.

The heuristic virtue of functionalist psychology is that it enables us to proceed with the study of cognition without having solved the problem of how human beings actually carry out their cognitive activities. We know from examples such as tag that at least some human activities involve rule systems, which can be studied independently of their physical manifestation. The limitation of this kind of psychology is that once our theories have been liberated from the reductionist constraint, they may spin off into irrelevant speculation about humanly impossible models. This raises one of the oldest questions in the study of behavior, the nature of the relation between body and mind.

5. What Is the Physical Basis of Mind?

What is the physical basis of knowledge? The answers to this question range between materialism and dualism. According to materialism, for every mental state there is a corresponding physical state of the human brain. According to dualism, mental states and brain states do not necessarily have direct correspondences. Materialism would seem to be the only position compatible with a true science of behavior. Human beings are obviously material objects: the claim that a human being could have a nonmaterial structure uniquely his own is tantamount to the claim that we have bodies and souls. The study of souls might seem to be outside of scientific inquiry, but only if one rejects functionalism. Functionalism imposes no restriction on theories about the computational basis of the behavior of hobbits, gryphons, or angels. The functionalist is concerned solely with the scientific description of the organizational system underlying behavior – not with the discovery of any physical correspondence to that system. Though the world as we understand it scientifically seems to be totally mechanistic, we do not have to commit our psychological theories to such a mechanism in order to pursue them.

Pursuing a psychological theory without some sort of commitment to a mechanistic basis might seem pointless, since the theory would be developed in the absence of methodological constraints that reflect the nature of the human brain. We run the risk of constructing formal models that are computationally adequate to behavior but incompatible with human brains. There is no problem here concerning our description of the initial data – as long as we build our theories on observed behavior only (including introspections). Then we will never propose a theory that initially describes something other than possible behavior.

At issue here are the notions of "natural class" and "natural extension" specified by a theory. That is, in describing data, a theory classifies behaviors according to how they are related. Reductionist materialism requires that the existence of such separate and overlapping classes be explicable by some form of physical relatedness in their material representations. Given our current understanding of computational devices, such a requirement seems too strong. Often we may not find a constant physical manifestation of the similarity between two particular rules in a computer program, even though we know the rules to be similar or even, in the limiting case, identical. We can maintain only the weak form of materialism sketched above: every mental state corresponds to some physical state. This allows for the possibility that regular organizational laws of behavior exist even though they are not materially represented in any particular way, and even though their formal nature is not explained by their material basis.

If the form of certain organizational laws is not explained in general by their material representation, what is the cause of such laws? This raises the last question we will consider, concerning the ontological status of forms of reason.

6. Why Is What Humans Know the Way It Is?

When an organism is said to "know" a particular thing or to add a skill, we can determine separately what causes that thing or skill to be what it is. We know, for example, that the moon reflects energy from the sun towards the earth. But nothing about human beings or their planetary knowledge causes this state of affairs. The sun would radiate energy, and the moon reflect it, with or without human beings to analyze why. The same may be true for more abstract entities. For example, the fact that five is a prime number is not caused by human knowledge of that fact. It was a prime number before any mathematician recognized the importance of such a category. It will continue to be a prime number after all intelligent species in the universe disappear. Realism, the position that certain formal entities are uncaused, is associated with the views of Plato. It is particularly plausible in dealing with the constancy of formal properties across their physical manifestations. The standard examples involve categorical properties such as triangularity or necessary truth. No accumulation of specific images or contingent truths can account for such categorical concepts.

One could argue that Platonism is an illusion of human cognition: it only seems that truths about numbers are categorical and without material cause. In the view of psychologism, numbers are caused by human cognition: whatever properties they seem to have are the result of how we think, and might well be different if we thought differently. There are various formal arguments against this posi-

tion, but it serves our present purposes to distinguish at least two potential forms of psychologism, corresponding to the two forms of empiricism we discussed above:
• modality-specific psychologism, and
• linguamental psychologism.

Modality-specific psychologism is clearly appropriate for an understanding of a structured capacity such as color vision. Human color vision has certain organizational regularities that may be entirely unique but are clearly rooted in the physiology of the eye and the optical nervous system. Accordingly, the properties of color vision are the result of modality-specific psychological structures.

Numbers, however, are different. Even if their properties were caused by human cognition, the kind of causation would be clearly of a different kind. At the very most we might argue that if such entities are not real, they are the result of deep properties of human cognition, so deep that cognition itself would break down if we perceived number differently. Such linguamental psychologism is in sharp contrast with the claim that there is a modality-specific cognitive cause for numbers, for example, a number sense.

As in the case of empiricism and nativism, the distinction between modality-specific and general cognitive causes of what we know has received greater interest. Recently, in parallel with the linguistic syllogism discussed above, language has been invoked as a structure like color vision, specifically the way it is just because human beings are the way they are. No one can question this, insofar as actually attested languages are concerned. But we can attempt to turn this problem into an empirical one by the distinction between modality-specific and linguamental causation for language and other cognitive capacities. In each case the question becomes,
• How specific is the cause of our knowledge?
and correspondingly,
• How independent of ourselves is the structure of what we know?

Is There a Cognitive Science?

The underlying goal of much of what psychology is taken to be is to ensure that theories are so constructed as to be ultimately amenable to reductionist materialism. The doctrines of empiricism, behaviorism, associationism, reductionism, materialism, and psychologism complement one another in this regard.
• Empiricism is consistent with this goal by ensuring that what the child learns is limited to what is physically observable and quan-

tifiable. This would seem to guarantee that any theory of knowledge would also be limited to such physically realizable mechanisms.

- Behaviorism rigidly ensures this characteristic in the scientific theories of knowledge.
- Associationism guarantees that the postulated mental operations will be limited to a particular kind – contiguity – which itself is transparently modeled physically.
- Materialism guarantees the relevance of mechanistically constrained reductionist explanations.
- Psychologism is the complementary position to behaviorism for the nativist functionalist. That is, it presupposes that the child creates, on the basis of internally structured mechanisms, any mental structures not accounted for in the external physical world.

Modality-specific psychologism, though not strictly compatible with behaviorism and empiricism, can serve as a redoubt for the behaviorist and empiricist faced with the alternative possibility that certain aspects of knowledge might be Platonically uncaused.

Acceptance of certain internal structures has always been a part of empiricism and behaviorism, in general restricted to obviously inherited physiological sensory systems. Modality-specific psychologism can expand the number of such systems that are inherited with minimal compromise of the basic empiricist and behaviorist position about the inductive basis for learning. Further, strict empiricism is entirely compatible with Platonic realism: if the child can learn only about actual events and properties in the world, then discovering mental categories is at least possible, if they are real. It is not possible, however, if one maintains that the only available learning principle is induction.

The reader can apply the matrix of positions on these issues while reading through this book. Each chapter grapples with one or more of these issues. We think that each of the disciplines represented – psychology, linguistics, and computer science – has a contribution to make towards an integrated solution. We expect

▶ from psychology a richer theory of learning as it applies to formal knowledge;
▶ from linguistics a better understanding of the nature of language;
▶ from computer science the development of physical models that can deal in part with the kinds of knowledge that human beings exhibit.

The form this integrated solution may take, however, seems entirely unclear at the moment. Periodically in behavioral science a movement emerges that presupposes an integrated solution to be implicit in the correct combination of contemporary disciplines. The current instantiation of that position is "cognitive science," a superset of the disciplines represented in this book. One program for this enterprise is clear: cognition should be pursued in the image of linguistics. Unlike traditional psychologists, many adherents to this position are nativist, mentalist, and relationalist, although none of these positions is necessary for them. It could be that everything turns out to be learned by induction, to be directly observable, and to be a compounding of associations, without invalidating the program of current cognitive science. Materialism is an innocuous hope that pervades all scientific positions without having any particular theoretical implications for the description of behavior. But current cognitive science does appear to presuppose explanatory reductionism and psychologism concerning the basis of mental processes and structures. This is a considerable commitment: it presupposes that each of the separate disciplines is necessarily about human knowledge rather than about what is known.

At one time it was thought that logic was the scientific inquiry of human reason – that a correct theory would account for errors in reasoning and would not lead to counterintuitive results. Yet logic flourished only after Frege tersely, and Husserl exhaustively, destroyed the connection between logic and thought. Today we see similar potential in linguistics. Artificial intelligence and cognitive science may be holding back the discovery of the real properties of language by requiring linguistics to account for all observed grammars and barring it from exploring grammars unlearnable by human beings. Suppose that computational laws are real in the Platonic sense. Then we are similarly hampering what may be the true potential of artificial intelligence: the explanation of laws governing intelligent systems. Finally, as functionalism implies, there may be real laws of thought, independent of the ability of human beings to master them. (Perhaps these would turn out to be a naturally definable subset of the hypothetical computational laws, but not necessarily.) Restricting ourselves to human thinking may obscure the nature of thought, and therefore make a true understanding of thought all the more difficult.

Of course, cognitive science can allow for these possibilities while pursuing its own goal: the achievement of an integrated picture of language, thought, and behavior in human beings. Cognitive science, however, is coherent only because there is a common descriptive target: human knowledge and behavior. It is not necessarily a monolithic science in itself. We expect that each of the component

disciplines has much to learn from the others. But if past developments are any indication, it seems most likely that the fruitful
interactions are impossible to predict or to legislate by scientific
fiat.

Thomas G. Bever
John M. Carroll
Lance A. Miller

Philosophy and Linguistics

AN OUTLINE OF PLATONIST GRAMMAR[1]

Jerrold J. Katz

I want to raise and answer a question that it will appear strange to be asking in the first place and whose answer will seem obvious to almost everyone. The question is, *What is a grammar, a scientific theory of a natural language, a theory of?*

The considerable progress in formal grammar that has taken place in linguistics over the last three decades makes it seem strange to be asking what a grammar is a theory of. We couldn't, it is felt, have gotten all this far without knowing what we were doing. This is true in some sense of "know," but the real question concerns our explicit knowledge of what we were doing it to. It is not uncommon in science for theories to develop rapidly while the understanding of their foundations remains at a standstill. Quine once observed that "Ancient astronomers knew the movements of the planets remarkably well without knowing what sorts of things the planets were." He added that, although such a situation is not untenable, "it is a theoretically unsatisfactory situation."[2]

The answer to the question will seem obvious to the vast majority of linguists, philosophers of language, psycholinguists, and computer scientists familiar with the Chomskyan revolution. The seemingly obvious answer is that a grammar is a theory of something psychological. There are disagreements about what kind of psychological theory a grammar is, but almost everyone agrees that it is some kind of psychological theory. But, despite its seeming obviousness, this answer is mistaken. In this paper I will try to show why, and present the answer I think correct.

All scientific concepts that have significantly shaped their field seem obvious for some time after. It is well to recall that this is even true of concepts that are then superseded. Einstein once wrote:

> Concepts that have proved useful for ordering things easily assume so great an authority over us that we we forget their terrestrial origin and accept them as unalterable facts. They then become labelled as "conceptual necessities." The road of scientific progress is frequently blocked for long periods by such errors. It is therefore not just an idle game to exercise our ability to analyse familiar concepts, and to demonstrate the conditions on which their justification and usefulness depend.[3]

The concept of grammars as psychological theories had a central place in the thinking that brought about the Chomskyan revolution in linguistics. This concept was an enormous improvement over American structuralism's concept of grammars as theories of disturbances in the air produced in speaking. Chomsky demonstrated that the psychologistic concept has impressive advantages over its predecessor in leading to more comprehensive, abstract, and precise theories of natural languages. After the revolution, as the psychological concept of grammars was handed down to new generations of linguists, this once revolutionary doctrine attained the obviousness of orthodoxy.

The absence of an alternative to the psychological concept was another significant factor responsible for its seeming obvious. The discredited structuralist concept could hardly be expected to make a comeback so soon after being overthrown, and no other concept of what grammars are theories of was available. But the absence of an alternative to the concept of grammars as psychological theories was only a matter of historical accident. Logically, an alternative concept of what grammars are theories of, one that does not take the discredited position of American structuralism, was always around. On this concept, grammars are theories of the structure of sentences, conceived of as abstract objects in the way that Platonists in the philosophy of mathematics conceive of numbers. Sentences, on this view, are not taken to be located here or there in physical space like sound waves or deposits of ink, and they are not taken to occur either at one time or another or in one subjectivity or another in the manner of mental events and states. Rather, sentences are taken to be abstract and objective. They are entities whose structure we discover by intuition and reason, not by perception and induction.

Given the possibility of a Platonist position, the situation at this point is as follows. Chomsky's choice of a psychological concept with which to replace the physical concept of the structuralists may have been the only reasonable choice in the circumstances, but there is nothing necessary about this choice. Platonism exists as a real, if undeveloped, alternative. Whatever defects Platonism may have, they are surely not those that made the structuralist's concept of grammars subject to Chomsky's criticisms. The structuralist concept of grammars as theories of sound waves and marks represents grammars as insufficiently abstract to account adequately for the grammatical properties and relations of sentences in natural languages.[4] Since the Platonist concept allows grammars a maximum of abstractness, Platonism cannot be faulted on the same grounds as the structuralist concept. New and independent reasons have to be found if Chomsky's choice of a psychological concept is to be justified.

While Chomsky launched his attack on American structuralism and developed his new theory of generative grammar with its psychological ontology, he showed no sign of recognizing the necessity for such further justification. Recently, however, under the prompting of Montague grammarians,[5] Chomsky[6] has presented an argument against the possibility of Platonist alternative. He claims that a theory of universal grammar in such a purely mathematical sense – one that "attempts to capture those properties of language that are logically or conceptually necessary" – is merely "an inquiry into the concept 'language'," and that such an enterprise is "unlikely to prove more interesting than an inquiry into the concept 'vision' or 'locomotion'."[7]

Is this argument good enough to provide a reason for rejecting not specifically the approach of Montague grammarians but any approach on which linguistics is a branch of mathematics? The argument has a defect that makes it useless against Platonism generally: there is no reason to restrict the Platonist approach to the study of the concept "language" in Chomsky's narrow sense. There are *two notions* of "concept of." On the one that figures in Chomsky's formulation of the Platonist position, "concept of" means "lexical definition of." Thus, the concept of "vision" is something like "the power to form mental images of objects of sight," and the concept of "locomotion" is something like "movement from place to place." On this sense of "concept of," what Chomsky says about the triviality of the view that linguistics is realist mathematics is certainly true, but use of this sense of "concept of" in his formulation of the Platonist position is surely unfair, because Platonists would not use it in their formulation. On its other sense, which is the one that I, and I expect other Platonists, would use in the formulation of the Platonist position, "concept of" means "concept of the nature of the thing itself."[8] Here one is referring to the thing rather than the meaning of the word that names it. An inquiry into the concept of vision, locomotion, number, language, or natural language in *this* sense is no trivial matter of everyday lexicography, but a highly interesting theoretical enterprise. Granted that, on the Platonist view, the enterprise will not be empirical, still – judging just on intellectual interest, which is the basis of Chomsky's argument – this ought not matter in the slightest. Pure mathematics is surely not devoid of intellectual interest. The interest of an inquiry into the structure of the sentences of a language and into the invariants of all languages comes from the richness of structure revealed by the principles that account for the structure of the sentences, in the one case, and the invariants in the other. Chomsky's arguments, although successful against the Platonist position he sets up, fail against real Platonism.

A recent set of criticisms of Platonism by Fodor elaborates on this theme of Chomsky's that Platonism is uninteresting. Fodor writes: "The only thing against Platonism, so construed, is that, deep down, nobody is remotely interested in it."[9] On one way of taking Fodor's remarks, he is simply saying: "Go ahead, be a Platonist if you like. But the action is all at the other end of the town."[10]

If this is the claim, the reply is straightforward. The issue of what a grammar is a theory of, or what linguistics is about, does not turn on what Fodor or anyone else thinks is interesting. It turns on the ontological status of languages. Even if everyone were to share Fodor's relish for the science of psychology and exhibit the same disinterest in the question of whether linguistics is mathematics or psychology, this would not make the question itself any the less a question, any the less interesting inherently, or any the less linguistically or philosophically important. Disinterest in mathematics itself coupled with a widespread craze for the psychology of human mathematical ability would have not the slightest bearing on the issue of what mathematical theories are theories of, or what mathematics is about, or whether Gödel's Platonism is important.

There is, however, another way of taking Fodor's remarks. This way results from the manner in which he construes Platonism. On this way, he is quite right about nobody being interested, and would have been right had he gone further to claim that nobody ought to be. But the Platonism that he is right about is only Platonism-as-Fodor-construes-it, which has no serious relation to Platonism as actually held.

Fodor's misconstrual of Platonism begins when he says that the position I call Platonism is unassailable in the unflattering sense that it says that anything goes in linguistics. He writes: "What [Katz] thinks is that linguistics is part of mathematics, and (I suppose) in mathematics you can stipulate whenever you are so inclined."[11] This is, in the first place, a bizarre view of mathematics. Try stipulating your way out of trouble when you are caught dividing by zero or stipulating your way into a complete and consistent formalization of arithmetic.

It is also a bizarre view of the philosophy of mathematics. While it may be that Wittgenstein[12] and the logical empiricists hold something like the view of mathematics that Fodor has in mind, Platonists don't.   Ascribing this view to Platonists is like ascribing the verifiability principle to metaphysicians. Those in the philosophy of mathematics who advanced this conventionalist view introduced stipulation in the hope of thereby obviating the Platonist view. Platonists in the philosophy of mathematics have no need for stipulation in their account of the nature of mathematics, since they hold that numbers and systems of numbers are part of what is real and that mathematical truth is correspondence between mathematical statements and these abstract objects. Platonists in the philosophy of linguistics likewise have no need for stipulation, since they hold that sentences and systems of sentences (languages) are part of what is real and that truth in linguistics is correspondence between linguistic statements and these abstract objects.   On the Platonist account, mathematicians and linguists neither invent such objects, nor stipulate truths about them; mathematicians and linguists merely discover and describe them.

Fodor says

> there is no particular reason why, in choosing a domain for his theory, the Platonist needs to attend to those of the speaker/hearer's capacities that are left when you eliminate contamination from memory limitations and the like. In principle, he might just as well attend to the construction of grammars that predict only intuitions about sentences with more than seven vowels, or sentences whose twelfth word is "grandmother," or sentences that happen to be uttered on Tuesday.   Once you start to stipulate, it's Liberty Hall.[13]

Fodor *assumes* that there is some compelling reason why linguists ought to give their professional attention to competence and that it is to the discredit of Platonism that it does not endorse this reason. But this assumption is just what is at issue! Platonists in linguistics deny that such a reason exists – just as Platonists in mathematics deny that mathematicians ought to give their professional attention to human arithmetic capacities.   Platonists contend that grammars are theories of abstract objects (sentences, languages). Hence, the implication that it is to the discredit of Platonists that they do not endorse the view that the linguist *qua* linguist ought to pay special attention to the "speaker-hearer's capacities" begs the question. It can no more be to the discredit of Platonism that it doesn't pay attention to psychological capacities than it can be to the discredit of Fodor's psychologism that it doesn't pay attention to abstract objects.

These remarks of Fodor's also confuse the issue with respect to the question of what Platonists take as the framework for linguistic research. Fodor equates Platonism with absolute freedom of choice in what can be studied in linguistics, which is almost true, but he suggests that adopting Platonism will inaugurate an era of licentiousness in linguistics, which is false. First, since Platonists constrain the choice of what can be studied in linguistics only in the minimal way that they constrain the choice of what can be studied in mathematics, any possible language *may* be taken as an object of study in linguistics, just as any possible system of numbers *may* be taken as an object of study in mathematics. This rules out the counterparts of systems with division by zero but leaves quite a lot. This seems to be a worrying prospect for some, but it is not clear why. It does not impose any priority on what is studied when or any restriction on how much. It does not preclude the linguist from emphasizing the study of natural languages any more than it has precluded mathematicians from emphasizing the study of natural numbers. Moreover, given that things that look at one time to be not worth study often turn out to be highly important in unexpected ways, one would have thought that freedom of the kind Platonism offers is a virtue rather than a vice. Thus, Fodor's idea that there is benefit in limiting the linguist's freedom of inquiry has little to recommend it to those who are not already convinced that linguistics is a psychological science.

Second, Fodor's insistence on restricting the domain of linguistics to a psychological reality is, in fact, insistence on a policy whose acceptance would, depending on contingent and presently unforeseeable circumstances, *commit* linguists to just the absurd grammars (e.g., ones with sentences whose twelfth word is "grandmother") that Platonism merely *allows*. For, since it's an empirical question, it could turn out that the mental or neural structures responsible for the "speaker-hearer's capacities" instantiate grammatical principles that do indeed introduce "grandmother" into the deep structure of every English sentence (deleting it at various derived syntactic levels). As I shall argue in more detail below, this is merely one of an indefinitely large number of absurd possibilities – some of which are not farfetched at all – that linguists let themselves in for in adopting the view that grammars are psychological theories.

The irony is that Fodor should raise the spectre of such absurd grammars when it is *his* position that is haunted by the prospect of embracing them. If the human mind or brain turns out to contain such absurd grammatical structures, Fodor's doctrine about the subject matter of linguistics would force linguists to adopt absurd grammars, and hence it would be Fodor's position that deserves the blame. If the doctrine that linguistics is psychology would saddle linguistics with absurd grammars in a myriad of contingent cases, it ought to be regarded as far less attractive, other things being equal, than a doctrine that runs no such risks.

It should also be mentioned that Fodor is wrong in suggesting that only his view "defines the goals of linguistics *ex post facto,* in the light of the theories now in the field." Platonism, too, does this. Theories can be viewed, within the Platonist framework, as explications in the sense of Chomsky:[14] grammars projected from early intuitions are revisable in the light of later intuitions and canons of theory construction; goals are refined, added, and dropped in the process.[15]

It must now be clear that Fodor's claim that "the right view [Fodor's euphemism for his own view] is the right view *so far as we can now make out*"[16] is supported solely by arguments that either assume Fodor's view or replace Platonism with Platonism-as-Fodor-construes-it.

One final point. Consider Fodor's comment on the prospect of present (he supposes) psychologically inspired attempts to construct grammars turning out to have been totally on the wrong track:

> In that case, there will be a residual philosophical question whether we ought to say that linguistics was misconstrued by the Right View or that there is no such science as linguistics. I, for one, won't much care.[17]

The "residual philosophical question" that arises in the event of a theoretical disaster is a facet of the perennial question at issue between conceptualists and Platonists from at least the time of Plato. The question of the ontological status of theories in linguistics is merely a special case of the classical philosophical question.[18] For Platonism is an existential claim: it asserts that there are abstract objects. Hence, until the case of linguistics is settled, the classical philosophical question cannot be decided against Platonism. Fodor's "I, for one, won't much care." is the declaration of a philosopher who has hung around psychologists so long that he's gone native.

Chomsky also has taken the position that a Platonist linguistics is not a study of anything. This is because, as he puts it, "'language' is no well-defined concept of linguistic science."[19] Chomsky's grounds for this position are that no clear principles have yet been formulated to distinguish languages from one another. But this is no support for his claim about Platonist linguistics. The absence of clear principles distinguishing virtue and vice is not grounds for abandoning ethics, but only reason to make more of an effort to define such principles. Indeed, in the case of conceptualist linguistics, there are no clear principles to distinguish linguistically relevant mental states from linguistically irrelevant ones. This, however, does not lead Chomsky to say that conceptualist linguistics is not about anything. Surely, Chomsky would take the position that specifying the linguistically relevant states (competence) is not something we can expect to have handed to us at the outset, but something that our inquiry aims at achieving in the long run. But, then, the same thing can be said about specifying languages.

The arguments of conceptualists against Platonism in linguistics have little force. If Platonism in its turn can mount a successful argument against the psychological concept of grammars, then, coupling this argument with Chomsky's argument against the structuralist concept, we obtain a strong case for the Platonist view that grammars are theories of abstract objects. The reason is that nominalism, conceptualism, and Platonism exhaust the ontological possibilities. One can take the objects of a theory to be concrete, physical particulars, as the nominalist does, or take them to be psychological, mental, or biological particulars, as the conceptualist does, or deny they are particulars at all and take them to be atemporal, aspatial objective entities, as the Platonist does.

We might dwell for a moment on the special interest of our question for the disciplines concerned: linguistics, philosophy, psychology, and computer science. In linguistics, the question "What is a grammar a theory of?" is pivotal. Any answer to this question is also an answer to others:

"What is linguistic theory a theory of?"
"What kind of science is linguistics?"
"What is a natural language?"
"What sort of object is a sentence?"
"What is the object of study in linguistics, and what are proper methods for studying it?"

If it can be shown that theories of natural languages are about abstract objects, then linguistic theory, being about natural languages collectively, is also about abstract objects, linguistics is a mathematical science, and its objects of study, sentences, are abstract objects.

Even practically minded linguists will have to face the fact that ontological questions are relevant to decisions they have to make between grammars and linguistic theories. I give two examples of how the ontological issue bears on the concerns of a working linguist. The first illustration comes from the controversy between Chomsky[20] and Postal[21] over whether Chomsky's Extended Standard Theory or Postal's version of Generative Semantics is "the best theory." The controversy is slightly dated, since Chomsky has moved on to his Revised Extended Standard Theory and Postal to his and Johnson's Arc-Pair Grammar, but it is a well-known controversy and the underlying issues are anything but resolved.

Postal has argued that Generative Semantics, at least in his version, is the best theory because, in stating grammatical rules in the form of derivational constraints, it provides a completely "homogeneous" statement of them. Postal argued that a more homogeneous grammar is preferable on standard methodological grounds in science (Occam's razor) because, in requiring less apparatus to explain the same facts, it is a more parsimonious account. Chomsky replied that Postal might be right if the issue were as simple as Postal assumes. But Chomsky argued that the issue is not merely a matter of parsimony. Chomsky saw the issue as going beyond the question of whether a linguistic theory makes descriptively adequate grammars available for each language. From Chomsky's viewpoint, the issue also encompasses the question of selecting descriptively adequate grammars on the basis of primary linguistic data. Given that a linguistic theory concerns how a speaker acquires grammatical competence, Chomsky is correct in claiming that

> the matter is considerably more complex. Given two theories T and T', we will be concerned not merely with their simplicity or homogeneity, but also with their *restrictiveness*. If T and T' both meet the condition of descriptive adequacy but T permits only a proper subset of the grammars permitted by T', then we may well prefer T to T' even if it is more complex, less homogeneous. Postal regards it as obvious that we would prefer T' to T in this case, but this conclusion is plainly false in general, if our concern extends to explanatory adequacy.[22]

This is a big "if." Linguistic theory concerns questions of explanatory adequacy in Chomsky's technical sense only if Chomsky is correct that a linguistic theory is a psychological theory about the initial competence of a human language learner. Only then is restrictiveness relevant. Faced with the fact that a child learns an extremely complex and abstract system of rules rapidly, under difficult stimulus conditions and with little variation with respect to intelligence, it seems plausible, other things being equal, to prefer the theory that represents the child's choice as a selection from the narrowest set of possible grammars. Such a maximally restrictive theory best fits the facts of language acquisition as we know them. But if Chomsky's assumption about the psychological character of linguistic theory is incorrect, Chomsky's reply to Postal collapses.

Here is where Platonism bears directly on the concerns of the working linguist: it denies that linguistic theory is a psychological theory of the competence underlying human language learning. On the Platonist view, linguistic theory is no more than a theory of the common structure of the sentences in all natural languages,[23] and so an argument that we ought to severely restrict the class of grammars from which the child selects would belong to psychology rather than linguistics. Therefore, if Platonism can be shown to be preferable to conceptualism, Chomsky cannot claim that the issue between Postal and himself goes beyond the question of whether linguistic theory makes descriptively adequate grammars available for each language. Thus, even on Chomsky's account on the matter, Postal is right in preferring the most homogeneous theory. In short, Postal can exploit Platonism to claim that, although Chomsky's more restrictive theory may be better psychology, his less restrictive but more parsimonious theory is better linguistics.

The second illustration of the relevance of the ontological issue to the working linguist is up to date. Langendoen and Postal[24] have recently argued that, if Platonism offers the best answer to what a grammar is a theory of, then every theory of grammar in which grammars have the form of constructive systems is wrong.

Langendoen and Postal argue that, ontological considerations to one side, there is no basis for imposing any size constraint on the sentences of natural languages and, as a consequence, the existence in natural languages of unbounded coordination subject to a natural closure principle entails that their sentences are more numerous than countable infinity. The argument against imposing any size constraint is a generalization of an argument showing that the sentences of a natural language cannot form a finite set as some linguists once claimed in connection with, for example, *very* long sentences and multiple center-embedded sentences.[25] The argument was that, for any upper limit on sentence length, there are strings exceeding the limit whose syntactic structure is exactly the same as strings that do not exceed the upper limit and these longer strings must *ipso facto* count as grammatical, since grammaticality is a matter of well-formed syntactic structure. No finite number of morphemes can determine that a string is too long to be a grammatical sentence. Langendoen and Postal generalize this argument by showing that nothing changes when the issue changes to strings of *any* size that exemplify a well-formed syntactic structure.

A linguist who wishes to resist Langendoen and Postal's argument might try to show that considerations outside of pure grammatical theory provide a basis for drawing the line to exclude non-finite sentences. Here the appeal might either be to nominalist scruples or to conceptualist ones. That is, either it is claimed that non-finite strings can't be grammatical sentences because they cannot be realized physically or because they cannot be generated even by the ideal speaker-hearer. But if Platonism can be shown to provide a better account of what grammars are theories of than either nominalism or conceptualism, then neither of these responses to Langendoen and Postal's argument is possible, and their conclusion about the non-constructiveness of grammars seems to go through.

The interest of our question for philosophers is straightforward. The realist's claim that there are abstract objects is the existential claim that there is at least one special science whose theories are about such objects. Thus, if it can be shown, as I shall argue here, that theories in the special science of linguistics are theories about abstract objects, then – given standard views of ontological commitment – quantifying over abstract objects in the pursuit of true theories in linguistics *ipso facto* commits one to the existence of such objects. Therefore, our question about grammars is relevant to the traditional philosophical controversy about universals: an answer showing that grammars are theories about abstract objects provides a basis for Platonic realism in ontology.

The interest of our question for psychologists and AI scientists has to do with the desirability of a clear-cut division of labor among the several disciplines that in one way or another concern themselves with language. I think many unfortunate quarrels are a consequence of confusion about where the line should be drawn between linguistics and cognitive science. I also think that this confusion exists largely because of a widespread acceptance of the view that linguistics is a branch of psychology. If, as the Platonist view of linguistics claims, linguistics is rather a branch of mathematics, as different from the psychology of language as number theory is from the psychology of arithmetic reasoning, there is a clear boundary between linguistics and psychology that, one may reasonably expect, will provide as clear-cut a division of labor here as exists between mathematics and the psychology of mathematical reasoning.

Let me illustrate how a conception of linguistics as psychology gives rise to such boundary problems. Given this conception, the only thing to separate the linguist's task from that of psychological scientists is the distinction between competence and performance. But competence, as Chomsky has stressed, is a component of performance; it is the knowledge of the language applied in the use of language. "A theory of performance (production or perception), Chomsky writes, "will have to incorporate the theory of competence – the generative grammar of a language – as an essential

part."[26]   But, as psychologists and computer scientists have observed, it has hardly been proved beyond all reasonable doubt that
the performance system underlying production and comprehension
operates on linguistic knowledge *in the form it takes in grammars
written in linguistics.*   It might even be, as some claim, that no
component in the performance system is modeled by standard
transformational grammars.   This is the line taken by Winograd[27]
and by Wanner and Maratsos.[28] Dresher and Hornstein[29] accept the
terms of the argument but respond that all that has been shown is
that one account of the performance system is not constructed to
incorporate the theory of transformational English syntax.   Both
sides have enough of a point to keep the disputes going.[30] The
anti-transformationalist side can press their point by claiming that
the account in question is not just any account but the best account
of the processing underlying production and comprehension.   The
transformational side can press theirs by producing internal evidence from grammatical intuitions to support the theory of transformational English syntax.   Considering the strength of the evidence on each side, how different in nature such evidence is, how
committed each side is to its position, and how much weight each
side puts on its own evidence, this controversy promises to go on
interminably.

But why accept the terms of the argument?   That is, why accept
that grammars in linguistics, written as theories to explain evidence
about the grammatical structure of sentences, are theories of the
knowledge that underlies the speaker's use of the language?   The
only reason is that conceptualism says grammars are psychological
theories.   Thus, if Platonism is right in positing that grammars are
not psychological theories, the two sides on this issue have been
talking at cross purposes.   Each side can be right and the issue
dissolves.   Therefore, for psychology, AI, and the related cognitive
sciences, the question of what a grammar is a theory of is important
because its answer can resolve troublesome issues about where the
linguist's work ends and the cognitive scientist's begins.   A Platonist answer to this question would clearly divide linguistics and
cognitive sciences so that the wasteful and unnecessary quarrels of
the past can be put behind us.[31]

The major developments in linguistics over the last thirty or forty
years have been concerned in large part with the question of what a
grammar is a theory of.   The most significant event of this period,
the Chomskyan revolution, was basically a new answer to this
question.   The dominant view before this revolution was American
structuralism.   Under the influence of a neopositivist picture of

science, it espoused a straightforward form of nominalism for linguistics.[32] The idea, as Bloomfield stresses in many places, is that a grammar is a theory of the physical disturbances in the air resulting from articulatory movements (secondarily, deposits of graphite, ink, etc.). Bloomfield wrote in one place, "Non-linguists (unless they happen to be physicalists) constantly forget that a speaker is making noise, and credit him, instead, with the possession of impalpable 'ideas.' It remains for linguists to show, in detail, that the speaker has no 'ideas' and that the noise is sufficient."[33] Linguists collect recordings or descriptions of such acoustic phenomena and classify distributional regularities in them. Taxonomic grammar was the structuralist theory of the proper type of classification of such regularities. The theory imposed constraints on grammatical description to ensure that there would be no backsliding into mentalistic concepts or other concepts not reducible to constructions out of a material corpus.

The main thrust and most important consequence of Chomsky's revolution was to replace this nominalist scheme for interpreting grammars with a conceptualist scheme based on the idea that grammars are theories of competence – the idealized speaker-hearer's knowledge of the language. Chomsky's idea that grammars are theories of competence makes the object of study in grammar an idealized mental state; hence the nominalist view of the structuralists was replaced with the conceptualist view that grammars are psychological theories.

Popular culture has it that the Chomskyan revolution introduced transformational grammar into linguistics. However, although Chomsky convinced linguists of its superiority over phrase structure grammar, transformational grammar was invented by Zellig Harris[34] well before the Chomskyan revolution. Chomsky himself made this clear in his first paper on the transformational approach to syntax. He states that this approach

developed directly out of the attempts of Z. S. Harris to extend methods of linguistic analysis to the analysis of the structure of discourse. This research brought to light a serious inadequacy of modern linguistic theory, namely, its inability to account for such systematic relations between sentences as the active-passive relation. There had been no attempt in modern linguistics to reconstruct more precisely this chapter of traditional grammar, partly, perhaps, because it was thought that these relations were of a purely semantic character, hence outside the concern of formal, structural linguistics. This view was challenged by Harris, who has since devoted a good deal of research to showing that distributional methods of linguistic analysis can be broadened and developed in such a way as to include, in a rather natural manner, the study of formal relations between sentences, and that this extension yields much additional insight into linguistic structure.[35]

Transformational rules, on Harris's version of the theory, were a way of describing distributional regularities at the sentence level. Harris wrote:

> Given a number of sentences in a kernel form, which have among them a particular acceptability ordering or differentiation.., all successions of transformations which are permitted, by the definition of their argument will produce sentences to preserve the same acceptability ordering.... If a sequence of words is not decomposable by transformation into one or more kernel sentences ... then that sequence is ungrammatical. If it is so decomposable, then it has a certain kind and degree of acceptability as a sentence, which is some kind of reasonable sum of the acceptabilities of the component kernel sentences and the acceptability effects of the transformations that figure in the decomposition.[36]

The nominalist interpretation of transformational theory as an account of the distribution regularities that determine acceptability orderings greatly restricts the degree of abstractness with which grammatical transformations can be stated. Chomsky showed how Harris's transformational theory could be significantly improved if the formal theory of transformational structure is stripped of its nominalist interpretation and refitted with a conceptualist interpretation on which the theory represents the internalized tacit principles constituting a speaker's competence. By separating transformational theory from its nominalistic interpretation, Chomsky could make the theory abstract enough to overcome a wide range of explanatory problems that are essentially unsolvable within the structuralist framework.[37]

Except for the differences due to its generative form, Chomsky's early transformational theory is essentially the same mathematical theory of sentence structure as Harris's, only under a radically different ontological interpretation. Thus, the comparison of Harris's transformational theory with Chomsky's is of special interest here because it can give us a picture of how a formal mathematical theory of grammatical structure can be stripped of one ontological interpretation and refitted with another without its account of grammatical structure undergoing fundamental change. Such a picture will be useful to us in showing how the conceptualist interpretation of theories in current linguistics can be stripped off and replaced with a Platonist interpretation. Such a picture also enables us to see the Platonist proposal as in a direct line of development with earlier nominalist and conceptualist stages in American linguistics. The picture will enable us to construct the argument in favor of replacing the conceptualist interpretive scheme with a Platonist one as a special case of a pattern of argument appropriate to determining the proper ontological interpretation for theories in a special science. Finally, it will enable us to see that, since the basic theory of sentence structure is preserved throughout changes of interpretation, accepting the argument for the new interpretive scheme sacrifices nothing essential in the theory of sentence structure.

Let me flesh out the claim that Harris's transformational theory is, in all essential respects, the same theory as the early version of Chomsky's transformational theory of syntactic competence. The parallels I shall draw clearly show that we have here the same formal theory of transformational structure which, from the different ontological perspectives of Harris and Chomsky, says different things about the nature of language. The version of Harris's theory in question is that in "Discourse Analysis"[34] and "Co-occurrence and Transformation in Linguistic Structure".[38] The version of Chomsky's theory in question is that in *Syntactic Structures*[14] and "A Transformational Approach to Syntax".[35]

The principal parallels between Chomsky's theory and Harris's are these. First, both theories draw a fundamental distinction between *kernel* or *underlying sentence structures,* which serve as the base for the application of transformational rules, and the *derived sentence structures,* which constitute a transformation level superimposed on this base. Second, both theories use the same notion of "transformational rule": a structure-dependent mapping of abstract representations of phrase structure onto abstract representations of phrase structure. True, Harris's transformational rules are less abstract, and even at that, their abstractness was an embarrassment to his structuralist principles; but structuralists have long been accustomed to invoking instrumentalist philosophy of science to explain away their embarrassing use of abstraction.[39]

Third, both theories classify transformational rules into *singulary transformations,* which take a single representation of phrase structure into a single representation of phrase structure and *generalized transformations,* which take two or more representations of phrase structure into a representation of compound phrase structure. Fourth, both theories treat grammatical transformations as constructions out of *elementary transformations,* such formal operations on strings as deletion, permutation, copying, substitution for dummy elements, and insertion.

Fifth, in both theories, the transformational level is the place at which the variety of sentence types found in the language is introduced and also the place at which the indefinitely great syntactic complexity within sentences of a given type is produced. Sixth, even the particular types of transformations are largely the same. Harris had worked out, in the domain of singularies, the passive transformation, various question transformations, negation transformation, ellipsis (zeroing), and so on, and in the domain of the generalized transformations, the coordinating or conjunctive transformations, relative clause transformations, nominalization transformations, and so on.

Seventh, Harris's theory also takes the kernel or underlying level to be the place at which co-occurrence restrictions are stated, and transformations to be structure-preserving mappings. Thus, both theories enable the grammar to state such restrictions in the simplest way by putting them at the earliest point and having subsequent rules preserve structures that meet them. Finally, Harris's theory also contains ordering restrictions on the application of transformations in derivations, thus providing a form of the distinction between *obligatory* and *optional* rules.

Now, although there is this strong parallelism between Harris's formal theory of transformations and Chomsky's, Harris interpreted his formal theory as a device for predicting the relative acceptability of utterances. As a consequence, for Harris there is no sharp line between well-formed and ill-formed sentences, just a gradient of acceptability, determined distributionally. Furthermore, for him the generative capacity of grammatical rules has absolutely no psychological significance. Harris wrote:

> Even when our structure can predict new utterances, we do not know that it always reflects a previously existing neural association in the speakers (different from the associations which do not, at a given time, produce new utterances). For example, before the word *analyticity* came to be used (in modern logic), our data on English may have contained *analytic, synthetic, periodic, periodicity, simplicity,* etc. On this basis, we would have made some statement about the distributional relation of *-ic* to *-ity,* and the new formation of *analyticity* may have conformed to this statement. But this means only that the pattern or habit existed in the speakers at the time of the new formation, not necessarily before: the "habit" – the readiness to combine these elements productively – may have developed only when the need arose, by association of words that were partially similar as to composition and environment.... Aside from this, all we know about any particular language habit is the probability that new formations will be along certain lines rather than others, and this is no more than testing the success of our distributional structure in predicting new data or formulations.[40]

The contrast between nominalist and conceptualist interpretations of the same transformational theory is nowhere more striking than in the comparison between this remarkable claim of Harris's and the opposite claim that Chomsky made on behalf of generative capacity, namely, that the creative aspect of language use is *the* proof that speakers of a language have enduring neural structures that contain an infinite number of sentences in their generative potential. Chomsky stressed that

> The normal use of language is innovative, in the sense that much of what we say in the course of normal language use is entirely new, not a repetition of anything that we have heard before and not even similar in pattern.... The number of sentences in one's native language that one will immediately understand with no feeling of difficulty or strangeness is astronomical.[41]

Indeed, Chomsky held that the

> inadequacy of traditional grammars is [that] although it was well understood that linguistic processes are in some sense "creative," the technical devices for expressing a system of recursive process were simply not available until more recently. In fact, a real understanding of how a language can (in Humboldt's words) "make infinite use of finite means" has developed only within the last thirty years.... Now that these insights are readily available it is possible to return to the problems that were raised, but not solved, in traditional linguistic theory, and to attempt an explicit formulation of the "creative" processes of language.[42]

The heart of Chomsky's conceptualism is the idea that these new systems of recursive processes – particularly in their most linguistically sophisticated form, transformational grammar – account for "the creative aspect of language use" when taken as a theory of the competence underlying such use. Creativity is formally modeled in the way that recursive rules of a transformational grammar "make infinite use of finite means." The understanding of novel sentences is reflected in the grammatical description that such rules assign the infinitely many sentences they generate.

The Chomskyan revolution also eliminated the nominalist interpretation of linguistic theory as a discovery procedure, that is, a procedure for mechanically producing taxonomic grammars when applied to a rich enough corpus, replacing it with a conceptualist interpretation on which linguistic theory is an evaluation procedure for "selecting a descriptively adequate grammar on the basis of primary linguistic data."[43] Linguistic theory is now seen as a theory of how children acquire the competences represented in grammars of natural languages.[44] Thus, linguistic theory

> offers an explanation for the intuition of the native speaker on the basis of an empirical hypothesis concerning the innate predisposition of the child to develop a certain kind of theory to deal with the evidence presented to him.[45]

I want to argue that the conceptualist interpretation of grammars and linguistic theory should be replaced with an interpretation on which grammars are theories about abstract objects, sentences of a natural language, and linguistic theory is about invariances over all such abstract objects. We should note a few things before beginning this argument. First, although I have referred, and will refer, to Chomsky and to transformational grammar, my focus is *not* Chomsky *per se* and my concern is *not* with transformational grammar *per se*. I realize that Chomsky is far from being the only conceptualist in linguistics at present and that transformational grammar is far from being the choice of linguists everywhere. Rather, my focus is conceptualism of any stripe, and my concern is with the interpretation of any grammar that can lay claim to being a scientific theory. I have focused on Chomsky and transformational grammar because they have an overwhelming historical and systematic position in the field, but my argument is not restricted to them.

Second, Platonism denies that theories in linguistics are about psychological states, processes, etc., but does not deny the existence of such states, processes, etc., or the legitimacy of their study in psychology, computer science, neurophysiology, etc. The Platonist in linguistics no more denies the existence of linguistic knowledge or the legitimacy of its study in empirical science than the Platonist in mathematics or logic denies the existence of mathematical or logical knowledge or the legitimacy of their study in empirical science. Thus, no one should object to Platonism on the grounds that it prevents us from making use of grammatical theories in the explanation of the human ability to acquire and use languages. The use of these theories in such explanations is like applied mathematics. The issue at hand is whether linguistics concerns a realm of grammatical objects beyond psychology.

Platonism draws a fundamental distinction between the *knowledge* speakers have of their language and the *languages* that speakers have knowledge of.[46] The distinction is simply a special case of the general distinction between knowledge and its object. No one confuses psychological theories of how people make inferences with logical theories of implication, or psychological theories of how people perform arithmetical calculations with mathematical theories of numbers. Yet, in the exactly parallel case of linguistics, conceptualists do not make the distinction, conflating a psychological theory of how people speak and understand speech with a theory of the language itself. Platonism is in part an attempt to be consistent in our treatment of the special sciences by drawing the same distinction between knowledge and its object in the case of linguistics that we draw, as a matter of course, in the parallel cases of logic and mathematics. Platonism claims that the subject-matter of linguistics is, in this sense, independent of psychological sciences – just as the subject-matter of logic and mathematics is independent of the sciences concerned with people's logical and mathematical ability.

The issue between Platonism and conceptualism (and also nominalism) is an a priori issue, and the competing claims of the Platonist and the conceptualist (and the nominalist) are a priori claims. It makes no sense to construe *these* claims as a posteriori claims about empirical matters, insofar as the issue between these ontological claims decides the logically prior question of whether empirical matters are relevant to linguistics at all. How could empirical evidence decide between the claim that a discipline is empirical and the claim that it is not? Because this is an a priori issue, it would make no difference if by some miracle the grammarian's theory of a natural language were to satisfy perfectly the empirical demands on a psychological model of the speaker's linguistic knowledge. Such an extraordinary coincidence would be a stroke of luck for cognitive scientists, whom it would provide with a ready-made formal theory to serve as one component of their overall account of cognition; but it would not have the least relevance to the issue of whether the discipline from which the theory was borrowed is or is not a part of psychology. Such a hypothetical coincidence is comparable to the actual coincidence between the extension of "creature with a kidney," and the extension of "creature with a heart." Just as the actual coincidence of the extensions of these expressions is compatible with an a priori, logical difference in their meaning, so the hypothetical coincidence of a grammar and a psychological model of competence is compatible with an a priori, logical difference between the domains of linguistics and of psychology.

In its most general form, Chomsky's argument for conceptualism showed that a nominalist scheme for interpreting grammars and linguistic theory puts too low a ceiling on their abstractness for them to qualify as fully adequate by the traditional explanatory standards in the study of grammar. Taxonomic constraints on the admissibility of constructs – imposed to ensure that everything at higher grammatical levels can be reduced back down to the physical events at the lowest – precluded grammatical categories that are required to satisfy even minimal standards of grammatical explanation. Chomsky writes[47] that he tried for over five years to formulate explicit data-cataloguing procedures that, when applied to a corpus, mechanically produce the appropriate sets of phonological, morphological, and syntactic classes, but found it impossible to characterize the inductive step necessary for general phonological, morphological, and syntactic classes. He came to realize that there is no inductive basis on which such classes can be built out of the physical material in the corpus, and that the generality required for defining grammatical classes could be attained only if nominalist constraints were eliminated so that grammars, instead of having to be built up from a corpus, could be, as it were, dropped down from above. Chomsky thus conceived grammars, in analogy to formal deductive systems, as generative systems whose principles and categories are directly postulated. Although "dropped down from above," grammars can be empirically justified on the basis of whether their predictions about sentences are confirmed by the judgments of fluent speakers.

Two features merit special attention in constructing a parallel argument for Platonism. One is that Chomsky's argument is basically a demonstration that the nominalist constraints ensuring a physical interpretation for taxonomic grammars are responsible for the inadequacy of these grammars as theories of natural languages. The other feature is that the standards of adequacy Chomsky uses to judge taxonomic grammars are the ordinary standards of grammatical description, namely, conformity of the description to facts about the sound pattern of sentences, word-formation processes, well-formedness, ambiguity, ellipsis, sentence types, agreement, and so on, as reported in speaker's intuitions.[48]

Now, in the light of these features, we can identify one direction to look in for an argument against conceptualism in linguistics. Although the psychological constraints that conceptualism imposes on theories in linguistics are tame by comparison with the physical constraints that nominalism imposes, the conceptualist's constraints are not negligible. In requiring conformity to a concrete reality, psychological reality conditions impose constraints of a kind different from the requirement that grammars correctly describe the sound pattern, well-formedness, ambiguity, and other structural features of sentences. Psychological reality conditions in linguistics do not concern the grammatical structure of sentences but concern particulars of subjective experience or human biology. Since conceptualism imposes constraints requiring grammars to reflect some concrete reality, it could, in principle, prevent grammars from achieving the degree of abstraction necessary for satisfying traditional descriptive and explanatory standards.

Thus, with conceptualism, as with nominalism, there is a possibility of conflict between a demand that grammars satisfy an extrinsic, ideologically inspired constraint and the traditional demand that grammars meet intrinsic constraints concerning the successful description and explanation of the grammatical structure. If such conflicts can exist, then linguists cannot adopt extrinsic, psychological constraints. Linguists, like other scientists, must always try to choose the best available theories, and hence cannot adopt an ontological policy that would select worse theories of natural languages over better ones.

These conflicts can arise on a conceptualist metatheory but not on a Platonist one because the latter imposes *no* restriction on the degree of abstraction in grammars. Conceptualists have to construct grammars as theories of the *knowledge* an ideal speaker has of the language, whereas Platonists construct grammars as theories of the *language* that such knowledge is knowledge of. Therefore, the conceptualist's theories address themselves to the *internal cognitive representation* that humans have of such things as well-formedness, ambiguity, word-formation, ellipsis, and synonymy, whereas a theory of the language should address itself to well-formedness, ambiguity, word-formation, ellipsis, and synonym themselves. Because the mental medium in which human knowledge is internally represented can materially influence the character of the representation, there can be a significant divergence between what a theory of such an internal representation says and what is true of the language. Hence, only in the case of conceptualism is there the possibility of conflicts between ideologically inspired, extrinsic constraints and intrinsic constraints.

I now give a number of such conflicts. The first class of such conflicts contains cases in which the character of human cognitive representation makes the speaker's tacit linguistic knowledge take the form of one rather than another strongly equivalent rules. For example, the character of human cognitive representation might make the speaker's tacit linguistic rules take a form differing from other possible forms just in the way that a propositional calculus with only conjunction and negation as primitive connectives differs from an equivalent one with only disjunction and negation. This is surely a possibility. But now conceptualism would have to say that the psychologically real version of these explanatory equivalent theories is *the* true theory of the language because it is the psychologically real one. This seems obviously wrong: the theories are equally simple, equally adequate from a descriptive and explanatory viewpoint. Since the theories make exactly the same prediction about the grammatical properties and relations of every sentence in the language, they are just different ways of expressing the same claims about the language. Since the theories are equally simple, neither has an edge in how the claims are expressed.[49]

Consider a slightly different case involving notational variants instead of different but strongly equivalent systems. We are now talking about a case in which the character of human cognitive representation causes the speaker's tacit linguistic rules to have a form that differs from other possible forms in only the way that a system of propositional calculus expressed in Polish notation differs from one expressed in *Principia* notation (e.g., "KCpqCqp" versus "p ⊃ q & q ⊃ p"). Here there can be no linguistically relevant difference between the theory that conceptualism prescribes and the theory it forbids. Therefore, if one accepts conceptualism, one could be committed to claiming that, say, a grammatical counterpart to the calculus in Polish notion *is* the true theory of the language and a grammatical counterpart in *Principia* notation is not, even though they are mere notation variants, since the human mind could be constructed in such a way as to represent its grammatical knowledge in the one form rather than in the other. This is comparable to claiming that a Polish notation propositional calculus is preferable *as a theory of propositional logic* to a *Principia* notation propositional calculus when both express the same theory.

Things get even worse. The psychologically preferable theory might not only be on all fours with theories disallowed by conceptualism, but it might even be outright inferior to them on either methodological or explanatory grounds. A methodological difference would exist if, say, the psychologically preferable theory is less parsimonious than some disallowed theories but otherwise the same. It is surely possible that the human mind is so constructed that its representations of grammatical knowledge use more theoretical apparatus than is necessary to formulate the grammatical rules of a language. For example, let us suppose that the grammar of English is transformational and that there are transformations in English, such as the passive or dative movement, in which lexical material is moved from one position to another. Transformations are formulated out of a fixed class of formal operations on strings like deletion, permutation, copying, substitution for dummy elements, etc. One can imagine a grammar of English, Gi, in which some movement transformations are constructed out of an operation of permutation that, as it were, picks up a constituent and puts it somewhere else, whereas other movement transformations are constructed out of an initial operation of copying a constituent into the new position and then an operation of erasing the copied occurrence. We can also imagine another grammar of English, Gj, without permutation, in which all movement is accomplished by copying and deletion, but which is otherwise identical with Gi. Since the effect of permutation can be obtained by a combination of copying and deletion, and both these operations are in both grammars, Gi is less parsimonious because it uses more theoretical apparatus to do a job that can be done with less (with a proper subset of the apparatus in Gi). Hence, by Occam's razor, the preferable scientific theory of the language is clearly the more parsimonious grammar, Gj. But it could certainly happen that the child is genetically programmed for knowledge of a language in which formal operations are overdetermined with respect to the construction of movement rules. Accordingly, speakers acquire a competence system corresponding to Gi. Therefore, in the situation in question, conceptualism requires linguistics to prefer the more complicated grammar, Gi, over the simpler but otherwise identical grammar, Gj. Whereas in the preceding case conceptualism would force us to make a completely arbitrary choice among linguistically indistinguishable theories, in the present case it would force us to choose the less scientifically desirable theory over the more scientifically desirable one. Surely, abandoning conceptualism is preferable to committing ourselves to such methodologically perverse choices.

But not only could adopting conceptualism in linguistics force us to make choices that run counter to sound methodological practice in science, but it could force us to choose false theories where true ones are available, and known, and nothing else stands in the way of their acceptance. Let me make the point by way of an analogy. Major calculator companies, such as Texas Instruments and Hewlett-Packard, construct some calculators on the basis of principles that incorrectly determine the values of a function for a range of arguments that, for empirical reasons, can never be inputs to the device. Companies do this because such "incorrect principles" are either less complicated to build into the device, hence less expensive for the company, or more efficient in on-line computation, hence less costly to the customer. Since computations that produce the incorrect values of the function will never take place, these savings are free and clear. Now, it is plainly absurd to suppose that God, Nature, or Evolution would find it impossible to do what Texas Instruments and Hewlett-Packard can do. Hence we may imagine that, for essentially similar reasons, such heuristic principles have been built into the human brain as internalized competence rules for language processing, that is, as its knowledge of the language. In this best of all possible worlds, we have been provided with a language mechanism that requires less brain utilization and is more efficient in on-line processing. But for all such benefits, and not withstanding the fact that these internalized rules give the correct results for all sentences that can occur in performance, the rules *falsely* predict grammatical facts about sentences that can never occur in performance (because they are, say, too incredibly long or complex). For example, the internalized rules might convert all strings of words above a certain very great length, *n,* into word-salad, so that the best theory of the speaker's competence falsely predicts that strings of English words exceeding length *n* are ungrammatical. Or, the internalized rules might turn out to be nothing but a huge, finite list of *n* sentences, each of which is paired with a structural description. If this is what turns out to be in our heads, a psychologically real grammar must falsely predict that English contains only finitely many sentences, and only *n* of them at that. Given that no acceptable metatheory for grammars ought to allow us to be committed, even contingently, to false theories of natural languages when they are avoidable, it follows that, in committing us to these and indefinitely many further potentially psychologically real but linguistically false grammars of natural languages, conceptualism is unacceptable.[50]

Finally, some grammatical properties of sentences are not explainable in grammars taken as psychological theories. Sentences like (1)–(4) have the property that Kant called "analytic":

(1) Nightmares are dreams.

(2) People convinced of the truth of Platonism believe Platonism to be true.

(3) Flawed gems are imperfect.

(4) Genuine coin of the realm is not counterfeit.

The meanings of the words in these sentences and their syntactic arrangement guarantee the satisfaction of their truth conditions.[51] Two things are clear. First, analyticity is a semantic property, since it is determined by meaning, and hence it must be accounted for at the semantic level of grammars. Second, analyticity is a species of necessary truth. Sentences (1) through (4) express propositions that are true *no matter what,* unlike the synthetic sentences (5)–(8) which, though in fact true, could be false if circumstances were different:

(5) Nightmares usually take place at night.

(6) Few are convinced of the truth of Platonism.

(7) Flawed gems would be more valuable with less flaws.

(8) Genuine coin of the realm exists.

Theories of natural languages ought not preclude explanation of the grammatical properties of their sentences. At the very least, a theory of natural language ought not rule out the possibility of accounting for necessary truths like (1)–(4) which owe their necessity to the language. But this is exactly what conceptualist theories of natural language do in treating grammars as theories of psychological principles and in treating linguistic theory as a theory of the innate basis for internalizing such principles. Conceptualist theories are limited to accounting for necessary truths like those expressed by (1)–(4) as nothing more than consequences of principles that human beings, by virtue of their psychological or biological make-up, cannot take to be false. Such necessary truths come out on the conceptualist's account as merely what human beings are psychologically or biologically forced to conceive to be true no matter what. But this is a far cry from what *is* true no matter what. On the conceptualist's account, impossible objects like *genuine coin of the realm which is counterfeit* are nothing worse than something humans cannot conceive. Conceptualists must treat such *impossible* objects as four-dimensional space was once treated, inconceivable by us but for all we know quite possible.

If we raise the prospect of beings different from us whose psychology makes them take (1)–(4) to be false, the conceptualist must embrace relativism. The conceptualist must say, "We have our logic, they have theirs." The Platonist is the only one who can say, as Frege said in a similar connection, "We have here a hitherto unknown type of madness."[52] Only Platonism enables us to say that such necessary truths are true no matter what – no matter even if we discover that *human* cognitive apparatus is built to take (1)–(4) to be false.

I have described a number of ways in which theories of the competence underlying human linguistic ability are not abstract enough to be adequate theories of the grammatical structure of a natural language. Linguists, like other scientists, are obliged to prefer the best available theory. Thus, linguists cannot adopt a general policy for interpreting their theories that would lead to their preferring worse theories over better ones. Hence, linguists cannot adopt the conceptualist policy.

We come now to what linguistics is like without conceptualism. The psychological view of linguistics has been so prevalent that even the present attempt simply to outline an alternative must consider some of the questions that will undoubtedly arise concerning whether we stand to lose anything valuable in relinquishing conceptualism.

One such question is whether, in eliminating constraints on the psychological reality of grammars, we are dropping constraints that we need in order to choose among theories. Pointing to the proliferation of theories in recent linguistics and the trouble linguists have had in obtaining consensus on which theory is closest to the truth, some conceptualists say we ought to welcome the introduction of new constraints that narrow the range of theories, and they will surely complain that, in rejecting psychological constraints, the Platonist is looking a gift horse in the mouth. But it makes no sense to insist on constraints *just* because they narrow the range of theories. After all, constraining the range of theories about a natural language by requiring them to be theories of hiccups or the origin of life does a pretty good job of narrowing. There is the prior question of establishing that the constraints are the right kind. This is the question begged when Platonism is criticized on these grounds.

Underlying the conceptualist's demand for psychological constraints to narrow the range of theories of a language is the further assumption that it is desirable to narrow it so drastically. Why ought we welcome such new constraints solely because they reduce the number of theories that have survived confrontation with the grammatical evidence? It is a common fact of scientific life that evidence underdetermines the choice of a theory, even given methodological criteria like simplicity. Presumably, then, the conceptualist wishes to say something stronger, namely, that, even assuming we had *all* the evidence about the grammatical properties and relations of sentences in the language, there would still be a choice remaining between equally simple (and otherwise methodologically equal) theories for which the new constraints are needed. But why suppose that such a further choice is substantive? Theories that are equivalent in grammatical description, and on all methodological grounds, are completely equivalent theories of *grammatical* structure. So at least the Platonist claims. One question that divides Platonists and conceptualists is thus whether there is a *linguistically significant* choice between theories of a language that do not reflect a difference either in what grammatical properties and relations they predict or in how methodologically well they predict them.

All such equivalent theories of a language can be taken as optimal grammars of the language because, on the most natural definition, an "optimal grammar" is *a system of rules that predicts each grammatical property and relation of every sentence in the language and for which there is no simpler (or otherwise methodologically better) such predictively successful theory.* The fact that more than one theory of a language will count as an optimal grammar just puts the situation in linguistics on a par with the one familiar in logic and mathematics.

Platonism also offers a natural conception of the notion "correct linguistic theory." Linguistic theory, on the Platonist view, is a theory of the invariances in the grammatical structures of all natural languages: the relation between linguistic theory and grammars of natural languages is like the relation between topology and the geometries whose invariances it studies.[53] A "correct linguistic theory" states all invariances and essential properties of natural language in the simplest way.

Another question concerning whether we stand to lose anything in replacing conceptualism arises in connection with the three fields that came into existence with the Chomskyan revolution: linguistic semantics, formal properties of grammars, and cognitively oriented psycholinguists. These have become important research fields, and no one would suggest giving up any of them. But there is no risk of that. Though they came in with the conceptualism ideology, they would not go out with it since none of these fields depends on conceptualism.

Linguistic semantics did not exist within structuralism, because concepts in the theory of meaning are not reducible to features of the acoustic material in a corpus. But, insofar as Platonism does not replace the extrinsic constraints it removes by others, the liberalization that brought linguistic semantics into existence is not jeopardized by Platonism.

The field of formal properties of grammars came into existence with the Chomskyan revolution because the revolution provided the stimulus for various new kinds of grammar and because of the special attention Chomsky gave to the study of formal properties. But since the field of formal properties of grammars never concerned itself with more than the mathematical structure of grammars, it has no investment in the conceptualist ideology.

Finally, cognitively oriented psycholinguists, too, would continue without alteration under Platonism. Platonism makes no criticism of the new psycholinguistics. Platonism leaves this discipline in its proper place, namely, in psychology.

Nothing of value is lost in Platonist linguistics and much is gained. Linguistics proper gains a conception of what its theories are theories of that is free of inherent conflicts between ideology and its commitment to descriptive and explanatory aims. On the Platonist conception, theories in linguistics are subject only to traditional descriptive and explanatory aims and the methodology of science generally. Grammars thus are under no constraints that force linguists to choose arbitrarily between equivalent theories or notational variants, to settle for uneconomical theories, or, worst of all, to accept false theories when true ones can be had. Nor is linguistics forced to rule out the possibility of explaining necessary truths in natural languages. In fact, Platonism in linguistics offers an explanation of the necessity of truths like (1)–(4) in terms of its conception of sentences and their senses as abstract objects.[54]

Philosophy gains a new approach to the long-standing issue over the existence of abstract objects.[55] Moreover, in coming at the issue from the perspective of the ontological status of languages, the approach is particularly timely in the light of recent nominalist contributions to the issue which assume that a nominalist reconstruction simply can take the status of language for granted.[56]

Psychology, artificial intelligence, neurophysiology, etc. gain a clear, sharp boundary between where the work of the linguist ends and the work of the cognitive scientist begins. This boundary makes the division of labor between the linguist and the psychologist, artificial intelligence scientist, and neurophysiologist as clear as that between the mathematician and the empirical scientist.

One final thought. The conceptualist criticized the nominalist for confusing competence and performance: the speaker-listener's *knowledge* of the language with the *speech* resulting from the exercise of this knowledge. The Platonist criticizes the conceptualist for confusing the speaker-listener's *knowledge* of the language with the *language* that the speaker-listener has knowledge of. The nominalist's constraints require faithfulness to the facts of speech; the conceptualist's require faithfulness to the facts of knowledge. Only Platonist constraints require faithfulness to just the facts of language.

REFERENCES

1. The Platonist conception of language outlined here is developed more fully in Katz, *Languages and Other Abstract Objects*. Totowa: Rowman and Littlefield, 1981.

2. W.V.O. Quine, *From a Logical Point of View*. New York: Harper and Row, 1953, p. 47.

3. G. Holton, *Thematic Origins of Scientific Thought*. Cambridge, MA: Harvard University Press, 1973, p. 5.

4. N. Chomsky, *The Logical Structure of Linguistic Theory*. New York: Plenum Press, 1975, pp. 30-33.

5. R. Montague, *Formal Philosophy*. New Haven, CT: Yale University Press, 1974, pp. 1-69.

6. N. Chomsky, *Rules and Representations*. New York: Columbia University Press, 1980, pp. 29-30.

7. Ibid., pp. 29-30.

8. This is the distinction between narrow and broad concepts in J.J. Katz, *Semantic Theory*. New York: Harper and Row, 1972, pp. 450-462.

9. J.A. Fodor, "Some Notes on What Linguistics is About." In *Readings in Philosophy of Psychology*, N. Block, ed. Cambridge, MA: Harvard University Press, 1981, p. 205.

10. Ibid. p. 206.

11. Ibid. p. 205.

12. L. Wittgenstein, *Wittgenstein's Lectures on the Foundations of Mathematics*, E. Diamond, ed. Hassocks: Harvester Press, 1976.

13. Fodor, op. cit. p. 205.

14. N. Chomsky, *Syntactic Structures*. The Hague, Holland: Mouton and Company, 1957, pp. 13-17.

15. J.J. Katz, "The Real Status of Semantic Representations." *Linguistic Inquiry* 8 (1977): 571-574.

16. Fodor, op. cit. p. 206.

17. Ibid., p. 206.

18. Another example of the failure to appreciate the philosophical nature of the question that linguistic Platonism raises is found in J. Higgenbotham's "Is Grammar Psychological?" [in *How Many Questions?* L.S. Cauman, I. Levi, C. Parson, and R. Schwartz, eds. Indianapolis: Hackett Publishing Co., 1983, pp. 170-179.]. Higgenbotham is replying explicitly to my *Language and Other Abstract Objects*. He accuses it of merely stipulating that linguistics is not psychology (pp. 172-174). What is peculiar about the accusation is that Higgenbotham ignores the arguments that the book gives for this thesis, while his own case for the opposite thesis itself rests on nothing more than a stipulation. Higgenbotham says, "Defense of this thesis Katz appears to take as entirely straightforward, once we distinguish between theories of a domain D and theories of the *knowledge* of D." (p. 172) He seems not to have looked beyond the first section of Chapter III, particularly, the next section of that chapter and Chapters V and VII, which contain the fuller form of the arguments at the end of the present essay.

    Higgenbotham's stipulation that linguistics is "an empirical inquiry into the identity of human languages" begins with the quite true statement that "one may also be interested in questions like (1): For which (S, S') is Jones's language = (S, S'), and why?" (p. 172). This is no more objectionable than saying that one may be interested in questions about the identity of human systems for arithmetic calculation. But then the unobjectionable statement is superseded by a full-blooded stipulation when Higgenbotham claims that "it is only by seeing the consequences of the attribution of such systems [(S, S')] to persons that linguistic theory can be tested" (p. 174). This only makes sense if we assume already that the principles being tested are principles about "the identity of human languages". If not, then it is a flat *non-sequitur*. Could one sensibly claim against a Platonist in the philosophy of mathematics that it is only by seeing the consequences of the attribution of mathematical theories to persons that mathematical theories can be tested? Neither mathematical intuition nor linguistic intuition presuppose that mathematical or linguistic theories are attributable to people in the sense required for claiming that linguistics is empirical. (See *Language and Other Abstract Objects,* Chapter VI.)

The confusion that runs through Higgenbotham's reply is between the sense of abstractness in which we speak of the objects in an empirical idealization being reached by abstracting away from certain aspects of real situations and the sense of abstractness in which Platonists speak of abstract objects. The former depends on empirical reality while the latter does not. Here, I think, is the reason for the failure to appreciate the nature of the question that the linguistic Platonist is raising: confusing these two notions of abstractness makes Higgenbotham and others think that they can do justice to the Platonist's stress on the abstractness of linguistic theories while still maintaining that linguistic theories are empirical.

19. Chomsky, *Rules and Representations,* p. 217.

20. N. Chomsky, "Some Empirical Issues in the Theory of Transformational Grammar." In *Goals of Linguistic Theory,* S. Peters, ed. Englewood Cliffs, NJ: Prentice-Hall, Inc., 1972, pp. 63-130.
      N. Chomsky, "Chomsky." In *Discussing Language,* H. Parret, ed. The Hague, Holland: Mouton and Company, 1974, pp. 47-49.

21. P. Postal, "The Best Theory." In Peters, ed., op. cit. pp. 131-170.

22. Chomsky, "Chomsky," p. 48.

23. This neglects the Platonist's conception of what the essence of language is, but the omission does not affect the argument in the text. See Katz, *Language and Other Abstract Objects,* pp. 221-240.

24. D.T. Langendoen and P.M. Postal, *The Vastness of Natural Languages.* Oxford: Basil Blackwell, 1984.

25. J.J. Katz, *The Philosophy of Language.* New York: Harper and Row, 1966, p. 122.

26. N. Chomsky, "The Formal Nature of Language." In *Biological Foundations of Language,* E. Lenneberg, ed. New York: Wiley, 1967, pp. 435-436.

27. T. Winograd, *Understanding Natural Language.* New York: Academic Press, 1972.

28. E. Wanner and M. Maratsos, "An Augmented Transition Network Model of Relative Clause Comprehension." Cambridge, MA: Harvard University (unpublished manuscript).

29. B.E. Dresher and N. Hornstein, "On Some Supposed Contributions of Artificial Intelligence to the Scientific Study of Language." *Cognition* 4 (1967): 321-398.

30. An overview of this debate is found in V.V. Valian, "The Wherefores and Therefores of the Competence–Performance Distinction." In *Sentence Processing,* W.E. Cooper and E. Walker, eds. Hillsdale: Lawrence Erlbaum Associates, 1979, pp. 17-19.

31. An attempt to exhibit the relevance of Platonism for language acquisition can be found in T.G. Bever, "Some Implications of the Non-specific Basis of Languages." In *Language Acquisition State of the Art,* L. Gleitman and E. Wannar, eds. Cambridge, MA: Cambridge University Press, 1982, pp. 429-449.

32. L. Bloomfield, "Linguistic Aspects of Science." In *International Encyclopedia of Unified Science, 1,* O. Neurath, R. Carnap, and C. Morris, eds. Chicago: The University of Chicago Press, 1938, pp. 219-232.

33. L. Bloomfield, "Languages or Ideas?" *Language* 12 (1936): 93.

34. Z. Harris, "Discourse Analysis." *Language* 28 (1952): 1-30.

35. N. Chomsky, "A Transformation Approach to Syntax." In *Proceedings of the Third Texas Conference on Problems of Linguistic Analysis in English, 1958,* A. A. Hill, ed. Austin, TX: The University of Texas, 1962, pp. 124-158.

36. Z. Harris, "Transformational Theory." *Language* 41:3 (1965): 363-401. Reprinted in *Papers in Structural and Transformational Grammar.* Dordrecht, Holland: D. Reidel Publishing Co., 1970, p. 555.

37. For further discussion, see Katz, *Language and Other Abstract Objects* (pp. 21-44), and also the earlier discussion in J.J. Katz and T.G. Bever, "The Fall and Rise of Empiricism." In *An Integrated Theory of Linguistic Descriptions,* T.G. Bever, J.J. Katz, and D.T. Langendoen, eds. New York: T.Y. Crowell, 1976, pp. 11-64.

38. Z. Harris, "Co-occurrence and Transformation in Linguistic Structure." *Language* 33 (1957): 283-340.

39. Bloomfield saw the practical need to order grammatical rules, but such ordering was an embarrassment since ordering is too abstract to be *in* the corpus. Hence he claims that it is mere fiction. See L. Bloomfield, *Language.* New York: Henry Holt and Co., 1933, p. 213.

40. Z. Harris, "Distributional Structure." *Word* (1954): 146-162. Reprinted in *The Structure of Language: Readings in the Philosophy of Language,* J.A. Fodor and J. J. Katz, eds. Englewood Cliffs, NJ: Prentice-Hall, Inc., 1963, p. 37.

41. N. Chomsky, *Language and Mind.* New York: Harcourt, Brace, and World, Inc., 1968, p. 10

42. N. Chomsky, *Aspects of the Theory of Syntax.* Cambridge, MA: The MIT Press, 1965, p. 8.

43. Ibid. p. 25.

44. Ibid. pp. 18-59.

45. Ibid. pp. 25-26.

46. See Katz, *Language and Other Abstract Objects,* pp. 76-93.

47. Chomsky, *The Logical Structure of Linguistic Theory,*, pp. 30-33.

48. In *Language and Other Abstract Objects* (pp. 64-73), I develop this observation into a conception of a neutral framework for evaluating competing ontological positions.

49. Someone might object that it makes a difference what the primitives of a theory are insofar as the primitives express a theory's conception of the fundamental notions in the domain. But the objection begs the question

because in the present case such a difference can only be significant from a psychological viewpoint. From a mathematical viewpoint, which set of notions from equivalent sets is chosen as primitives matters no more than which of the true statements of a deductive system are chose as postulates. Asking which states should rank as postulates, as Quine once said, is "as meaningless as asking which points in Ohio are starting points." *From a Logical Point of View,* p. 35.

50.   It does no good to reply that false rules cannot appear in competence because competence is knowledge, since then, in the case in question, grammars are not about anything.

51.   Katz, *Semantic Theory,* pp. 171-200.

52.   G. Frege, *The Basic Laws of Arithmetic,* M. Furth, trans. and ed.   Berkeley, CA: University of California Press, 1967, p. 14.
      Also, Katz, *Language and Other Abstract Objects,* pp. 160-173.

53.   For further discussion, see Katz, *Language and Other Abstract Objects,* pp. 221-240. Platonist linguistic theory formulates an account of the nature (or essence) of natural language in logical rather than in psychological terms. Chomsky and Halle [*The Sound Pattern of English.* New York, Harper and Row, 1968, p. 4] give a psychological account in which the essential properties of natural language are those contributed to all competences by the child's innate endowment for language acquisition. Such an account will, of course, contain the same problems noted above with a psychological account of grammars because, on conceptualist theory, universal grammatical structures must reflect the mental characteristics of the medium of representation. Such problems are eliminated when the conceptualist interpretation of linguistic theory is abandoned and a psychological account of the essential properties of natural language replaced with a logical one. One such account is that the essential properties of natural language are the invariants of the sentence/meaning correlations in particular natural languages that are necessary in order for natural languages to be expressively unrestricted, that is, effable.

54.   Katz, *Language and Other Abstract Objects,* pp. 179-186. Furthermore, it offers an explanation of *a priori* knowledge of analyticity and other grammatical properties and relations of sentences in terms of a new theory of intuition. Ibid. pp. 192-216.

55.   And a more comprehensive and viable Platonist position; see Katz, *Language and Other Abstract Objects,* pp. 12-17, 192-220.

56.   For example, H. Field, *Science Without Numbers.* Oxford: Oxford University Press, 1981.

SENSE AND REFERENCE IN A
PSYCHOLOGICALLY BASED SEMANTICS[1]

Ray Jackendoff

My paper "Toward an Explanatory Semantic Representation"[2] describes a wide-ranging class of grammatical and lexical generalizations for which there is no apparent grammatical source. Several semantic fields of verbs, having to do with possession, ascription of properties, and relation to activities, show close parallels to verbs of spatial motion and location with respect to their lexical realizations, their prepositional patterns, and the inference rules appropriate to them. In that paper and a succeeding one,[3] I argued that the most attractive explanation of these generalizations is that they are linguistic reflections of deeper generalizations rooted in the structure of cognition. In short, grammatical and lexical distribution appears to have revealed something about the nature of thought.

The idea that language mirrors thought goes back to the most ancient philosophy, but by present-day standards most work attempting to demonstrate it would be considered hopelessly speculative. Further, the tradition of semantics in which most of us were educated traces its roots back to mathematical logic – Frege, Russell, and Carnap, for instance, were interested primarily in mathematics – and this tradition shows no interest in the psychological foundations of language. Nor (with the possible exception of one offshoot, Montague grammar) does it show interest in finding a particularly enlightening relationship between semantics and the grammar of natural language.

Thus the tradition of formal logic was of little help in my attempts to forge an argument from grammatical form to psychological structure. Rather, I was forced to examine a number of fundamental assumptions about semantics that stood in the way of grafting my results onto an existing framework. The present paper concerns some of the most basic ways in which my current way of thinking about semantics differs from tradition.

1. Criteria for Semantic Theory

I take the goal of semantic theory to be a description of the class of meanings that human language can express, and of the principles by which these meanings are related to the syntactic structures of particular languages. Within the theoretical paradigm I assume, this goal is to be met by the construction of a theory of *semantic well-formedness rules,* which describe the class of possible meanings, and a theory of *projection rules* or *correspondence rules,* which relate meanings to syntactic structure. As in the theory of syntax, it is of the utmost importance to determine which aspects of each rule type are innate and which are language-specific, and to characterize the range of variation among languages. Since children manage to learn a language, the language-specific aspects of the rules must be plausibly learnable.

Most theorists assume that at least the following four conditions must be met by an adequate semantic theory.

▶ First, it must be able to express unambiguously all the semantic distinctions made by natural language.

▶ Second, in order to account for the fact that languages are (largely) intertranslatable, the stock of semantic expressions available to particular languages must be universal; that is, the semantic well-formedness rules must be universal. (This does not mean that every language is necessarily capable of expressing every possible meaning.)

▶ Third, a semantic theory must provide some principled way for the meanings of the parts of a sentence to be combined into the meaning of the whole sentence. This requirement of compositionality may be taken more or less strongly, according to whether one requires each constituent (as well as each word) of a sentence to be provided with a well formed interpretation.

▶ Fourth, a semantic theory should be able to account formally for the so-called "semantic properties" of utterances, such as synonymy, anomaly, analyticity, and presupposition. In particular, the notion of valid inference must be explicated.

These generally accepted criteria, however, do not bear on the question raised by the grammatical generalizations reported in my 1976 paper:[4] How does the syntactic form of the language reflect cognitive structure? In order to address this issue, it is necessary to adopt two further criteria on the adequacy of semantic theory, which I will call the Grammatical Constraint and the Cognitive Constraint.

The *Grammatical Constraint* says that one should prefer a semantic theory that explains otherwise arbitrary generalizations about
the syntax and the lexicon. As one motivation for this constraint,
consider the task of the language learner, who must learn the mapping between syntactic form and meaning. Wexler and Hamburger[5]
have shown that the syntax of a language is *formally unlearnable*
unless the learner makes use of information from the meaning of a
sentence as well as information from the surface string.[6] That is,
the language learner cannot acquire syntax without use of the
correspondence rules: (s)he must be independently guessing the
meaning of utterances from context and putting it to use in determining syntax. Reinforcing this result, Macnamara[7] shows the
fundamental importance of innate aspects of meaning in the very
early stages of language acquisition, and how they help shape the
development of syntax. One major point of my 1972 book[8] is that
many apparently syntactic constraints follow from semantic constraints, so that once a language learner has learned the meaning of
the construction in question, the observed syntactic distribution will
follow automatically. Finally, one should prefer a semantic theory
that relates apparently distinct readings of a polysemous word,
since this would make it easier for the language learner, given one
reading, to acquire another.

This constraint on semantic theory is addressed by Fodor's speculation that

> the resources of the inner code are rather directly represented in the
> resources of the codes we use for communication. The least that can be
> said in favor of this hypothesis is that, if it is true, it goes some way
> toward explaining why natural languages are so easy to learn and why
> sentences are so easy to understand: The languages we are able to learn
> are not so very different from the languages we innately know, and the
> sentences we are able to understand are not so very different from the
> formulae that internally represent them.[9]

The force of Fodor's suggestion goes beyond language learning to
include facts about language universals. Under the reasonable
hypothesis that language serves the purpose of transmitting information, it would be perverse not to take as a working assumption
that language is a relatively efficient and accurate encoding of the
information it conveys. To give up this assumption is to refuse to
look for systematicity in the relationship between syntax and semantics. Any deviation from efficient encoding required by a
particular semantic theory should be rigorously justified, for what
appears to be an irregular relationship between syntax and semantics may turn out merely to be a bad theory of semantics. (See
Vendler[10] for arguments to this effect with respect to natural lan-

guage quantifiers; Goldsmith and Woisetschlaeger,[11] with respect to progressive aspect; and Jackendoff,[12] with respect to sentences about temperatures.)

For a familiar example of a theory that violates the Grammatical Constraint, consider quantificational logic in its traditional form. The sentence *Floyd broke a glass* translates into $\exists x$(glass(x) & break(Floyd, x)), or, in the notation of restricted quantification, $\exists_{glass(x)}$(break(Floyd, x). In either case, the syntactic constituent *a glass* does not correspond to any semantic constituent; rather, its interpretation forms several discontinuous parts of the logical expression. (Russell[13] observed this lack of correspondence and didn't bat an eyelash. Since then tradition has sanctified it.) Furthermore, the logical translation severely distorts the embedding relationships of the sentence, since the existential quantifier, the outermost operator in the logical expression, is a semantic contribution of the indefinite article, one of the most deeply embedded constituents of the sentence.

Naturally, there are reasons for adopting the formalism of quantificational logic, having to do with solving certain aspects of the inference problem. But one could hardly expect a language learner to learn the complex correspondence rules required to relate the quantificational formalism to surface syntax. The logician might respond that this aspect of the correspondence rules is universal and therefore need not be learned. But then we could ask on a deeper level why language is the way it is: Why does it display the constituent structure and embedding relations it does, if it expresses something formally so different?

In short, under the Grammatical Constraint, the use of quantificational logic as a model of natural language semantics cannot be taken for granted. A model that accounted for the same inferences but preserved a simpler correspondence of syntactic and semantic structure would be preferable.

Nor are logicians the only offenders in this regard. A sizable segment of the artificial intelligence community (e.g., Schank[14] and Wilks[15]) seeks to process natural language – that is, to relate texts to semantic structures – without especially detailed reference to the syntactic properties of the texts. While I agree that syntactic structure alone is insufficient to explain human linguistic abilities, and that human beings do not process language by doing all the syntactic analysis first, I do not agree that syntactic structure is a trivial aspect of human linguistic capacity, and that it is merely incidental to language processing. One reason why such attempts may have seemed plausible is that the syntax of the sentences used as examples is invariably rather trivial, and there is little attempt to explore the grammatical and lexical generality of the patterns used for analysis. That is, this work is concerned on the whole only with the observational adequacy of the system and with such descriptive adequacy as the system happens to provide; the notion of linguistically significant generalization plays no role in this research. Thus this work inevitably meets the Grammatical Constraint only occasionally and by accident.

It is my contention that the Grammatical Constraint must be imposed on semantic theory in order to make semantics an empirically interesting enterprise. Linguistic research has shown that syntax is not the chaotic, unprincipled mass of individual facts it was once thought to be; rather it is a system of remarkable complexity and subtlety. Moreover, its organization cannot be predicted in any simple way from general principles of cognition, semantics, pragmatics, communicative convenience, or ease of processing. In studying natural language, one ignores or denigrates syntax at the risk of losing some of the most highly structured evidence we have for any cognitive capacity. It is the Grammatical Constraint that sanctions the attempt to extend this evidence into the domain of semantics. Without it, one will never try to discover anything of interest in the relationship between form and meaning.

But the Grammatical Constraint alone is not sufficient for constructing an argument from grammatical generalization to the nature of thought. One needs a further constraint, which has received attention recently through the work of Clark and Chase,[16] Fodor,[17] and Miller and Johnson-Laird.[18] This constraint has been occasionally acknowledged by linguists and in certain kinds of work on artificial intelligence; but it has not played a significant role in recent philosophical discussion or in most AI work on text processing. We may call this constraint the *Cognitive Constraint:* There must be levels of mental representation at which information conveyed by language is compatible with information from other peripheral systems, such as vision, nonverbal audition, smell, and kinesthesis. If there were no such levels, it would be impossible to use language to report sensory input. Likewise, to account for the fact that people can carry out orders, there must be a level at which linguistic information is compatible with information eventually conveyed to the motor system.

A satisfactory theory of psychology obviously requires interfaces between nonlinguistic modalities as well. For instance, in order to use vision to help tell the organism where to go, there must be a visual-motor interface; to know that visual and auditory sensations occur simultaneously, there must be a visual-auditory interface; and so forth.   In principle, there could be a different form of mental representation for each of these interfaces.   However, it is reasonable to make a simplifying assumption that, if true, places interesting constraints on the theory of mental processing.   We may call it the *Conceptual Structure Hypothesis:* There is a *single* level of mental processing at which linguistic information, sensory information, and motor information are compatible.   Let us call this the level of *conceptual structure.* I emphasize that there is no necessary reason for there to be such a unified level – as there is for the existence of individual interfaces between modalities.   But at worst, the Conceptual Structure Hypothesis is a plausible idealization; at best, it is a strong unifying hypothesis about the structure of mind.

As Fodor[19] points out, conceptual structure must be rich enough in expressive power to deal with all things expressible by language. It must also be rich enough in expressive power to deal with the nature of all the other modalities of experience as well – obviously no simple matter.   In order to give some formal shape to the problem, I will assume that the possible conceptual structures attainable by a human being are characterized by a finite set of *conceptual well-formedness rules.* It seems reasonable to assume that these rules are universal and innate – that is, that everyone is born with essentially the same capacity to develop concepts.   However, the concepts that one *does* develop must depend to some extent on experience – including possibly linguistic experience, so that there is room for a certain amount of "Whorfian" variation in concepts due to linguistic experience if that should prove necessary.

On the other hand, the position that conceptual well-formedness rules are innate is not consistent with what I take to be the strongest version of Piagetian developmental theory, which could be construed in the present framework as a claim that certain conceptual well-formedness rules, such as those having to do with measurement and amounts, must be learned.   Rather, the development of the child's conceptual ability must be attributed either to increasing richness and interconnection of concepts, or to growth either of the well-formedness rules or of computational capacity, over which the child and the environment have little or no control.   The kind of growth I have in mind is akin to the growth of bones and muscles: the environment must of course furnish nourishment, and the person can stimulate growth by exercise, but these inputs hardly can be said to control the interesting aspects of structure.   For example, the same nutrients build bird wings and human fingers; it is the innate structure of the organism that determines which of these actually develops. (See Chomsky[20] and Fodor[21] for more discussion of this point.)

Returning to the Cognitive Constraint: the point of imposing it on semantic theory is clear. It is a specific statement of the psychological reality of linguistic information, and it serves as a link between linguistic theory and cognitive theory. Thus the two relatively novel constraints on semantics, the Grammatical Constraint and the Cognitive Constraint, serve to make semantic theory responsible to the facts of grammar and of cognitive psychology, respectively. It is precisely these two constraints that are lacking in the traditional logical program of research on the semantics of natural language, and that are necessary in evaluating a theory that purports to use linguistic evidence to study the nature of thought.

One can understand why the Grammatical Constraint played little or no role in semantics at the turn of the century, since so much less was known about grammar than now. Today it is harder to condone research in semantics that lacks proper attention to syntax. Similarly, it is perhaps excusable that little serious attention has been paid to the Cognitive Constraint, even by those who espouse a mentalistic theory of language, because it is so difficult to see how to apply it in any useful way. Our notions of the information conveyed by nonlinguistic peripheral systems are if anything feebler than our understanding of the linguistic information. But though there is little useful *theory* of the end product of visual perception, there is certainly a great deal of highly organized evidence that can be brought to bear on such a theory, and, given the Cognitive Constraint, on semantic theory as well. A large-scale attempt to integrate the power of perceptual and linguistic systems appears in Miller and Johnson-Laird.[22] More than any other piece of work I know of, this book exemplifies the sort of integration I have in mind, even if many of its specifics are open to question.

There are in principle two ways in which conceptual structure could be related to the linguistic system. First, conceptual structure could be a further level beyond semantic structure, related to it by a rule component that corresponds to what most people call rules of *pragmatics*. This appears to be the view of Katz and Fodor[23] and Katz,[24] for example. Alternatively, conceptual structures could be simply a superset of semantic structures; that is, semantic structures would be just those conceptual structures that happen to be verbally expressible. This view would claim, then, that the correspondence rules effect a direct mapping between syntactic structure and conceptual structure, and that rules of inference and pragmatics are mappings from conceptual structure into conceptual structure. This is the view assumed in most work on artificial intelligence; it is argued for in Fodor, Fodor, and Garrett[25] and Jackendoff.[26] In the present paper, I assume this view without argument – though the choice is not especially relevant to the immediate concerns here.

In the rest of this paper I want to show what happens to the theory of natural language semantics if one takes the Cognitive Constraint really seriously.

2. The Real World and the Projected World

We begin by stating two basic questions of semantics: First, what is the information that language conveys? Second, what is this information *about?* The first question can be identified with the traditional philosophical concern with *sense* or *intension;* the second with *reference* or *extension.* Naïve introspection yields these answers: The information conveyed consists of ideas – entities in the mind; the information is *about* the real world. A great deal of the philosophical literature has been concerned with debunking one or the other of these answers, and proposing (and debunking) alternatives. The first answer in particular has come under strong and steady attack. In fact, even the first *question* has sometimes been argued to be illegitimate or irrelevant, often in concert with general attacks on the notion of mind as a legitimate subject for empirical or theoretical inquiry.

The view I will take here, of course, is that it is indeed legitimate to question the nature of the information conveyed, and that the answer of naïve introspection is in some sense correct. That is, I assume that there is a level of human organization that can plausibly be termed *mental,* that this level is causally connected, but not identical, with states of the nervous system, and that the function of this level can be treated, at least in part, as processing of information. Furthermore, the Cognitive Constraint in effect states that certain aspects of this mental information constitute the information encoded in language.

On the other hand, I want to take issue with the naïve (and nearly universally accepted) answer that the information language conveys is about the real world. To see why, we need to step back from language for a while and talk about some very basic issues at the foundations of psychology.

Perhaps the most significant general result of the school of gestalt psychology (e.g. Wertheimer,[27] Köhler,[28] Koffka[29]) was its demonstration of the extent to which perception is the result of an interaction between environmental input and active principles in the mind that impose structure on that input.   Two trivial and well known examples appear in Figures 1 and 2.

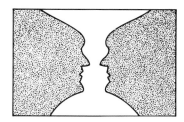

Figure 1   **Figure 2**

In Figure 1 the four dots are quite naturally seen as forming a square, although no linear connections are present on the page. Why?   Furthermore, why these particular linear connections and not, say, an X, which is logically just as possible an organization? And why is the organization of the four dots in Figure 3 into a square so much less apparent, even though they are in exactly the same spatial relations?

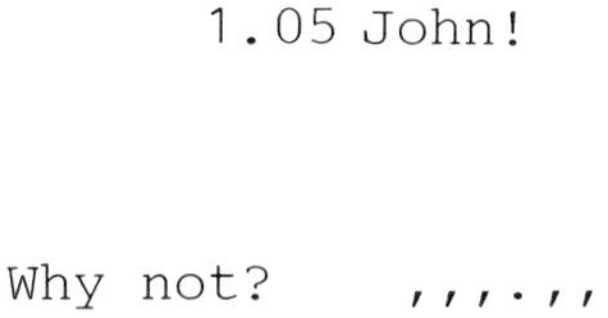

1.05 John!

Why not?   , , , . , ,

Figure 3

Figure 2 is one of the famous ambiguous figures. Wittgenstein's[30] "duck-rabbit," Figure 4, is another, and many of the same arguments apply. As is well known, Figure 2 can be seen as a profile of a vase against a black background or as two profiles of faces against a white background.   If fixated, the example usually switches periodically from one interpretation to the other; that is, the environmental input does not change at all, but what is seen does change.   Moreover, though the example is a diagram in the plane, in the "vase" interpretation the two black areas are seen as constituting a unified background that extends behind the white

Figure 4

area; in the "faces" interpretation the white area is seen as extending behind the two black areas.

These examples show that what is seen cannot be solely environmental in origin, since the figures are imbued with organization that is not there in any physical sense, that is by no means logically necessary, and that, in the case of the depth in Figure 2, is inconsistent with the physical facts. This organization, which involves both segmentation of the environmental input and unification of disparate parts, must be part of the *mind's encoding* of the environmental input in preparation for presentation to awareness. All of this is demonstrated by the gestaltists in great detail, and is probably somewhat familiar to most readers. I want, however, to examine the consequences of this argument for semantics; so it is worth following further.

The mental processes that perform this organization of the input are both automatic and unconscious. They are susceptible to voluntary control only to the extent that one can, for example, choose to see the "faces" rather than the "vase" in Figure 2. But the choice is at best between different organizations, not between organized and unorganized input; and some organizations (e.g., the disparity of lengths in the Müller-Lyer illusion, Figure 5) are notoriously difficult or impossible to overcome willfully. Thus the world as experienced is unavoidably influenced by the nature of the unconscious processes for organizing environmental input. One cannot perceive "the real world as it is."

What makes this last assertion so repugnant to common sense is that the organization of the input is experienced not as part of the act of thinking, but as part of the environment. The square in

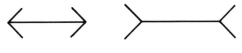

Figure 5

Figure 1 is not in my head, it is out there on the page. The vase and the faces in Figure 2 are out there on the page too, though not both at once; and, disturbingly, they have mutually inconsistent properties. Moreover, as Wittgenstein observes,[31] "I describe the alternation [between the two ways of seeing it – RJ] like a perception; quite as if the object had altered before my eyes." That is, the change in its nature is out there too, not in my head at all.

It does no good to explain the presence of this organization on the basis of its utility in dealing with the world. That does not explain it *away;* the burden still falls on psychology to provide an account of it. Nor are we at liberty to dismiss examples such as Figures 1-5 as mere psychologist's tricks and to say that perception of the ordinary *real* world is quite different. Why should the perceptual process arbitrarily distinguish between inputs that happen to be used by psychologists as examples and inputs that are "ordinary" (as seems to be implied by the Gibsonian view of research on perception)? A more reasonable position is that all inputs are organized by the same processes, and that perceptual ambiguities, constructions, and illusions, in and out of the context of psychological experiments, are cases in which what is experienced is noticeably different from what we believe *ought* to be experienced. The deliberate examination of examples that result in out-of-the-ordinary perceptual judgments thus serves as one important tool in developing a theory of the mental processes that organize perceptual input. The use of such examples is altogether comparable to the linguist's examination of unusual sentences in studying grammatical competence. In short, illusions are not wrinkles to be added into the theory after "ordinary experience" is accounted for.

Such a view, however, seems to compel us to claim that potentially vast areas of our experience are due to the mind's contribution, even though the experience is of things "out there in the real world." The only way out of this apparent conflict between theory and common sense is for the theory to include "out there" as part of the information presented to awareness by the unconscious processes organizing environmental input. That is, "out-thereness" is as much a mentally supplied attribute as, say, squareness.

That this solution is not simply an escape hatch, an unfalsifiable way of defining oneself out of the problem, is shown by dreams and hallucinations, where "out-thereness" is part of an experience for which there is *no* environmental input. According to this account, then, the reason it seems counterintuitive to ascribe so much of the organization of experience to the mind is that a part of this organization is the ascription of the organization itself to the world. We are programmed normally to be unaware of our own contribution to our experience.

The necessity of adopting such a view toward perception was brought home to me by my work with Fred Lerdahl on musical cognition.[32] In order to account for the kinds of intuitions people have about music – from elementary intuitions about phrasing and meter to more subtle intuitions such as the relation between a theme and its variations – one must ascribe to pieces of music an elaborate abstract structure. Intuition tells us, and the standard tradition of musical analysis takes for granted, that the structure inheres in the music itself. But if one starts to look for musical structure out there in the real world, it vanishes. What reaches the ear other than a sequence of pitches of various intensities, attack patterns, and durations? More pointedly, how do we locate something like Beethoven's Fifth Symphony in the real world? One may be tempted to tie such an entity somehow to the written score, as Goodman does.[33] But this is clearly unsatisfactory, since there are many *unwritten* musical traditions in which pieces can be named and identified. Even in a written tradition, as every musician knows, a large part of what goes into a performance of a piece is not in the score, but resides in the performer's unwritten (and perhaps unwritable) understanding of the style. This suggests that the term "Beethoven's Fifth Symphony" refers to an abstract structure which the experienced listener constructs in response to a performance of the sequence of events partially represented by the score, and which he attributes to that sequence of events, out there. Beethoven wrote the particular notes he did in order to evoke from the listener this structure, which he had in mind in advance, perhaps unconsciously. (One can see in Beethoven's sketchbooks his painstaking efforts to fit the notes intuitively to an underlying conception that is unstated but evidently clear to him.)

What makes the musical evidence for the nature of perception more unequivocal than the usual visual evidence is that, though one might conceivably claim that the structure of visual experience ordinarily models something pre-existing in the real world, musical structure must be thought of ultimately as a product of the mind. Nonetheless, musical structure is *experienced* as part of the world out there; here it is even clearer than in the visual case that we are programmed to be unaware of our own vast contribution to the experience.

If indeed the world as experienced does owe so much to mental processes of organization, it is crucial for a psychological theory to distinguish carefully between the source of environmental input and the world as experienced. For convenience, I will call the former the "real world" and the latter the "projected world" ("experienced world" or "phenomenal world" would also be appropriate). The term "projected" is borrowed from psychotherapeutic usage, where "projection" denotes an aspect of one's personality that for some reason is not experienced as one's own, but attributed to the environment and experienced as an aspect of it – for instance in paranoia, where one's own aggressive tendencies are experienced as emanating from others and directed against oneself. This term thus simultaneously captures the importance of one's mental contribution to experience and one's lack of awareness of this contribution. I deviate from the psychotherapeutic sense of the term in regarding projection not as an aberration but as part of the normal mental process of constructing conscious experience. (Cases in which projection leads one astray, as in paranoia or hallucination, might then be spoken of as "illegitimate projection.")

This distinction between the real world and the projected world is hardly new; something much like it appears as early as Kant. What I think is relatively new here is the systematic application of the distinction to the semantics of natural language.

Note well that the projected world does *not* consist of mental images. Experiencing a horse is one thing; experiencing an image of a horse is another. They correspond to different, though probably related, projections of mental constructions. There is much more one could say about images; for the moment, it is sufficient to observe that though they are surely among the denizens of the projected world, they are far from the only ones. To forestall another possible misunderstanding, I should mention that the projected world is much richer than the "percepts" of psychology: it embraces not only direct perceptual experience but also all sorts of abstractions and theoretical constructs, as will be seen.

At the beginning of this section, I took issue with the naïve position that the information conveyed by language is about the real world, and it should now be clear why. We have conscious access to only the projected world – that is, the world as organized by the mind; and we can talk about things only insofar as this organization has been imposed. Hence *the information conveyed by language can only be about the projected world.* Furthermore, we can explain the naïve position as a consequence of our being programmed to treat the projected world as the real world.

It should now also start to become evident that we must be suspicious of the traditional philosophical notions of *truth* and *reference* as central to natural language semantics. Truth is regarded as a relationship between a certain subset of sentences (the true ones) and the real world; reference is regarded as a relationship between expressions in a language and things in the real world that these expressions refer to. If we reject the direct relevance of the real world to language, we cannot take these notions as starting points for a theory of meaning, as many logicians do. At best, we may ask what the words "truth" and "reference" mean in English, and why truth and reference are intuitively so important.

I should mention a natural objection to the claim that language conveys information only about the projected world. This claim implies that people could interpret environmental input differently, and hence it should be in principle impossible to be sure that any two people are talking about the same things. How can language be that subjective? (This objection is essentially Quine's[34] doctrine of "indeterminacy of radical translation," applied now to each individual.)

The answer has two parts. First, the only way to guarantee that we are talking about the same things is to guarantee that the processes by which we construct the projected world are the same in each of us. For a wide range of our experience, this seems plausible. A theory that allows for this possibility must claim that part of one's genetic inheritance as a human being is a set of processes for constructing a projected world, and that these processes are either largely independent of environmental input or else dependent on kinds of environmental input that a human being cannot help encountering. Current research in human and animal psychology strongly supports the claim that much of the organizing process is indeed innate; this innateness can account for our apparent abilities to understand one another.

On the other hand, the projected world has some aspects whose construction is underdetermined both by universals of human heredity and by common environment, and here we do find wide interpersonal and/or intercultural differences. For example, people have differing abilities to understand mathematics or music or chess; ethical, political, and religious notions too are open to considerable (though probably constrained) variation. In these areas we find situations in which people in fact *cannot* convey information to each other, because their construals of experience are incompatible. Hence the objection that, according to the present theory, language must be subjective may be granted without damage. It *is* subjective, but the fact that we are all human beings, with similar mental structure, guarantees that in a vast range of useful cases our projections are for most purposes compatible. Thus we can reasonably operate under the assumption that we are talking about the same things, as long as we are careful about detecting misunderstanding.

3. The Fictive Metalanguage and Some Examples

Meanwhile, we are in a terrible bind. If language talks about only the projected world and not the real world, it is impossible to coherently *claim* that this is the case, for the real world and the projected world spoken of in the claim are both projected world entities. And since language is all we've got for making claims in, we're stuck.

In order to continue, we must resort to the fiction that we can use a metalanguage in which it is possible to speak of both the real world and the projected world. In this language, I will designate real-world entities in ordinary type, but will enclose references to projected-world entities in # #. In effect this usage acquiesces in the illusion that what you and I are talking about is reality; it's only our experimental subjects who talk about their projections. We conveniently overlook the fact that we are necessarily among our own experimental subjects. This arrangement has the virtue of feeling like fairly natural discourse, but it is important to guard against being insidiously lulled into confusion. I will do the best I can.

To give the reader a feel for the metalanguage, let us examine a fairly clear example that distinguishes real-world entities from projected-world #entities#, having to do with color. In our present terms, the physical and biological sciences (as carried out by our experimental subjects) can best be said to be attempts to develop #entities# and #relations# whose structure is as close as possible to an isomorphism with entities and relations in the real world. If successful, they can be said to be getting as close as is humanly possible to the structure of the real world. If physics is right, for instance, the real world contains, among other things, electromagnetic radiation of various wavelengths and energies traveling in various directions; the properties of electromagnetic radiation are isomorphic to the #properties# of the theoretical construct #electromagnetic radiation#.

Psychology, on the other hand (again as carried out by our experimental subjects), is concerned with the structure of the projected world. In the projected world, the counterpart of certain (real) radiation is #light# of various #hues#, #brightnesses#, and #saturations#; the counterpart of certain other radiation is #heat#; and much of electromagnetic radiation (e.g., X rays) has no projected counterpart at all except as a theoretical construct. The structure of #color# can be characterized by the #color solid#, a well known construct of psychological theory.

Psychology is also concerned with two sorts of links between the real world and the projected world. First, it seeks the principles that establish the correspondence between real-world phenomena and projected-world #phenomena#. In this example these principles include the account of color perception, color constancy, and so forth. The correspondence is nontrivial, involving complex contextual considerations; it is not simply that a particular wavelength corresponds to a particular #color#. (Though this has been known for a long time and was investigated by the gestaltists, among others, it has been driven home in especially striking fashion by the work of Land.[35])

In addition, psychology is concerned with an account of the real-world nervous system correlates of the processes of mental organization that give rise to the projected world. In the present example, this goal has led to research on the chemical structure of retinal cells, on neural maps for the visual system, and so forth.

In the description just given, it is crucial to notice that there is no such thing as (real-world) light and color – only #light# and #color#. #Color# is part of an organism's projected response to the pattern of electromagnetic radiation impinging on the visual system. The nervous system brings about a nonisomorphic mapping between the real and projected phenomena.

To make the metalanguage sufficient for our purposes, we need one more notational device. Recall that #color# is not "in the mind," but projected "out there." In order to talk about the mental structures that give rise to the projection #color#, we must be able to refer to the mental information that is projected into awareness. I will designate this information in capitals. Thus the pattern of electromagnetic radiation is processed by neural mechanisms to yield, among other things, information of the form COLOR; COLOR may then be projected into awareness as #color#, or it may remain unconscious – that is, unnoticed or unattended.

Except for one stray remark about mental images, I may have given the impression that the projected world is experienced as completely outside the body. Now I want to correct this impression and at the same time sharpen what it means to say the projection is "out there."

Think about the perception of pain. Though pain is sensed as being localized in various parts of the body, it is well known that the brain mediates the experience of pain. This suggests that in the metalanguage being adopted here, we should speak not of pain but of #pain#: #pain# is a projection onto a part of the body, in response to a chain of neural events beginning with excitation of pain receptors or whatever. The projective nature of #pain# is especially well revealed by the phenomenon of phantom limbs, whereby amputees experience #pain# in body parts they no longer possess. We see therefore that the projected world must include #phenomena# within one's own #body#.

Next think about mental images, such as what one experiences when carrying out instructions like "Imagine a square," or "Imagine a major triad." Intuitively, they are evidently experienced as being "in the mind." It is a little harder to realize that mental images must be treated as projections too. But recall what has always been the decisive objection to the existence of mental images: there is no room in the head for a little projection screen and a little person to view it. So most recent research on mental images (cf. Kosslyn[36] and references cited there) has tried to eliminate this objection by treating mental images solely in terms of the processing of mental information. However, this leaves unexplained the fact that mental images are not experienced as information processing any more than ordinary sensation is. The right approach emerges if we add to the information-processing theories the claim that the experience of mental images, like the experience of ordinary sensation, results from the projection of information being processed by the brain. And just as with ordinary sensation, the projected #mental image# may bear no direct resemblance at all to the real-world phenomena that give rise to it.

4. The Ego, the Mind–body Problem, and Gestalten

The claim that some projected #entities# are experienced within oneself requires us to rethink our idea of projected #entities# being invested with the character "out there," which seems to imply exterior to the body. In light of the last two examples, a more appropriate term seems to be "outside of (or distinct from) ego." I intend here not the ego in Freud's sense, but something closer to Koffka's[37] notion of a particular mental subsystem with at least three important properties. First, the ego contains the "executive," the component that organizes and directs action. Second, the ego has partially variable boundaries; that is, it is capable of taking into itself or excluding certain aspects of mind, body, and external environment. Third, entities that at a particular time are within the ego-boundary do not at that time give rise to projected-world #entities#.

These last two properties may seem obscure, and I will not undertake any serious account of them; but a common sense example will make them intuitively clearer. The example is due essentially to Polanyi.[38] He points out that when one is hammering a nail, and is skillful at it, one feels not the impact of the hammer's handle on the palm, but the impact of the hammer's head on the nail. The hammer has temporarily become part of oneself; one invests oneself in it. (The language describing the phenomenon seems unavoidably mystical – but the experience should be altogether familiar.) Similarly for most tool-using tasks: in the ideal case, one feels the tennis ball hitting the racket, not the racket jarring the hand; one feels the road under the car, not some complex jiggling of the body; one produces music rather than pushing piano keys. The ego has in some sense expanded to include the tools, so as to come into more direct contact with the desired goal. In the process, the tool has temporarily disappeared from view. Of course, if mechanical difficulties arise in the use of the tool, one again becomes aware of the tool. A subsidiary goal has arisen, that of getting the activity back on the right track. The ego therefore "contracts" in order to externalize the region of difficulty, putting it back in the projected world where it may be attended to. Such expansion and contraction goes on constantly in carrying out ordinary tasks.

This transparency of the tool during skilled use is evident in a case more germane to the present context. In carrying on a conversation or lecture, one is most often aware only of conveying information, not of forming sentences. Likewise, as is well known, listeners or readers normally remember the information conveyed better than the actual sentences used to convey it. One becomes conscious of one's language only when having difficulty expressing oneself or comprehending someone else. In other words, the whole linguistic apparatus functions as a kind of tool for conveying information, and its relation to awareness during use is not so different from that of a hammer. The main difference is that a great part of the linguistic apparatus can never be brought into consciousness, whereas we can inspect hammers rather thoroughly.

We have seen how the ego can expand to include external objects. It can also contract to exclude parts of the body (say the fingernails one is cutting) and parts of the mind — not just certain aspects of language, but mental images, memories, and beliefs. Given this conception of ego, it seems plausible to attribute to all projected world #entities# the character "external to ego." They differ, in addition, as to whether they are, among other things, internal or external to the body, and internal or external to the mind.

As long as we are on mysterious issues, let me mention perhaps the biggest mystery of all: the mind-body problem. In the present framework the mind-body problem can be expressed this way: mental information (e.g. COLOR) is presumably reducible to some configuration of brain states. But the projected world (e.g. #color#) is not made up of brain states, it is made up of experiences; and nobody seems to have any idea at all what experience is, or how configurations of brain states are transmuted into it by the mechanism of projection. For example, we find it difficult even to imagine what it would mean to answer the question "Does a computer have experiences?" I suspect that the mind-body problem is one that human beings are congenitally unequipped to be able to answer.

We can sidestep this problem without jeopardizing the entire enterprise by making the reasonable assumption that the mapping between projected mental information and the projected world is an isomorphism. That is, the character of #color#, for example, is to be accounted for directly in terms of the information constituting COLOR. What makes the problem interesting, though, is that much of the *internal* structure of COLOR cannot be independently projected; that is, it is not accessible to consciousness. Hence one cannot determine the structure of #color# by mere introspection; we need a theoretical discipline of psychophysics to explicate it.

This situation, which I believe is typical of projected #entities#, provides an explanation in the present framework of the "gestalt" or "holistic" character of experience — that is, the fact that perceived #wholes# are often greater than or different from the sum of their #parts#. The reason for this is that, of the mental information that is projected as the #whole#, only the components that are *independently projectable* can result in perceived #parts#. The presence of the rest may be sensed intuitively through the disparity between the #whole# and the #parts#, but its nature cannot be revealed in any simple way by introspection alone. Such an account of the holistic nature of experience, I believe, removes some of the mystery surrounding the central doctrine of gestalt psychology as presented by, for example, Wertheimer[39] and Köhler.[40]

5. Cognitive Theory and Its Relation to Language

Since it is in the nature of experience not to wear its structure on its sleeve, we need a theoretical discipline to explicate it. I will use the term *cognitive theory* for this discipline. Essentially, cognitive theory in this sense is the study of mental information – Fodor's[41] "inner code" or Miller and Johnson-Laird's[42] "conceptual structure." The task of cognitive theory thus includes, among other things, seeking the structure of mental information and the principles by which computations are performed upon it. In effect, what is sought is the *grammar* (including the lexicon) of the inner code.

An especially important part of this grammar will be a specification of those expressions of the inner code which are projectable – that is, which give rise to projected entities in the world of experience. Both apparent regularities and apparent anomalies in the nature of the projected world should be explicated in terms of the nature of the inner code, in particular by the properties of the projectable expressions.

Let us now turn back to the two questions of semantics I raised at the beginning of Section 2, and see how all the intervening talk about psychology bears on them. We can now say that the information language conveys, the *sense* of linguistic expressions, consists of expressions in the inner code. What the information is about, that is, the *reference* of linguistic expressions, is not the real world as in most semantic theories, but the projected world. The *referring expressions* of natural language will be just those expressions that map into projectable expressions of the inner code.

What difference does this picture make for the study of semantics? One important difference is in the ontological presuppositions of natural language – what sorts of entities, in a very broad sense, language can be said to be talking about. Given the assumption that we are talking about reality, philosophy has always had difficulty justifying the existence of abstract entities like propositions, sets, predicates, numbers, and properties, all of which we talk about as if outside ourselves. The alternatives in treating these have never been really satisfactory: either claiming they are incorporeal Platonic entities to which we somehow have access; or claiming natural language doesn't *really* talk about them, because they don't exist, and that an adequate semantics must reduce them to concrete terms; or avoiding the psychological issues altogether.

In the present view, though, the ontological presuppositions of natural language are far less dependent on the nature of reality; rather, they are linked to the nature of *projected* reality and thus to the structure that human beings impose on the world. For example, it is perfectly satisfactory to posit #color# as the reference of color words, even though there is no such thing in the real world; #color# is a consequence of the structure of mind. Likewise, it is very difficult if not impossible to find a real-world counterpart of causality: one gets immediately caught up in problems about counterfactual conditionals and the like. Thus the question of the reference of phrases like *the cause of the accident* has been a troubling one. In the present theory, the notion of causality can be treated as a mentally imposed relationship between two perceived events, proceeding from the innate nature of conceptual structure. Much of the discussion about real-world correlates then falls into questions of psychophysics: what range of real-world inputs leads to an attribution of causality? (And it is not necessary that this class of inputs be particularly natural from a physical point of view. See the work along these lines by Michotte,[43] for example.) Similarly, Jackendoff[44] and Talmy[45] show that linguistic evidence leads one to postulate an ontology far beyond the limited one usually assumed in logic and much work in psychology; the present paper can be taken in part as an attempt to make sense of those results.

In general, then, this view of reference frees us of many of the philosophical conundra that are a consequence of assuming we talk about the real world. It does not immediately solve all the philosophical problems by any means, but it at least puts many of them into a category of empirical rather than merely speculative issues. I take that to be some sort of advance.

Furthermore, the Cognitive Constraint on semantic theory, from which this view of reference follows, encourages us – even forces us – to take seriously what evidence there is on the nature of perception and motor control in developing hypotheses about meaning in natural language. Conversely, the Cognitive Constraint in conjunction with the Grammatical Constraint enables us to use evidence from a serious examination of grammar to help us know what sorts of #entities# to look for in nonlinguistic modes of interaction with the environment; Miller and Johnson-Laird,[46] Talmy,[47] and Jackendoff[48] are examples of this approach. In short, I think the adoption of these constraints provides a way of integrating the study of language in all its wonderful detail more fully into psychology, and I find it reasonable to look forward to exciting results for both disciplines.

REFERENCES

1. This essay consists largely of excerpts from *Semantics and Cognition*. Cambridge, MA: MIT Press, 1983. This work was supported in part by a Fellowship for Independent Study and Research from the National Endowment for the Humanities, and I wish to express my deep gratitude for that support. Among the many people who have contributed to my thinking on these matters, I particularly want to thank John Macnamara.

2. R. Jackendoff, "Toward an Explanatory Semantic Representation." *Linguistic Inquiry* 7 (1976): 89-150.

3. R. Jackendoff, "Grammar as Evidence for Conceptual Structure." In *Linguistic Theory and Psychological Reality*, M. Halle, J. Bresnan, and G. Miller, eds. Cambridge, MA: MIT Press, 1978, pp. 201-228.

4. Jackendoff, "Toward an Explanatory Semantic Representation," op. cit.

5. K. Wexler and H. Hamburger. "Insufficiency of Surface Data for the Learning of Transformational Languages." In *Approaches to Natural Language*, J. Hintikka, J. Moravcsik, and P. Suppes, eds. Dordrecht, Holland: Reidel, 1972.

6. See also
    K. Wexler and P. Culicover, "The Semantic Basis for Language Acquisition." Social Sciences Working Paper 50. Irvine, CA: University of California, 1974.
    K. Wexler and P. Culicover, *Formal Principles of Language Acquisition*. Cambridge, MA: MIT Press, 1980.
    P. Culicover and K. Wexler, "Some Syntactic Implications of a Theory of Language Learnability." In *Formal Syntax*, P. Culicover, T. Wasow, and A. Akmajian, eds. New York: Academic Press, 1977.

7. J. Macnamara, *Names for Things*. Cambridge, MA: Bradford Books, MIT Press, 1982.

8. R. Jackendoff, *Semantic Interpretation in Generative Grammar*. Cambridge, MA: MIT Press, 1972.

9. J. Fodor, *The Language of Thought*. Cambridge, MA: Harvard University Press, 1975, p. 156.

10. Z. Vendler, "Each and Every, Any and All." In *Linguistics in Philosophy*. Ithaca, NY: Cornell University Press, 1967.

11. J. Goldsmith and E. Woisetschlaeger, "The Logic of the Progressive Aspect." *Linguistic Inquiry* 13 (1982): 79-90.

12. R. Jackendoff, "How to Keep Ninety from Rising." *Linguistic Inquiry* 10 (1979): 172-177.

13. B. Russell, "On Denoting." *Mind* 14 (1905): 479-493. Reprinted in *The Logic of Grammar*, D. Davidson and G. Harman, eds. Encino, CA: Dickenson.

14. R. Schank, "Identification of Conceptualizations Underlying Natural Lan-
     guage." In *Computer Models of Thought and Language,* R. Schank and K.
     Colby, eds. San Francisco, CA: Freeman, 1973.

15. Y. Wilks, "An Artificial Intelligence Approach to Machine Translation." In
     Computer Models of Thought and Language, R. Schank and K. Colby, eds. San
     Francisco, CA: Freeman, 1973.

16. H.H. Clark and W.G. Chase, "On the Process of Comparing Sentences
     Against Pictures." *Cognitive Psychology* 3 (1972): 472-517.

17. Fodor, op. cit.

18. G. Miller and P. Johnson-Laird, *Language and Perception.* Cambridge, MA:
     Harvard University Press, 1976.

19. Fodor, op. cit.

20. N. Chomsky, *Reflections on Language.* New York: Pantheon, 1975.

21. Fodor, op. cit.

22. Miller and Johnson-Laird, op. cit.

23. J.J. Katz and J. Fodor, "The Structure of a Semantic Theory." *Language* 39
     (1963): 170-210.

24. J.J. Katz, "Chomsky on Meaning." *Language* 56 (1980): 1-41.

25. J.D. Fodor, J.A. Fodor, and M. Garrett. "The Psychological Unreality of
     Semantic Representations." *Linguistic Inquiry* 6 (1975): 515-532.

26. Jackendoff, *Semantics and Cognition.*

27. M. Wertheimer, "Laws of Organization in Perceptual Forms." In W.D. Ellis,
     A Source Book of Gestalt Psychology. London: Routledge and Kegan Paul,
     1938, pp. 71-88.

28. W. Köhler, *Gestalt Psychology.* Mentor Books reprint, 1947.

29. K. Koffka, *Principles of Gestalt Psychology.* New York: Harcourt, Brace, and
     World, 1935.

30. L. Wittgenstein, *Philosophical Investigations.* Oxford: Blackwell, 1953.

31. Wittgenstein, ibid. p. 195.

32. F. Lerdahl and R. Jackendoff, "Toward a Formal Theory of Tonal Music."
     Journal of Music Theory (1977): 111-171.
          F. Lerdahl and R. Jackendoff, *A Generative Theory of Tonal Music.* Cam-
     bridge, MA: MIT Press, 1982.

33. N. Goodman, *Languages of Art.* New York: Bobbs-Merrill, 1968.

34. W.V.O. Quine, *Word and Object.* Cambridge, MA: MIT Press, 1960.

35. E. Land, "Experiments in Color Vision." *Scientific American* (May 1959), and
     "The Retinex Theory of Color Vision." *Scientific American* (December 1977).

36. S. Kosslyn, *Image and Mind.* Cambridge, MA: Harvard University Press,
     1980.

37. Koffka, op. cit.

38. M. Polanyi, *Personal Knowledge.* Chicago, IL: University of Chicago Press,
     1958, Chapter 4.

39. M. Wertheimer. "The General Theoretical Situation." In Ellis, op. cit., pp. 12-16.

40. W. Köhler, "Physical Gestalten." In Ellis, op. cit., pp. 17-54.

41. Fodor, op. cit.

42. Miller and Johnson-Laird, op. cit.

43. A. Michotte, *La perception de la causalité*. 2d ed.   Louvain: Publications Universitaires, 1954.

44. R. Jackendoff, "Grammar as Evidence..." and "An Argument on the Composition of Conceptual Structure," in *Theoretical Issues in Natural Language Processing*, D. Waltz, ed.   New York: Association for Computing Machinery, 1978. See also *Semantics and Cognition*, loc. cit.

45. L. Talmy, "The Relation of Grammar to Cognition – A Synopsis." In Waltz, op. cit.

46. Miller and Johnson-Laird, op. cit.

47. L. Talmy, "Rubber-sheet Cognition in Language." In *Proceedings of the 13th Regional Meeting of the Chicago Linguistic Society*. Chicago, IL: Department of Linguistics, University of Chicago, 1977. And "The Relation of Grammar...," loc. cit.

48. Jackendoff, "Toward an Explanatory...," "Grammar as Evidence...," "An Argument on...," *Semantics and Cognition*.

SOME THOUGHTS ON THE BOUNDARIES
AND COMPONENTS OF LINGUISTICS

Charles J. Fillmore

1

Anybody familiar with discussions in and around linguistics these days is accustomed to hearing people say things such as:
- "We've got to distinguish the properties of the language faculty in the species from facts about individual languages. What you've just presented as a fact about English is really a fact about Language." or
- "Those are not questions of grammar; they're questions of usage." or
- "Why do you persist in giving structuralist explanations for facts that have only social-historical explanations?" etc.

I want to examine two closely related problems here. The first is that of deciding what does belong to a properly constituted science of language and what does not. The second is that of deciding how the components or subdomains of such a science need to be separated from one another. In general, my approach is to look at certain classes of facts and to ask what are the proper sources of explanation for such facts. In many cases my problem seems analogous to that of deciding, for a given piece of furniture, whether it fits well in one room rather than in another, or whether we ought to throw it away or give it to someone else.

I do not intend, except in one or two cases, to try to resolve these border-drawing questions, but I at least wish to examine the ways in which such issues have been discussed in recent years by linguists and their allies. The questions that need to be asked are:
- What kinds of observation fall within the scope of a given discipline?
- What methodological choices seem appropriate for a given discipline or subdomain of a discipline?
- What is the accepted explanatory base – that is, the standard form for statements of explanation – that a given scientific theory makes available to its disciples?

It is well known that scholars working in what might broadly and vaguely be called "the science of language" differ importantly in respect to the cleanness with which they choose to define a central core of concern with language as such as opposed to questions about the use or context of language. Many linguists are motivated to make the circle small, liking to feel that they have closed off a territory that can be safely defended, around which a secure wall can be built, and within which everything can be known and labeled.[1] Many non-linguists too would like linguistics to be made clean and small, because that would make their own work more readily definable: if linguists could tell them precisely what "language" or "linguistic competence" is, then they in their turn could ask questions about how it is learned, how it is used, how it fits its contexts, and so on.[2] Linguists who choose to make the circle big, by contrast, might do so because their vision is grand, or because they enjoy the risk and excitement of having so many more things to keep track of.[3] Among those who draw the circle big are many who would not call themselves linguists at all, but are rather people who either work within a larger theory in which a science of linguistics is a proper part, or who hold to a theory that purports to deal with the data linguists concern themselves with but which finds no need for a well-defined science of linguistics within it.[4]

For ease of exposition, I shall refer to this broadly conceived "science of language" as "linguistics," including, just for now, even the work of those who explicitly reject "establishment linguistics" as a potential source of wisdom on the workings and structure of language.

My own interest in the resolution of these boundary-drawing questions does not come from territorial urges on my part, nor does it arise from a desire for neatness, from a love of tidily labeled boxes. Rather, I feel we need to ask: Are we free to draw borders in and around linguistics according to our taste, our generosity, or the grandness of our vision — or are there empirical bases for making the boundaries go one way rather than another? That is, we need to recognize the difference between the esthetic act of drawing a boundary — in ways determined by such measures as our sense of symmetry or the reach of our arms — and the scientific act of discovering a seam in nature and tracing its course. Using a different image, we need to distinguish the perspective of a butcher from that of an anatomy student, each confronting a pig's carcass. The anatomy student, in disassembling the pig, traces a muscle from one of its moorings to the other, because he is interested in learning how the animal is put together. The butcher, by contrast, makes his segmentations of the animal in accordance with the prevailing practices of local meat-eaters and his own inner urges. The point is that we need to decide whether the conceptual framework within which we articulate our beliefs about the workings of language follows the realities of language itself. In fact, we need to find out if there is such an object whose realities are in principle discoverable.

2

The problem of boundaries for the science of language is that of finding the proper sources of explanation for the various kinds of facts connected with human communication. The problem of sorting out these various sources of explanation can be equated with that of identifying the abstractions and idealizations legitimate to a science of language. The articulation of the full set of needed idealizations provides the makings of a theory of levels that may be more complex than anything ordinarily considered in linguistics. One of my goals is to try to begin to make explicit the outline of such a theory of levels.

Human speech communication gives us one of the most compelling cases of a domain of facts requiring multiple sources of explanation. Language as we know it is learned, and learnable, only by human beings: many of the facts of human language are doubtless to be explained from the reality that its users are all members of our species. Language is learned and used in a structured but changing matrix of social activity: the purposes and institutions of groups of social beings affect language behavior in ways obvious to everyone; they are bound to have a shaping effect on linguistic structure as well. Language is transmitted from person to person in such a way that output (the utterances) produced by one generation of speakers provides, in a context of personal engagement, the data out of which the next generation constructs for itself an equivalent or near-equivalent system: the interaction of the nature of language and the nature of the human language faculty must determine both the course of this transmission and the tolerance for transmission failures of the kind that, accumulated, result in the profound changes in language form that we see across the centuries. Language is both enabled and limited by the productive, memorial, perceptual, imaginal, and processual capabilities of human beings. And it is used by people who move in, and interact with, what we sometimes call the real world. The shape of language, and the facts about its employment, must be determined in many ways by each of these realities.

3

Let us imagine an indefinitely large *record* of the various kinds of facts we can gather about a given *speech sample*. We can say that this record is a set of *representations* of the speech sample, that the elements of each representation are determined by a set of *criteria,* and that each set of criteria characterizes a *level* of representation. We can, following Halliday,[5] define *rank size* as the size of the speech sample over which the criteria are to be applied, such as word or sentence or discourse.

I intend these notions to be taken as broadly as possible, assuming nothing in advance about which facts are linguistic or about which level-defining criteria are going to turn out to be linguistically relevant. By my definitions, then, one conceivable representation of a text is a tracing of all the places at which the speaker yawned while producing it. Another is a detailed phonetic representation using just the contrasts implicit in some given segmental or featural notation system. Another is a tracing of pitch contours for the sample. It is less easy to find explicit criteria for what might be called a cognitive representation – defined according to the kinds of images, associations, awareness of fit with real world situations, etc. – that could be assumed to appear in the comprehension of an ideal interpreter.

Let us assume, then, that we can have an unlimitedly large and detailed set of representations of speech samples, or texts, in any language. We can then assume that a great many of the questions that need to be answered if we are to construct a science of language can be asked about this set. For example,

• What determines the occurrence of phenomena at given levels of representation?
• What determines the structuring of the phenomena at given levels of representation?
• Which questions get answered differently for different languages?
• Which questions get answered in the same way for all languages?

In some cases, the questions might get answered by a straightforward appeal to phenomena on another level. Thus the reason the speaker used the phoneme /m/ in a particular place in a particular English utterance is that he used the word MOTHER, as shown in the lexemic representation of the same utterance, and the word MOTHER "contains" the phoneme /m/. Some other questions can be answered only by appealing to a language specific set of formation rules – mastery of which can be imputed to the speakers of that language – governing the kinds of structures to be found in representations at a particular level. English phonotactics allows word-initial /kr/, but does not allow word-initial /kt/. Still other questions require the discovery of sets of rules for linking one level of representation with another, in the way that a linguistic-phonetic representation can be predicted or derived from a phonological representation of the same text. And many other answers will come from knowledge of either constant or changing aspects of the context of use.

4

As a way of exploring some of these questions, I would like to set up various distinct kinds of articulations or relationships between different levels of representation. In many cases we will be able to see a nonrandom relationship between the phenomena and structures on one level of representation and those on another level.

A first type of relation – called *part to whole* – is between representations of the same text. Here one representation of an utterance is part of another representation of the same utterance. A trivial example can be seen in the relation between a record of all the vowels in an utterance and a record of all the phonetic segments in the utterance.

A second kind of relationship – *taxonomic* – links units to categories of those units. The relationship between a representation showing word tokens and one showing part-of-speech tokens of the same utterance is taxonomic.

A third kind of relationship – *hierarchical* – is the one most commonly discussed. In it, sequences of units on one level correspond to individual units on another level. Morphemic and lexemic representations have this kind of relationship, since a "lexeme" or word is made up of a sequence of (one or more) morphemes. Lexemic and phrasal representations are related in the same way.

In a fourth kind of relationship we can say that the units on one level provide the tools, or the means, for units on another level. Here I would like to say that the nature of the relationship is *instrumental.* Thus a level of syntactic representation might be said to have an instrumental relationship to a level of representation of *illocutionary* acts. Linguists and speech-act theorists who are careful about this relationship encourage us to use a different terminology for each level, as when they distinguish "interrogative sentence" from "question," "indicative sentence" from "statement," etc. Thus, if we regard a relationship as instrumental, we can say that at such-and-such a point the speaker *used* an interrogative sentence *as* a question.

My fifth and sixth types of relationships, which show systematic rule-like relationships, differ in the structure of their rules. In the fifth relationship, the rules are "autonomous" – that is, they are independent of external influences. We can regard one level as an *idealization* of the other level, an idealization from which the influences of external factors – noise, production, disturbances, etc. – have been taken away and can be resupplied once those factors are again taken into account. In the sixth relationship, we can regard one level as an *abstraction* of the other level, an abstraction from which the details, the redundancies, have been removed and to which they can be resupplied by a completely regular systems of rules.

I refer to the one as *internal-regular* and to the other as *external-regular,* for want of more perspicuous terms. I see an internal-regular relationship between a phonological and a linguistic-phonetic representation, with linking rules of the standard allophonic type. I see an external-regular relationship between a linguistic-phonetic representation and what might be called an absolute phonetic representation, in which certain distortions in the signal can be seen as explainable by the facts that, say, the speaker was a young boy who yawned during the first ten seconds of the utterance and was being tickled during the final three seconds.

These notions do not exhaust the possibilities, since several different representations might well be jointly responsible for the phenomena in another representation. In explaining one representation, we might say that other representations, in a cluster, *interact,* and that the relationship between the one representation and the cluster might be either internal-regular or external-regular. One view of the prosodic contours in English is that they are determined by an interaction among phonological, lexical, syntactic, semantic, and pragmatic representations.

5

Many issues in the organization of the science of language can be formulated within my descriptive framework. We can examine the usual kind of embedding hierarchy for linguistics by which, for example,

- units at the morphemic level combine hierarchically to determine units at the lexemic level,

- recursive combinations at the lexemic level define a hierarchical articulation between lexemic and syntactic representations, and so on.

The theory of deep structures and meaning-preserving transformations provides two syntactic levels of representation linked in an internal-regular way.

We can ask whether the relationship between traces of prosodic features in English and morphemic representations is of a part-to-whole type, as would correspond to the theory of grammaticized intonation contours and stress superfixes,[6] or whether, as seems the more current view, phonological representations containing prosodic information are derived from phonological representations in which such information interacts with syntax at least, and doubtless with semantics and pragmatics as well.[7]

If there is such a thing as semantic representation, we could ask if its relation to a cognitive representation of the utterance is instrumental or external-regular – that is, whether semantic structures provide tools for the comprehension process or stand as idealizations of it.

And we can ask certain extremely important questions about the relation between sentences and texts. If the relationship is hierarchical, then sentences are the constituents of texts, and it makes sense to talk about a grammar of texts;[8] but if the relationship is instrumental, then a text can be seen as an activity in which the producers of the text are engaged, and the sentences can be seen as the means of performing certain acts within that activity.

6

At this point I would like to take up a number of boundary issues in linguistics, beginning with the speech end of "speech communication," and discuss the questions of the proper treatment within the conceptual framework introduced above.

The raw observations of speech are made up of the actions of the bodies of the communicating partners, the acoustic events that accompany those actions, and the perceptual experiences, on the hearers' part, that follow from those actions and events. As a first-level abstraction, then, we need to separate the patterns that belong to human speech from those of other noise-creating events such as belching, laughing, crying, sneezing, whistling, and coughing.

Events of these types may occur independently of speech, in which case we can, so to speak, resplice the tape after cutting out these events, thus ignoring them completely. When they occur simultaneously with speech, we will not look to our science for an explanation of their occurrence, but we may indeed be interested in examining their signal-distorting effect in mapping out the external-regular relationship between a linguistic-phonetic representation and an absolute phonetic one. (A sustained yawn markedly affects vowel quality.) The controlled performance of some of these events can be used as part of a conventional communicative act, as when one clears one's throat to draw attention to some impropriety; but we will doubtless find that this conventionalized use fails to articulate in a general way with the more clearly linguistic levels of representation, and that the orderliness we find in the occurrence of these events or in their acoustic effect can be explained (if at all) by principles quite different from those we independently need for a science of language.

A second but related kind of data separation needed at the speech end is that by which we identify speech patterns given conventional values for the language community as a whole, in contradistinction to aspects of the speech signal that are determined by properties of the individual speaker. Here I have in mind the size and shape of the speaker's vocal tract, the length of the speaker's vocal cords, or the speaker's articulatory skills, processing speed, changing mental and emotional states, and so on. Again, and again quite obviously, the reason we are willing to exclude such matters from the central task of describing a language is our belief that whatever orderliness there is to be found here is to be explained with reference to differences among individuals and their changing states, and has little direct bearing on the character of the language they speak.

Coughing and yawning, and the rest, usually occur independently of speech and can generally be left out of consideration altogether. But voice quality, pitch range, tempo and its changes, and so forth are with us always and can be removed from the speech signal only by processes of abstraction. The usual phrasing for this abstraction has it that the linguist observes patterns, contrasts, oppositions, features of articulation type, etc., rather than the phonetic events directly. I think my description is equivalent to the standard one, the difference being that in my account one speaks of recognizing an idealization rather than of selecting the data.

7
Digression

The position I have taken is that differences in the bodies of the speakers affect language performance but not language structure – that they figure, in short, only when one is articulating the relation between an idealized phonetic and an absolute phonetic representation of the same utterance. While facts about human bodies might indeed figure in explanations about the character of language in general, *differences* between bodies of individuals, or set of individuals, cannot figure in explanations about differences between languages.

There is a conceivably different position we could take that bears on the way in which a language fits, and is employed by, the bodies of its users, something that ought to be mentioned because it raises another issue of external boundaries. If not just individuals but communities of individuals should have saliently different physical apparatuses for producing language, then it might be the case that different languages have been adapted to the different physical systems that their users make available to them. The claim might be made that certain languages differ from others precisely because of underlying physical differences between their users. Differing characteristics of human bodies could then be said to figure in the explanation of structural differences between languages. This would raise extremely interesting questions of whether language could be characterized independently of these bodily differences.

There are folk views that hold to a fairly direct explanatory connection between bodies and languages. There are views that particular languages have, or lack, certain properties because their native speakers have certain racially specific bodily features. One sometimes hears claims that the tongues of members of certain racial groups are inadequately shaped to deal with certain phonetic challenges. Such claims are invariably wrong, or at any rate inadequately defended; but if they were true, we would have a situation in which systematic physical differences between language users would partially explain systematic differences between languages.

There are in fact differences of the kind I have in mind, differences considerably greater than degrees of lingual agility. I am thinking of the differences between oral languages and manual-visual languages, such as the American Sign Language of the deaf. The physical apparatuses for these two types of communication system are different in obvious and striking ways, offering vastly different potentials for conventionalization. Whether a communication system like ASL, because of these extreme differences, is a "real" language is a question that has troubled otherwise polite and fruitful conversations about the education and language rights of the deaf. Thus this issue clearly has a place in a discussion of the boundaries of linguistics. That is, if we are forced to decide that the physical characteristics of speakers of oral languages figure directly in the explanation of the characteristics of language in general, the manual-visual languages are not real languages. On the other hand, if it is important to us to include them in the set of genuine languages, we need to discover those quintessential properties of Language (with a capital "L") that are independent of modality (yet certainly not general enough to encompass any semiotic system whatever) and then to explain how the modality differences make available different possibilities for conventionalization.

From here on I shall concern myself only with the familiar oral languages, but the serious issue raised about the character of manual-visual languages cannot be lost sight of in the larger picture.

8

British and American traditions of phonemic representation have differed with respect to the size of the rank within which the criteria for linguistic-phonological representations were to be formulated. In the British tradition, it tended to be that of the simple word;[9] in the American tradition, it was the utterance, variously defined. In the general British view, phonetic phenomena observable at word boundaries had to be thought of as belonging to a separate realm, not to phonemic analysis as such; the relation of a phonemic representation to a (for the most part, unexplored) representation of sentence phonology had to be thought of as internal-regular. American phonetic theorists, by contrast, developed various notions of phonemic junctures, having the twin advantages of (1) making it unnecessary to define the rank-size concept "word," and (2) allowing a place for internal sandhi phenomena in units that were clearly of word size. In the American scheme, then, a level of representation of word phonology, if that could be defined, had to have a part-to-whole relation to a representation of sentence phonology.

The consequences of these differences extend further still, in particular to questions of the interdefinability of elements of different levels. In the British tradition, prior identification of words made up part of the criteria for the phonemic level. In the American tradition, by contrast, phonological conditions were briefly thought of as essential to the correct definition of words.

9

A still different issue at the speech end has to do with the proper understanding of the relation between slow and fast speech. The question is: Should slow and fast speech each be described as variant phonological systems for the language? If so, are there just these two, or could there be more than two? If there can be more than two, is the number determinate? Or should we provide a single phonological system including all such variants? Or should we describe a kind of idealized maximally articulated speech style such that fast speech can be seen as derived from an idealized representation by means of a system of optional tempo rules?

There is an awkwardness in formulating these questions within my conceptual framework. Do we want to say that the record of the full set of representations of a fast-speech utterance contains a representation of a slow-speech version of that same utterance?

It is generally assumed that fast speech is derivable from (representations of) slow speech via processes of fusion, neutralization, and omission. Certainly nobody could propose a relationship in the opposite direction by which, for example, the maximally articulated version of "Did you eat yet?" can be derived by regular rules from [jiče?]. But the linking rules cannot be completely regular. In particular, such rules must take into account that fixed expressions have been subject to more exuberant kinds of phonetic play than other expressions, so that the mapping process must take such separate conventionalizations into account. (The style that allows "g'bye" for "good-bye" does not allow "g'boy" for "good boy.")

10

Among the various levels of phonic representations for given utterances, we have the problem of deciding on the nature of the relationship between word and sentence phonology, between phonological representations with and without prosodic features (in languages like English in which prosodic features do not have to be thought of as entering into the form of lexical items), and between representations of slow- and fast-speech versions of what is morphosyntactically the same text.

A different order of question arises when we consider possible explanatory links between phonological and nonphonological levels of representation. A clear problem exists with respect to the relative independence of phonology and morphology. We can recognize first of all a hierarchical relationship between phonemic and morpheme-alternant representations, and a taxonomic ("categorial") relationship between morpheme-alternant and morphemic representations. But, for English at least, it appears that there are more complicated relationships among these levels as well. For example, there are clear explanatory links between the phonotactic rules that constrain the possible structures of phonological representations, and the mapping between morphemic and morpheme-alternant representations – as is seen in the fact that many processes of allomorphy appear to be adaptations to English syllable structure. But there are also connections between morphotactic and phonotactic rules, as evidenced by the fact that some syllable-final sequences ending in /t/ or /d/, or /s/ or /z/, are possible only when that closing element represents a suffix of tense, number, or agreement.

11

So far I have been talking mainly about the speech end of communication. I now turn to the non-speech end, the "mental" end, if I can call it that, where we deal with meaning, conceptualization, expression, the transmission of messages.

The raw data at the speech end consisted of observations about physiological, acoustic, and perceptual events and experiences – observations from out of which various kinds of abstractions were required for sorting out the distinct levels of explanation. At the non-speech end the raw data, if we can call them that, are observations about the course of specific communication acts – observations about the intentions of the speakers and the comprehension of the hearers. One way or another, most directly of course when we ourselves are speakers or hearers, we observe something about what people have in mind when they talk, what they actually say, and how what they say gets understood.

At the this end, too, there are multiple sources of explanation for the data we observe. One dividing line, easy to state in principle but not always easy to find in real life, involves the familiar Chomskyan idealization of a language user not subject to failures of planning or execution; it is through this idealization that we have learned to recognize a difference between competence and performance. We can surely assume that whatever is orderly in communication, and that is to be accounted for by a science of language, should not include cases in which the speaker fails to express himself adequately because of interruption, memory failure, or planning failure, or cases in which the hearer fails to understand because of inattention, ignorance, or memory or process slippage. Here the difference between ideal and real-life communication is to be accounted for, at least partly, by considerations that fall outside the explanatory scope of a science of language.

I assume that, in principle, there is no room for controversy here as long as we acknowledge that your ability to understand me when I do not express myself well – and my tendency to misunderstand you even when you express your ideas perfectly – do not depend on principles that are not present when the process goes smoothly at both ends.

Not at all easy to exclude from the proper science of language are areas in which it looks as if what is going on should be explained by the assumptions of the communicating partners about what the world is like (including their assumptions of mutual rationality and cooperation among the communication participants), plus their informal knowledge of the principles of rhetoric or logic – or else it might be explained by what Schank and Abelson call informal psychology and informal physics[10] – or by what some workers call perceptual strategies.[11] All of these play a role in explaining some parts of communication behavior, but the nature of their position in the layering of linguistic representations is often a matter of serious dispute.

As with questions in the phonology area, there are likewise continuing disagreements in the non-speech end about matters that everyone agrees are clearly within the linguistics proper:

- What kinds of information should be assigned to the lexicon, as distinguished from the grammar proper?
- Do word-formation principles need to be stated independently of syntax?
- Are certain irregularities best stated as constraints on rules (hence, as information about those rules) – or as constraints on the behavior of specific lexical or phrasal items (hence, as information about those items)?

12

A simple and familiar kind of example can be introduced to make the case that questions of internal and external boundaries are

closely related. In early generativist work, two sources of explanation were introduced for native speaker judgments about the grammaticality and meaningfulness of sentences. These sources were
taken to be the internalized rule systems called *syntax* and
semantics. Roughly, syntax explained which linguistic products
speakers were capable of constructing by virtue of their linguistic
knowledge alone. This included, of course, infinitely many potential utterances that nobody would ever have the occasion or the
patience to produce. Semantics expressed, in some abstract way,
what it was that these syntactically constructed objects could be
used to communicate or express. The two systems were thought of
as analogous to the sets of a formal mathematical system – one for
forming well-formed formulas, the other for evaluating them. In
roughly the same way that only well-formed algebraic equations
could be evaluated as true or false, only grammatical – syntactically
well-formed – sentences could be taken as candidates for objects to
which semantic interpretations could be assigned.

In principle, this kind of fit between two levels of representation
seemed reasonable enough; but the principle is hard to pin down
when we are making decisions about borderline cases. A troublesome kind of example from the outset was a sentence like *Jimmy's
stories amused the doorknob.*

There are two facts connected with this sentence that need to be
assigned their separate places. One fact is that the sentence is in
some way bizarre, and that this bizarreness has something to do
with the wrongness of the fit between the verb *amuse* and its direct
object *the doorknob*. The second is that the sentence can indeed be
given some kind of interpretation; that is, it enjoys a kind of semantic coherence that the same string of words read backwards
cannot enjoy. (Both of these facts are vague and intuitive in the
extreme, but it is the purpose of a theory of language to make them
less so.)

The first generativist interpretation given to sentences of this type
was that they were not English sentences at all. The reason we
perceived the sentence as bizarre, then, is that we know the syntactic rules of English, and we know that those rules are incapable of
producing the sentence just encountered. If we want to account for
the interpretability of that sentence in spite of its oddity, we need
to appeal to some auxiliary theory or theories – in particular, a
theory of semi-sentences, a theory of the ability to produce approximations to English, and a theory that can account for our ability to
assign semantic interpretations to approximations of English sentences. That the proposed existence of such a theory was not

altogether far-fetched, the argument went, is seen from the fact that such a theory is needed to account for metaphor anyway.[12]

On this first accounting, then, the *oddity* of the sentence was accounted for by a theory of syntax; its *interpretability* fell in the domain of some auxiliary theory.

The solution required a syntax that systematically excluded sentences exhibiting the kind of selectional mismatch we find here. Verbs of the kind represented by *amuse* must be syntactically marked as requiring for their direct objects nouns taken from a syntactic class that does not include the noun *doorknob*.

The data, of course, do not in any way dictate that this is the correct solution. We could easily take the next step and say that the sentence is syntactically impeccable, and then offer a semantic explanation of its oddity, that explanation possibly taking the form that the verb *amuse* is semantically characterized as requiring a particular semantic class of direct objects, namely a noun phrase that can designate objects capable of certain cognitive experiences, and that the noun *doorknob* falls short of such conditions.

In this second solution, the *oddity* of the sentence is accounted for by the semantic component; the fact that it is not gibberish but has a form to which semantic rules can be applied is accounted for by the syntax. What is needed now is an account of its *interpretability*. One way of providing that would be to appeal to an auxiliary theory of language interpretation that *used* the semantic rules of a linguistic description for imposing an interpretation on sentences that were technically ill-formed. Another would be to construe a semantic theory in the first place in such a way that its role is to impose an interpretation rather than merely to accept or reject sentences according to their semantic well-formedness. In the former case, the *oddity* of the sentence is accounted for by the semantics, its *interpretability* by the auxiliary theory. In the latter case, both the *oddity* and *interpretability* of the sentence fall within the explanatory scope of a properly constructed semantic theory.

A third possible solution to the problem of the doorknob sentence is that it is both syntactically and semantically impeccable, and that its oddity consists entirely in our belief that anybody who could say this sentence in good faith must have a picture of the world that differs from our own in certain fairly interesting ways. In this third interpretation, a *linguistic* account of English contains no principles according to which the *oddity* judgment can be explained. The interpretability judgment, however, is straightforward. The sentence tells us that the doorknob in question got a certain kind of enjoyment out of hearing Jimmy's stories. In fact, we have to say that it is only by virtue of identifying precisely what the sentence could mean that its interpreter is able to figure out why what it says is so strange.

First we thought the bizarreness judgment was to be explained by the syntax. Then we turned it over to the semantics. In the end we took it away from the semantics too. Are we now ready to decide that it doesn't belong to linguistics at all?

Let us assume that we have two levels of representation for each meaningful utterance: *semantic* and *cognitive*. The semantic representation of our doorknob sentence is the one according to which it is seen as communicating something meaningful about a particular doorknob. The cognitive representation is the one that recognized that the utterance either is playful or assumes something unusual about the doorknob.

What, then, should be the nature of the relationships between the semantic and cognitive representations? Presumably we ought to be able to expect an external-regular relationship since the semantic representation is paired with both the context of situation and the background of beliefs, institutions, and practices shared by the speaker and the hearers.

We need to ask two crucial questions at this point. First, can the principles by which contextual information and semantic representations are integrated to construct cognitive representations be properly studied within a science of language? Second, does the final correct theory of language actually need a level of semantic representation distinct from the syntactic representations at one end and the cognitive representations at the other? My own suspicion is that there is probably no need for a level of semantic representation, but that if there is its role in determining the cognitive representation (of an ideal interpreter) should be regarded as studiable within linguistics, even if the external *facts* that contribute to that determination are not themselves facts that clearly belong to (that is, get explained by) the science of language.

No sensible person would claim that the fact about the deprived cognitive capacities of doorknobs needs to be incorporated into a theory of language – that is, to be explained by the principles of such a theory. But there may be a way of viewing the semantic end of a science of language as a system or apparatus that acknowledges facts, beliefs, models of the world, that are not themselves linguistic, and that provides interpretative principles that appeal to or build on such facts and beliefs. Workers in artificial intelligence, where this approach has been most explicitly developed, are not likely to claim that what they are doing is linguistics, but since some of them do claim that after they have done what they do there is nothing left that could be called linguistics, they are at least claiming that there is no line to be drawn between semantic and cognitive representations.[13] I wish to explore the value of that suggestions for linguistics.

13

Two traditions of semantics have arisen within, or have impinged on, linguistics: *ethnographic* and *formal*. In ethnographic semantics, a distinction between semantic and cognitive representations could not naturally occur, since that discipline looks at the phenomena of the world, or the life and institutions of a particular cultural group, and asks how the stuff of that world gets labeled, classified, described, and talked about by linguistic means. It would not make sense to ask an anthropologist who has just told us that a particular genus of edible berries has been given a particular name by the group being studied what the word means in independence of its fit with this botanical domain. In the tradition of ethnographic, or "lexical," semantics, such a question could not occur.

It is my belief that many of the words we use are like the names of things we know and have meanings that cannot really be talked about independently of reference to that knowledge. Some ideas, from what is coming to be called "frame semantics," seem most compatible with the point of view I have in mind. The idea is that words are learned and understood against the background of a particular topic or context, and that any use of them necessarily brings in associations with those contexts. One can speak of such an association with reference to a framing of the situation, and the framing contributes to the interpreter's construction of the world of the text.

To know the meaning of a word is necessarily to have access to at least some of the details of the associated schematization. The noun *land* does not simply designate the dry part of the earth's surface (in one of its meanings); it designates that part from the point of view of a schematization that divides land from sea. The noun *ground,* by contrast, also designates the earth's dry surface (in one of its meanings), but this time as part of a schematization that separates the earth from the air above it. Thus *being on land* evokes a context in which it is relevant to contrast being on land with being at sea, and hence suggests a stage in a sea voyage, a moment in the life of an amphibious animal, or the like, whereas *being on the ground* suggests a contrast with being in the air, and thus evokes a scene of an interrupted air trip, or of an alighted bird, or the like. Each of these expressions is, and is perceived as, a member of a particular integrated set of expressions whose meaning can be correctly perceived only by those familiar with the larger schematization of which the element is a part. It is common in linguistic semantics to speak of the associated *words* as defining a language-internal structure of some kind, whose elements are said to be paradigmatically opposed to each other by means of a system of contrasts and relations that can be fully stated independently of contact with any world. But that, it seems to me, is misleading.

For words that can be thus described, we can say that a word designates a point in a field – a point that in principle cannot be separated from its field. Some extreme statements of the difference between the linguistic meaning of a word and encyclopedic information about what the word designates assume that this separation is an abstraction essential to the proper determination of the boundaries of linguistics.[14]

Some time ago I had occasion to realize that I didn't know how to use the word *steeplechase*. I didn't know whether it was

- the name of a kind of place where a certain kind of horse racing takes places;
- the name of a sport (so that I could say *I enjoy steeplechase.*);
- the name of a particular contest within this sport (so that one could say *The final steeplechase of the day is about to begin.*);
- the name of the kind of horse that is trained to race in the way we associate with the concept of steeplechase – with hedges, wall, and ditches as obstacles.

I think I completely understood the brute and institutional facts underlying the meaning of the word, but I didn't know how the word "keyed" into the schema. I could allow myself to say that I knew the background against which the word was defined, but I didn't know what the word meant. I then wondered whether it would be possible to meet my counterpart, somebody who knew exactly what the word meant but was unfamiliar with the background of practices that motivated the existence of the word. It seems to me that such a person could not possibly exist.

14

I have been trying to think of an example in which it would be particularly difficult to draw a distinction between meaning proper and context of use, and one that I suggest works is *The menfolk returned at sundown.* It seems to me that the word menfolk is used to isolate adult males as a group from females and children in a human setting involving the activities of whole families. A natural setting for the sentence, then, would be one in which the men in a village went off for the day's fishing in the morning and returned to their families at the day's end.

A question we need to ask is whether such a sentence can be used appropriately in settings that depart from the one suggested by the word's primary schematization, and another is whether, independently of judgments of appropriateness, the sentence can be said to have a truth value in such alien settings. Consider an all-male community of workers on the Alaskan pipeline and a situation in which the workers returned to their dormitories at sundown. Clearly nobody would actually *use* the sentence in such a context, but what should you say if asked whether that sentence in that situation was *true?* A view of semantics that makes a sharp distinction between meaning and context of use would have to be able to answer that question one way or another, I believe. An ethnographic semantics view, by contrast, would simply allow us to say that the question of truth can't occur; the sentence has not been used in a situation in which it could directly convey anything that was either true or false.

Suppose, nevertheless, that we found somebody willing to say this sentence in the all-male community context described, and suppose too that people were able to interpret that sentence as meaning that the workers returned to their dormitories. We now have to deal with these facts: one, the sentence can be given an interpretation; two, the sentence is used inappropriately. A formal semantics view would have it that its interpretability is determined in a straightforward way by the theory of semantics for the language, but that judgments about its appropriateness are to be interpreted by a theory of usage, or register, or pragmatics. The ethnographic semantics account would see the bizarreness of the sentence in context as explained by a theory of semantics, since the background required by the meaning of *menfolk* is wrong. It would account for the interpretability of the sentence in spite of the framing failure as involving either some kind of construal principles of the sort needed for a theory of metaphor, *or* the recognition of an artificial sublanguage derived from English whose semantic principles have been deliberately limited to those congenial to the formulation of certain logical relationships.

15

Another important boundary issue for semantics centers on the contribution to linguistic semantics of the work of such scholars as Paul Grice and Oswald Ducrot.[15] In assessing and interpreting the data of speech comprehension, we have to keep in mind at least two sources of information: one the internally represented meanings of the lexical and grammatical forms at our disposal, the other a way of reasoning about why people say what they do. In Grice's case, this takes the form of principles of conversational cooperation plus a method for interpreting both adherence to and departure from these principles. In Ducrot's case, it takes the form of a series of laws of discourse.

Not many years ago, I kept at my fingertips a fine set of examples that I brought out for display whenever I wanted to impress people with the detail and richness of a native speaker's semantic competence. One of my favorites came from philosopher Stanley Cavell's discussion of the adverb *voluntarily*.[16] He suggested, and for many years I was only too willing to believe, that part of the meaning of *voluntarily* was that there was something fishy about what was being talked about in the predicate that the adverb modified. The adverb carried with it information about the type of event or situation that it could be used to qualify, and this quite independently of what the use of the adverb directly communicated. One of his examples was *Do you dress that way voluntarily?* Another example might be *English people drink warm beer voluntarily.*

Influenced by Grice and Ducrot, today's semanticist would be more likely to say that we should not be misled by an ability to distinguish stages in the comprehension process. Though we can indeed recognize an assumption of fishiness in these utterances, we are nowadays more likely to believe that it comes not from semantic information contained in the sentence but from our assumptions about why the speaker might question whether an action was performed voluntarily or under duress. If there wasn't something fishy about the action in the first place, such a question would be pointless. A fact once thought of as belonging to lexical semantics got taken over by a theory of rhetoric.

James McCawley has recently suggested applying Gricean principles to settle a long-standing issue about the putative observation that no two expressions can mean exactly the same thing, in particular that a word cannot mean the same thing as any of its proposed definitions. On the face of it, it should seem reasonable to say that *kill* means nothing more or less than "cause to die"; yet sentences in which these proposed equivalents are substituted for each other persist in giving different impressions. One possibility is that the proposed definition is simply wrong and that, with a little work, we should be able to come up with one that performs as a true definition ought to perform. A second possibility is that perfect defining paraphrases will never be found, simply because in principle no two expressions ever will or ever could mean the same thing. The doctrine expresses a kind of faith in the efficiency of language: a language would never allow itself to have different expressions unless it had different meanings to express with them.

The solution that McCawley favors is that a word and a phrase expressing its semantic analysis might indeed mean the same thing, but speakers can be assumed to have good reasons for choosing the more analytic expression when a simple and well-known word could have been used just as well. Such a choice can be taken as amounting to a violation of a Gricean obscurity-avoidance maxim and must therefore be seen as an attempt to convey some special impression. To put it intuitively, if a concept has been "lexicalized," that must be because it defines a category within a particular kind of framework; ignoring the lexicalization in favor of a paraphrase can be heard as a denial of the relevance of the categorizing framework.[17] ("I admit that what I did caused Smith's death." – "Are you then telling the court that you killed Smith?" – "No, that's not what I said at all.")

Once again we have our familiar situation of looking at two facts and trying to figure out which part of the explanatory apparatus of our science can be called upon to explain each. One fact is our judgment that *kill* and *cause to die* mean essentially, if not exactly, the same thing. The second is that sentences in which the two are interchanged seem to convey slightly different messages. The two non-Gricean views agree in rejecting the first fact, attributing the judgment to a misperception of the sort that is not surprising in naive native speakers. The first of these views accepts the possibility that a more accurate defining paraphrase can eventually be found; the second insists that there is at best similarity, never identity, to be found between two expressions. The Gricean view was that the synonymy judgment was a matter of semantics, and therefore clearly a part of linguistics; and that the subtle-difference judgment is to be explained with respect to people's sensitivity to the effect of rhetorical choices.

The Gricean view I have just characterized is compatible with the assumption that there is a difference between a level of semantic representation (the level on which *kill* and *cause to die* mean the same thing) and a level on which belief structures, knowledge of context, and rhetorical selections have made their influence felt, a level that is (or is closely related to) the level of cognitive representation discussed earlier.

I think the "convincingness" of the *kill* case needs to be countered with examples that are less abstract and general purpose. As I said earlier, in many cases a full description of lexical meaning requires some sort of schematic understanding of the background or frame of reference within which a particular cognitive category has been assigned a lexical form. The point can be made more strongly with *murder* than with *kill*. I believe there is no way to capture the meaning of the word *murder* without presenting (or taking for granted) the background of values and institutional knowledge within which it makes sense to categorize certain (but not all) actions of taking life as *murder*. In short, for some words it may indeed be impossible to provide a complete linguistic paraphrase with which the Gricean solution could even be tried out. I see a difference between *explaining* what something means and *presenting* what it means.

16

Many of my points have been that, in opposition to the view that there is a separate representation of semantic structure that can be abstracted away from general features of context and topic, respect should be given to an alternative view that locates meaning fairly directly with potential context. Scholars who wish to maintain the separate abstract semantic level are also motivated to keep that level as pure and simple as possible – uncluttered, in particular, with such troublesome notions as *presuppositions*. I have only the shallowest understanding of all the issues connected with presuppositions, but there is one on which the use of our fact-parceling strategy can be demonstrated once again. I have in mind the arguments for and against reliance on the so-called "negation test" for presuppositions – which I think fails to cover all cases of what one might want to call presuppositions, but I suspect that certain kinds of arguments against the test deserve critical examination.

The negation test, intended to distinguish logical entailment from presupposition, works like this. If P either entails or presupposes Q, then whenever P is true, Q is also true. But if P entails Q, not-P no longer commits one to the truth of Q. If P presupposes Q, not-P continues to commit one to the truth of Q.

Let me use the vague word "impression" for what can be understood from a statement. From the sentence *Lucille made John read the letter,* we get two impressions: that John read some specified letter, and that Lucille somehow forced John to read it. From the sentence *John regretted reading the letter,* once again we get two impressions: that John read the letter, and that John felt bad about having read it.

Now consider putting each of these sentences under negation. With *Lucille didn't make John read the letter,* we form the impression that Lucille didn't force John to read the letter, but we are left opinionless about whether John read the letter or not. With *John didn't regret reading the letter,* the proposition about John's feeling bad after reading the letter is denied, but we are still left with the impression that he did read the letter.

Inferences that can be drawn from an affirmative sentence and that survive when that sentence is replaced by its negative counterpart, the argument goes, are the presuppositions of that sentence.

Ruth Kempson has questioned this distinction.[18] She instead bases a different kind of argument on judgments of contradiction and interpretability. Let us consider the results of appending the sentence *In fact, he didn't read the letter* to each of our four sentences.[19] First, the two affirmative sentences:

Lucille made John read the letter. In fact, he didn't read the letter.
John regretted reading the letter. In fact, he didn't read the letter.

The first of these two-sentence texts contains a contradiction, since the second sentence denies what the first sentence asserts by entailment. The second text too presents a contradiction. A presuppositionist would characterize the contradiction by saying that what the first sentence presupposes, the second sentence denies. One who denies a distinction between entailment and presupposition could just as happily see both texts as presenting contradictions of the same type.

Next look at the two negative sentences with the appended sentence. In the first case, we get

Lucille didn't make John read the letter. In fact, John didn't read the letter.

There is nothing wrong with this text at all, just as you would expect if the relation we have been examining is one of entailment. But now the critical text:

> John didn't regret reading the letter. In fact, he didn't read the letter.

This text can be read as communicating the information that John, who was innocent of having read the letter, did not − because he could not − feel bad about it.

When a sentence is negated, its entailments are neither affirmed nor denied. Thus, if we make both the *make* sentence and the *regret* sentence simple matters of entailment, everything we have seen is automatically explained, and no distinction remains between entailment and presupposition.

There is a problem with this last two-sentence text, however, and this is where Kempson and the presuppositionists assign facts to different theoretical domains. The little text,

> John didn't regret reading the letter. In fact, he didn't read the letter.

elicits two judgments. First, it is interpretable in the way Kempson suggests. Second, it is definitely an odd thing to say. The theoretical dispute then concerns whether it is the oddity of the text or its interpretability that belongs to the realm of semantics. To Kempson, its *interpretability* is a matter of semantics, requiring nothing more than the well-established and independently-motivated theory of logical entailment; its *oddity* is to be accounted for by some auxiliary theory such as the theory of Gricean implicatures. (It is not relevant, nor informative, to deny feelings of regret for deeds one has not done.) For the presuppositionists, on the other hand, it is its *oddity* that is to be explained by semantic theory; its *interpretability* requires some presuppositions: the text is odd because the second sentence denies what the first sentence presupposes. Its interpretability makes it necessary to analyze the first sentence as a kind of metalinguistic statement, possibly a correction of what some previous speaker has said. Under that interpretation, the extra emphasis given to the word *regret* in the most natural rendering of the text would be explained. The sentence can be taken as a comment on the inappropriateness of the word *regret* in that context, something that could be signaled graphically by putting quotation marks around the word.[20]

Once again we have two facts such that putting either one in semantics requires putting the other somewhere else. One solution seems to make semantics simpler and better behaved than the other does. But it is no easy job to figure out which solution looks better for the whole theory. The presuppositionist view is more compatible with the position I have been taking: words have meanings and uses that can only be properly understood against some motivating background. The word *regret* "names" a part of a particular kind of "script" or "scenario" involving deeds and feelings about one's own deeds. The presuppositionist view recognizes that its meaning cannot be divorced from its background.

17

The problems I have looked at so far have been big and important ones, I think, but they pale before the ones I am going to turn to next.

It is commonly assumed in linguistics that, as a matter of methodological privilege, we can treat a speaker's competence in a language as a coherent, self-contained system with properties that can be considered, in principle, at a moment in time. This is the idealization of the *synchronic slice.* According to it, we sometimes allow ourselves to say that variation consists in a speaker's having access to more than one such complete and coherent system, and to say that language change consists in replacing one such system by another, either in the life history of an individual speaker or in the transmission of linguistic systems from one person to another in the changing generations.

A commitment to the methodological necessity of the synchronic slice may force us to take a completely unrealistic picture of linguistic knowledge. In a way, every idealization does that; but this idealization does not easily integrate with other idealizations or sources of explanation in a useful way.

A more realistic view might be one that sees the child's acquisition of linguistic competence as analogous to the work of historical comparative linguistics, working toward the elaboration of a system of representations and rules capable of accounting for the variety of related idiolects that have provided the child's data. Not only does the child's own internalized linguistic system have a time depth, but it must be seen as changing all the time.[21]

The living speaker's internalized "reconstructed language" gives its users more things to say in more life-situations than any known reconstructed "protolanguage" possibly could. But this reconstructed system is likely to have holes, leaks, vaguenesses, and pieces that don't fit together, just as the familiar historically recon- structed languages have.

While a cautious reconstructor of the child's input data would come up with an incomplete system, it is generally assumed that the child automatically imposes a closure or integration on the system it is developing, and that the nature of this integration can be discov- ered by careful elicitation or by noticing the forms of the child's novel utterances. But such assumptions are derived from the method, not from the facts. It could be that novel utterances are on-the-spot solutions to problems, that similarities of such solutions across speakers is evidence for the naturalness of some solutions as compared to others, and that the really considerable variations across speakers with respect to details of syntax and morphology are testimony to the independence of these solutions from speaker to speaker. We may also allow ourselves to question the assump- tion that each speaker has created or reconstructed a language system that exists as an integrated whole, and that many surprising properties of this whole can be revealed by subtle kinds of elicita- tion. We need to ask, at least in many cases, whether the native speaker judgments that come up through such interviews should be seen as existing before the interview and merely being pulled into the open air, or as decisions made on the spot as a result of the interviewing situation and the fact that each person's jerry-built grammar has a lot in common with every other person's jerry-built grammar.

18

Related to the question of the coherence of a synchronic system is the problem of idioms. The central theoretical problem posed by idiomaticity is that of figuring out a way of describing certain forms as being *simultaneously analyzed and unanalyzed* – that is, as simul- taneously having a structure and being learned and used as wholes. An internal grammar with time depth might offer a resolution by attributing to certain semantically unitary words or phrases assump- tions, which in many cases will be historically accurate, about their word- or phrase-formational history. Wrong analyses of idioms give us some of the most interesting data on how this component works. There is pretty good evidence that speakers do assign morphosyntactic structure to idioms even if they have no reason to know anything about their component parts. Long idioms that are (from our point of view) misperceived and misanalyzed tend to be given morphological and syntactic structurings that account perfectly for their prosodic gestalts. That is, they are interpreted as lexical or phrasal structures capable of assigning correct stress patterns in just those cases in which no single lexical form could be given that prosodic rendering.

As William Safire has learned to his profit, it is often amusing to notice phrases that people have misperceived. Children often misperceive because they do not know what is meant by passages they have been asked to memorize. (Just who is the man Richard Stans that so many of us as children mentioned whenever we pledged our allegiance to the flag and to the republic for Richard Stans?) More interesting from a theoretical point of view are such adult misinterpretations as *for all intensive purposes* instead of *for all intents and purposes* or *it'll cost you a nominal egg* for *it'll cost you an arm and a leg.* These expressions are idiomatic; so the meaning of the whole is not a compositional product of the meanings of the parts. The problem is, why, when they are misperceived, they are not merely taken to be long, unanalyzed words.

The answer seems to be that it is only as constructs made up of morphemes and words that they can be pronounced – in particular, that they can be given the correct patternings of stressed and unstressed syllables found in these expressions that are characteristic of English phrases and complex words. A conjunction of two words with *and* generally assigns the phrase stress on the last lexically stressed syllable (*intents and PURposes, an arm and a LEG*). A structure consisting of an adjective followed by a noun, unless the adjective is used contrastively, generally requires that the phrase stress be assigned to the lexical stress on the noun (*intensive PURposes, a nominal EGG*). These expressions have been misperceived and mislearned, but in ways that assign the correct stress pattern. This phenomenon could exist only in a language in which it is perfectly normal for people to use expressions whose meanings did not have straightforward relations to their forms. The result of idiomatization is an inconvenient articulation between the morphosyntactic level and the semantic level, but a convenient and regular kind of relationship between the morphosyntactic level and the phonological level.

One way of viewing the functioning of set expressions and idioms in a language is to assume that one part of the theory-constructing activity in which a language learner engages while learning a language is constructing a history of word- and phrase-formation, something that could usefully be called "folk etymology" were it not that that phrase is used only for etymologies known to be historically wrong. It's not just that speakers *do* this informal etymologizing but that the stress rules of English force them to.

Idiomaticity is a big question for the theory of language. It involves knowing the difference between what we have to know before we can use our language, and what we are able to figure out while we are using it. In particular, it involves questions of the nature of the articulation between morphosyntactic representations on the one hand and semantic or cognitive representations on the other. To be sure, speakers need to know the generative rules that characterize the morphosyntactic representations, and they need to know the compositional semantic rules that relate these to semantic representations. But they also need to know a large number of superimposed conventions governing the meaning, function, and popularity of certain expressions that cannot be sensibly accounted for by these general rules. One could, of course, accept a methodological *commitment* to a compositional or internal-regular relationship between morphosyntactic and semantic representations, mediated only by a lexicon of morphemes and morphemically simple words. Then, however, all the information that troubles scholars about idioms would have to be assigned to the selectional and collocational apparatus of a theory of the lexicon. The resulting analysis, even where it worked, would seem unnatural and unmotivated.

19

All of this leads to another large question. The study of speech communication, or of language, is very different depending on whether, at the communication end, only the decoding direction is taken into consideration, or encoding also. Paul Kiparsky, some years ago, made what seemed to be a reasonable proposal for treating formulaic speech and other fixed expressions within transformational grammar.[22] It went something like this: Some formulaic expressions can be handled within the selectional apparatus of the lexicon, as long as we allow words with particular semantic features. Some will have to be listed in the lexicon as unanalyzed wholes, retried, and used as whole phrases rather than assembled from their constituents. The rest can be safely ignored: their literal meanings are accurately enough determined from the compositional principles of the semantic component, their folkloric base is sufficiently well-known, and their metaphoric base is transparent enough for hearers to be able to figure out what they mean.

It is the excluding third clause which, unlike the others, seems to favor the decoding point of view. Expressions like *bury the hatchet* can generally be understood without explanation, are freely translatable from language to language with their non-literal intentions preserved, and so on. They pose no problem for the decoder (let us say), but what about the encoder? If linguists had taken for granted from the start that the encoding operation also fell naturally within the scope of the linguist's responsibilities – that is, if it was thought that the linguist should have something to say about conventions governing what a speaker can say in particular situations to convey particular meanings – then an argument like Kiparsky's could not carry. There are many expressions whose meanings we can figure out when we encounter them, but which we could not know how to say on our own unless we were familiar with the particular conventions regarding their use. The standard answer is that this kind of knowledge belongs to folklore rather than linguistics, but one wonders how one can know in advance that this is the right attitude to take.

The fact is, not all linguists have made this assumption; so once again we are dealing with a boundary that is drawn in one way by some linguists and in another way by others. The stratificationalists in particular regard the encoding process as an essential part of the whole picture, and so do the large group of Soviet linguists who work on what they call *phraseologisms.*[23]

An attitude toward idioms that seemed reasonable fifteen years ago was that a semantic theory that fails to account for idioms has made the right choice. Idioms are by definition expressions that cannot be accounted for by compositional semantic principles or by the general principles of word formation and phrase formation that serve the language. A description of such a general system therefore has no responsibility to account for the form and meanings of idioms. If we could maintain that position about what we ordinarily think of as idioms, namely the *decoding idioms,* only then would it be self-consistent for us to maintain the same position with respect to *encoding idioms* (to use Adam Makkai's useful distinction).[24]

In the framework of a system of representations and rules linking representations that we have adapted here, we obviously cannot begin by ignoring the encoding aspect. We can certainly assume that in many cases a part of the conveyed meaning of an utterance comes from the interpreter's awareness of whether the speaker chose or avoided the conventional expressions. Since judgments of this kind can be relevant even when the expression is completely semantically transparent, we can see that a full account of the

encoder's knowledge is necessary to a full account of the decoder's
abilities.

20

It is common to propose a distinction between sentence meaning
and utterance meaning. An implicit instrumental or internal-regular
relation between the two levels is assumed to be capable of associating the semantic structure of a sentence to a particular instance of
the sentence's use and of constructing its literal meaning out of
that. We can speak of this as an anchoring operation by which, for
example, indexical elements are assigned their referents. We can
speak of sentence meaning as meaning in a zero context, as in the
case of the famous Katz and Fodor anonymous letter,[25] or of a
neutral context in some more recent writings. The assumption here
is that the sentence has a well-defined meaning that can be built on
by using material taken from the context of its use.

But what if we find cases in which the context not only provides a
disambiguating or an anchoring function, but also is capable of
providing the information for achieving a primary semantic integration in the first place?

It is generally assumed that any interpretable sentence has a literal
meaning on which its contexted meaning can be built. But maybe
there are sentences that have *no* coherent literal meaning at all, that
is, sentences requiring a context for their semantic interpretation
even to get started? I have in mind the kind of expression that
some people have called *contextuals,* as discussed in work by Geof-
frey Nunberg, Herb and Eve Clark, Paul Kay, Karl Zimmer, and
Pamela Downing.[26] If the customer who has ordered a ham sandwich is referred to by the waitress as the *ham sandwich* (Nunberg's
example), if the one tour bus in a multi-bus tour that is scheduled
to stop at a pumpkin farm is known briefly as the *pumpkin bus*
(Zimmer's example), it might seem reasonable for us to say that
these sentences do not *have* literal meanings outside of their context
of use. In the one case, of course, we could *classify* what happens
as *pragmatic metonymy,*[27] since it uses something associated with a
person to refer to that person, and in the other case we could allow
ourselves to appeal to the almost unrestricted ways in which elements in a noun compound can be related to each other. But
somehow we need to bring into our account of language the fact
that code-changing as well as code-exploiting creativity is an important part of linguistic competence, and that perhaps *ad hoc* name
creating occurs in everyday language on a large scale. To under-

stand a meaning, we have seen, requires understanding the contextual background within which that meaning has been codified. The difference between meanings that exist in advance and those that get created on the run is the difference between contexts known in advance and contexts presented to us as we go.

If the name-creating of the kinds just illustrated were made explicit – that is, if it were accompanied by announcements of the form *When I say 'ham sandwich'* (or *'pumpkin bus')*, *I will be referring to such-and-such* – then we would not think of informal name-creating as a part of semantic competence as such, but would include it in an auxiliary theory of metalinguistic competence. But in these and many other cases we are dealing with a class of expressions that, as I see it, have no literal meanings, are not being used metaphorically, and have no conventionalized meanings associated with them, but are nevertheless immediately and perfectly understood by everyone engaged in the situation in which they are produced. If we can recognize that the ability to produce and understand such expressions is a semantic skill, and if as I suspect contextuals play a very large role in everyday discourse, then it looks as if semantic theory will have to take into its scope the principles by which contexts figure in informal naming.

21

In all of the cases we have looked at that touch on the meanings of utterances, it has been clear that a theory of language needs the means for relating either morphosyntactic or cognitive representations with the use of contextual information of one sort or another. On several occasions we found ourselves asking whether we need, in addition to these two, an intervening level of semantic representations. And with the last set of examples we were concerned not with whether we *need* semantic representations, but with whether we can *have* them.

It is my opinion that the final correct theory of the semantics of ordinary language will find no need for a level of semantic representation, that the everyday notion of meaning is more naturally associated with elements of cognitive representations, and that the concept of semantics can be limited to notions of the mapping between forms and meanings.

For a semantic-representation-free theory of language to work, we will have to recognize a level of representation that provides syntactically structured lexical material together with semantic information that can be associated with particular lexical items, phrasal items (where necessary), and particular syntactic forms (where necessary). This representation, together with information from the context of use, can be used to construct a cognitive representation. There may be no need, in other words, to require that compositional processes be applied to such a representation independently of the context in order to construct a mediating representation that could correspond to *the* context-free meaning of the sentence.

The position of formal semantics within such a theory is problematical, of course. I repeat my suggestion that formal semantics takes as its subject matter a language that is *derived from* a natural language like English; that its formal properties are selected for reasons very different from those which concern the ethnographic semanticist; and that by successive modifications and enrichments it can be made to look more and more like the source language.

I am by no means confident that the position I have taken is the correct one to take. But after hearing for so many years that those of us who have been concerned with the study of language as it is engaged in everyday acting and thinking are working in the periphery of linguistics rather than in its core, I wanted to hear what it would sound like to say it the other way around.

22

Imagine with me that you and I have inherited a very large house and a great deal of furniture, paintings, carpets, appliances, etc., with which we can furnish it. We take the sheets off some of the furniture, unroll some of the carpets, and set to work. We begin by clearing out one room and finding furniture that seems to fit in it pretty well. Then we clear out another room, assemble some more furnishings, and decide to decorate it, too. We may find, while getting this second room ready, that one of the pieces we put in the original room looks better in this second room, and maybe we've found another piece or two that go well in the first room in its place.

As we continue decorating and furnishing the rooms of the house, we continue finding that, with each new room and each new collection of furnishings we uncover, the arrangements we made for the earlier rooms can be changed.

For a long time we live comfortably and conveniently in this house, and what's more, we feel fairly free to move things around now and then to suit our changing fancy, or to satisfy our differing tastes. We enjoy this flexibility because this is a very large house and we have managed to keep several rooms unused. Sometimes you take my two favorite chairs out of the parlor and put them into one of the storage rooms, and then move your favorite sofa from the living room into the parlor. When it's my turn to be satisfied with the decor, I drag the two chairs out of the storage room to bring to the parlor, put your sofa into storage, and ask you to find something else to take its place in the living room.

The main reason we enjoy this flexibility is that we don't care what we put into the storage rooms. But now suppose the day comes when we decide to put the whole house in order, including those hitherto unused rooms that we've only been using to get unwanted objects out of the way. It now makes a difference which paintings and chairs and rugs get put into those rooms, because they have to have a consistent and pleasing decor too. Now our decisions become more constrained. We can still have disagreements now and then, but we have by no means the same flexibility that we had when we had rooms we never used except to get things out of the way. We may even find that, in order to get the whole house furnished to our liking, we will have to remove a wall here and there, or subdivide some of the larger rooms, or even admit that some of the furniture we own doesn't fit in our house at all.

The parable isn't over yet. One day it occurs to us to draw the drapes! For the first time we notice the garden, the yard, and the mountains in the distance. Suddenly the decor in some of the outer rooms seems wrong. We now have to rearrange things to take into account the sunlight coming in the windows, we have to provide access to the garden, and so on. What our house looks like has to depend somewhat on what the surrounding world looks like.

I am talking about facts, not furniture, and about principles of explanation, not rooms and gardens. The house of language that we live in is a large house, with many rooms. We do not know yet how many rooms we have, or exactly what kinds of furnishings we will find. Until the house is completely explored and furnished, we need to be tolerant of competing plans for furnishing the small number of rooms we spend most of our time living in.

REFERENCES

1. See, for example, Bloch's and Trager's reasons for excluding meaning from linguistic inquiry [*Outline of Linguistic Analysis*. Baltimore: Linguistic Society of America, at the Waverly Press, 1942, p. 6], as well as Chomsky's differently motivated circumscription of "core grammar" [*Lectures in Government and Binding: The Pisa Lectures*. Dordrecht: Foris, 1982].

2. See the discussion of the effect of generative linguistics on psycholinguistic research in J. Greene, *Psycholinguistics*. Harmondsworth: Penquin, 1972.

3. One important "wide circle" linguist is Dell Hymes, whose "ethnographic" position is laid out most clearly in *Foundations in Sociolinguistics: An Ethnographic Approach.* Philadelphia: University of Pennsylvania Press, 1974.

    Dwight Bolinger's "wide circle" view of meaning is presented in *Meaning and Form.* London: Longmans, 1977.

    Perhaps the strongest statement favoring a widening of the field of linguistics is the "Preamble" to the Ablex *Language and Being* series by G.P. Lakoff and J.R. Ross [first appearance in *The Imagination of Reality: Essays in Southeast Asian Coherence Systems,* A.L. Becker and A.A. Yengoyan, eds. Norwood: Ablex, 1979, vii-viii.]

4. The language scientist best known for his independence from mainstream linguistics is perhaps Roger Schank. Numerous statements of this independence can be found in his *Conceptual Information Processing.* Amsterdam: North Holland, 1975.

5. Michael A.K. Halliday. "Categories of the theory of grammar," *Word* **17** (1961): 241-292.

6. See the section on "pitch morphemes" and "superfixes" in the "Morphemics" chapter of A.A. Hill, *Introduction to Linguistic Structures from Sound to Sentence in English.* New York: Harcourt, Brace and Co., 1958.

7. See, for example, M. Halle and S.J. Keyser, *English Stress: its Form, its Growth, its Role in Verse.* New York: Harper and Row, 1971.

8. One branch of linguistics that has most deliberately maintained a continuity view of sentence structure and discourse structure is the tagmemics school, especially under the hand of Robert Longacre. See, for example, Longacre, *Discourse Grammar.* Arlington, TX: Summer Institute of Linguistics, 1976, Part I, pp. 1-8.

9. See J.R. Firth, "The Technique of Semantics" [in *Transactions of the Philological Society,* 1935; reprinted in *Papers in Linguistics: 1934-1951,* London, 1957, pp. 7-33); but note also Trubetzkoy's claims concerning "Wortphonologie" [*Anleitung zu phonologischen Beschreibungen,* Gottingen].

10. See R. Schank and R. Abelson, *Scripts, Plans, Goals, and Understanding.* Hillsdale: Lawrence Erlbaum, 1977.

11. For representative statements on the role of perceptive strategies in limiting the explanatory scope of linguistics proper, see

    T.G. Bever, "The Influence of Speech Performance on Linguistic Structures." In *Advances in Psycholinguistics,* G.B. Flores-d'Arcais and W.J.M. Levelt, eds. Amsterdam: North Holland, 1970.

    D.T. Langendoen, "A Case of Apparent Ungrammaticality." In *An Integrated Theory of Linguistic Ability,* T.G. Bever, J.J. Katz, and D.T. Langendoen, eds. New York: Thomas Y. Crowell, 1976, pp. 183-193.

12. For an early statement on the semantic interpretation of ill-formed sentences, see J.J. Katz, "Semi-sentences." In *The Structure of Language: Readings in the Philosophy of Language,* J.J. Katz and J.A. Fodor, eds. Englewood Cliffs: Prentice-Hall, 1964, pp. 400-416.

13. This is certainly true of work using "Conceptual Dependency," as in R. Schank, "Identification of Conceptualizations Underlying Natural Language" [in *Computer Models of Thought and Language,* R. Schank and K.M. Colby, eds. San Francisco: W.H. Freeman, 1973] and in Schank, *Conceptual Information Processing.*

14. For a recent statement about this distinction, see the beginners' semantics textbook [J.R. Hurford and B. Heasley, *Semantics: A Coursebook*. Cambridge: Cambridge University Press, 1983], where we find (p. 184) the following:

> The linguistic semanticist is interested in the meanings of words and not in non-linguistic facts about the world. Correspondingly, he attempts to make a strict demarcation between a dictionary and an encyclopedia. ...
> A DICTIONARY describes the sense of predicates.
> An ENCYCLOPEDIA contains factual information of a variety of types, but generally no information specifically on the meanings of words.

15. See

H.P. Grice, "Logic and Conversation." In *Syntax and Semantics 3: Speech Acts*, P. Cole and J.L. Morgan, eds. New York: Academic Press, 1975.

O. Ducrot, *Dire et Ne Pas Dire*. Paris, 1975.

16. See S. Cavell, "Must We Mean What We Say?" Originally in *Inquiry*, 1958. Reprinted in *Ordinary Language*, V.C. Chappel, ed. Englewood Cliffs: Prentice-Hall, 1964, pp. 75-112.

17. See J.D. McCawley, "Conversational Implicature and the Lexicon." In *Syntax and Semantics 9: Pragmatics*, P. Cole, ed. New York: Academic Press, 1978, pp. 245-259.

18. On the elimination of presuppositions as special semantic rules, see

R.M. Kempson, *Presupposition and the Delimitation of Semantics*. Cambridge: Cambride University Press, 1975.

D. Wilson, *Presuppositions and Non-Truth-Conditional Semantics*. New York: Academic Press, 1975.

19. See the discussion in Kempson, ibid., pp. 62-66.

20. See the summarizing discussion of Kempson's rejection of "speaker-based" presuppositions in Kempson, ibid., pp. 79-84.

Wilson's rejection of the claim that "external negation can be seen as denials of appropriateness" is given in Wilson, ibid., p. 85.

21. See, for example, C-J.N. Bailey, "The Integration of Linguistic Theory: Internal Reconstruction and the Comparative Method in Descriptive Analysis." In *Working Papers in Linguistics, Vol. 2, No. 4*. Honolulu: The Department of Linguistics, 1970.

22. See P. Kiparsky, "Oral Poetry: Some Linguistic and Typological Considerations." In *Oral Literature and the Formula*, B.G. Scholz and R.S. Shannon, eds. Ann Arbor.

23. A survey of the Soviet phraseological literature can be found in H. Jaksche, A. Sialm, and H. Burger, eds. *Reader zur sowjetischen Phraseologie*. Berline: Walter de Gruyter, 1981.

24. His distinction is explained in Makkai, *Idiom Structure in English*. The Hague: Mouton, 1972.

25. See J.J. Katz and J.A. Fodor, "The Structure of a Semantic Theory." In Katz and Fodor, op. cit., pp. 479-518.

26. See especially

E.V. Clark and H.H. Clark, "When Nouns Surface as Verbs." *Language* 55 (1979): 767-811.

P. Downing, "On the Creation and Use of English Compound Nouns." *Language* 53 (1977):810-842.

K.E. Zimmer, "Some General Observations about Nominal Compounds." In *Working Papers in Language Universals,* Stanford University: 5 (1971) C1-21.

K.E. Zimmer, "Appropriateness Conditions for Nominal Compounds." In *Working Papers in Language Universals,* Stanford University: 8 (1972) 3-20.

27. See especially the discussion in C. Ruhl, "Idioms and Data." In *Six LACUS Forum.* Columbia, S.C.: Hornbeam Press, 1976, pp. 456-466.

Psychology

APPROACHES TO THE STUDY
OF THE PSYCHOLOGY OF LANGUAGE

Walter Kintsch

Psychology, linguistics, artificial intelligence, philosophy – these are some of the disciplines concerned with the study of language. I would like to examine the role that psychology plays in this multi-disciplinary enterprise. Such an examination can be approached from many different viewpoints. I have opted for a rather narrow perspective, but I hope that it will enable me to impose some order and structure on this potentially limitless discussion. I shall first sketch the current state of research on text comprehension, a topic that is of particular interest to me, and then use this material as the background for a more general analysis of some of the important issues in the study of language. Specifically, I shall consider the function of representations in the psychology of language, the evaluation of theories, and the relationship between theoretical and applied work.

Notice that I am using the term *psychology of language* rather than *psycholinguistics*. Psycholinguistics has come to stand for a particular approach to the psychological study of language, namely the work stimulated by the Chomskyan revolution in linguistics.

Revolutions always make for an interesting history. In our case, it is a history characterized by sharp discontinuities. An active early interest among psychologists in language, associated with such names as Wundt and Karl Bühler, was effectively interrupted by behaviorism in America and by the Second World War in Europe. About twenty years ago, at least in America, another discontinuity occurred when psychologists came under the influence of the Chomskyan movement. How much of a discontinuity this was is hard to appreciate today. Compare, for instance, two review chapters in the *Annual Review of Psychology,* one in 1960 by Rubenstein and Alvorn, one a decade later by Fillenbaum.[1] Of the five authors most frequently cited in the 1960 review, none was among the top five in 1971; indeed, the author with the second highest number of citations in 1960 was not mentioned in the later review at all.

This shift in personnel was accompanied by a shift in topics. Before 1960, psychologists were concerned with statistical properties of language such as word association, with the probability of letter and word sequences, and to some extent with meaning, which meant the semantic differential and the Whorfian hypothesis. None of these section headings in the 1960 review survived as main topics in Fillenbaum's review. Instead, the body of that review is concerned with syntactic factors: grammaticality, paraphrase, ambiguity, transformations, and surface and deep structure. The remaining topics were a mixed bag that included sentence comprehension and memory, lexical structure, reasoning, and communication. But there was no question that the work on syntax was the showpiece of psycholinguistics. Linguists were going to tell psychologists what to look for, and psychologists were going to find it sooner or later.

But this linguistics-gone-psychological disappeared from the scene almost as fast as it came. This was partly because the psychologists wanted to share the fun of theorizing and partly because many linguists between MIT and Berkeley kept changing their minds and contradicting each other. But the chief reason was that the linguists talked syntax and, from a psychological point of view, there seemed to be so many more significant, more pressing problems about which our linguistic mentors had much less to say.

If we now look at the *Annual Review* chapter that Danks and Glucksberg have prepared for the 1980 volume, we again find a startling discontinuity. But the break is not as complete as it was in the 1960s. It is true that of the five authors cited most in 1971 only one has retained his position in 1980, and that the main concern of 1971, syntax, has left few traces in the 1980 review. But what appeared in 1971 to be minor and peripheral work has continued strongly into the present decade. Semantic memory is a central theme of Danks and Glucksberg's review. Sentence memory and sentence comprehension are still important topics. There is a great deal of concern with subjective reasoning and inference making, and with the communicative, pragmatic function of language. All of these are carried over from 1971. And two new concerns have emerged: a lively argument about word recognition and units of processing in reading, on the one hand, and a burst of activity on discourse comprehension, schemata, and story grammars, on the other. It is with this second development and its implication for a psychology of language, linguistics, and artificial intelligence that I shall be concerned here.

1. Comprehension

Rather than attempt to review the literature on comprehension,[2] I shall compare three different approaches to the comprehension problem:

- ▶ a representative of the classical/psycholinguistic work on sentence comprehension,
- ▶ an artificial intelligence program that abstracts newspaper stories, and
- ▶ a psychological process model of text comprehension.

For the work on sentence comprehension, I have selected Clark and Clark as a prototype.[3] For AI, I discuss DeJong's newspaper-skimming program, conducted at the Yale laboratory.[4] Enough characteristic features of these approaches to comprehension will be discussed to establish a basis for future comparisons. The third, slightly more detailed, example involves the text comprehension research with which I have been associated.[5] By this comparison, I hope to show how these efforts differ and how they complement each other, thus illustrating and evaluating the various alternative positions that linguistics, AI, and psychology take on some important issues in the study of language.

1.1 The psycholinguistics of sentence comprehension

Psychologists currently share a certain consensus on sentence comprehension that is rather different from the earlier, linguistically based views held when psychological processing was thought to mirror directly steps in the linguistic analysis of a sentence (for example, the *derivational theory of complexity*[6]). The present consensus is less directly based on linguistics, though it still operates within that framework.

Specifically, the view I refer to is that expressed by Clark and Clark.[7] Although I am sure that many of the investigators who have contributed to the formulation of that view would argue with the Clarks about some of the details in their book, the overall view of sentence comprehension expressed there appears to be shared by enough psycholinguists to deserve to be called a consensus.

The principal claims of Clark and Clark's treatment of sentence comprehension are as follows. Comprehension is defined as the derivation of a meaning from some representation (say, a phonological one), and the subsequent use of this meaning in some way. The modularity implied by this definition is the familiar syntax-semantics-pragmatics distinction. The "parsing" problem is of central interest: a sentence first has to be parsed into a set of constituents from which the meaning is derived, in the form of a propositional representation. The final constituents are words; the intermediate constituents are syntactic units, such as noun phrases and verb phrases. A rough operational test is offered for the determination of a constituent: if you can replace a group of words with a single word without violating the rest of the sentence (though not necessarily conserving its meaning), that group is a constituent.

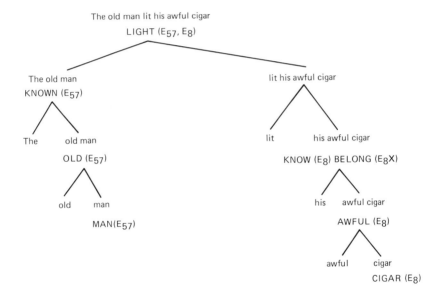

Figure 1.
The parsing of a sentence after Clark and Clark.[7]

Thus, in Clark and Clark's example (Figure 1),

The old man lit his awful cigar.

"The old man" could be replaced with "he" or "John," and hence forms an intermediate constituent. As "old man" could be replaced with "man", it forms another constituent; similarly for "awful cigar" and "his awful cigar." From "old man" one gets the propositions MAN (E_{57}) and OLD (E_{57}), where E_{57} is some specific entity. "The old man" goes to KNOWN (E_{57}); "awful cigar" introduces another entity, CIGAR (E_8) and AWFUL (E_8). "His awful cigar" leads to KNOWN (E_8) and BELONG (E_8 X) – X rather than to E_{57}, because from the constituent alone we don't know what "his" refers to. Finally we have LIGHT (E_{57}, E_8). The advantage of deriving constituents first, in accordance with this model, is that underlying propositions can then be determined with little or no reference to the rest of the sentence.

Most of the relevant experimental work is concerned with demonstrating the psychological reality of these constituents. On the whole, these demonstrations are successful in perceptual tasks. Other work is concerned with the way people determine the constituents of a sentence. Following Bever,[8] the dominant view is that this is not done through some linguistic algorithm but through the use of

▶ syntactic strategies – such as "A function word signals the beginning of a new constituent" and "Assume the first clause is the main clause unless marked." However, the experimental evidence for the use of syntactic parsing strategies is not overwhelming.

▶ semantic parsing strategies – where guesses of the meaning of the sentence are used to parse it. These are more promising. Examples of such strategies are "Use content words alone to build a proposition, and then try to parse the sentence accordingly," or "Assume that the first noun-verb-noun sequence corresponds to agent-action-object, unless otherwise marked."

The semantic strategies can be used to guide the parsing of the sentence, and this parsing can then be checked through a syntactic analysis of the sentence.

Under the topic of sentence use, Clark and Clark discuss single sentences with respect to the speech acts they represent: assertion, question, request, or indirect speech act.

Obviously I cannot do justice to all of this work with these few remarks. All I want to do is to indicate the nature of the work, so that I have a suitable background and contrast when I turn to the two text comprehension models.

1.2 An approach to text comprehension

I have chosen DeJong's FRUMP as an illustration of an AI program that comprehends texts.[9] Only some of the principles behind the program will be sketched, as was done for the psycholinguistic work on sentence comprehension.

The goal of FRUMP is to produce brief summaries of newspaper stories, nothing more or less. It comprehends a story when it manages to summarize its main points – a very restricted and a very ambitious goal. Its achievement is impressive: FRUMP summarizes correctly about 10% of the UPI news wires, and there is considerable possibility of improving it by simply giving it more knowledge structures to work with.

How is it done? First of all, by disavowing the relevance of the literature on sentence comprehension.[10] And, indeed, FRUMP often goes about its job in exactly opposite ways from the psycholinguistic model I have just discussed. Texts are processed almost entirely from the top down; there is no comprehension without knowledge – not just syntactic and semantic knowledge as in the parsing strategies of the psycholinguists, but solid doses of world knowledge. This comes in the form of fuzzy scripts – scripts very much like Schank and Abelson's,[11] but fuzzy because they contain less detail.

The system itself consists of two main modules: a Predictor and a Substantiator. The Predictor tells the Substantiator what facts to look for in a text. The latter tries to find them, and feeds its results back into the Predictor. The text analysis is thus driven by what the Predictor anticipates, rather than by the text itself. The Predictor may ask for a specific script or, at a lower level of analysis, for a specific conceptualization or filler for a role in a conceptualization; or it may merely specify some constraints on a script or conceptualization. Thus it is very different from a process of generating and testing a hypothesis of the kind used in some psychological models of concept formation. The Substantiator has these ways of confirming or disconfirming the Predictor: It looks at the text itself to see whether the requested piece of information can be found. If not, it sees whether that piece of information can be generated as an inference, using either its dictionary knowledge (in the form of a conceptual dependency representation) or its world knowledge (in the form of a script). Syntax plays a very minor role in all of this: it is merely used for some clues about where in a text certain filler variables might be found. For instance, if there is a request for the subject of a verb, look backward from the verb for a noun not preceded by a preposition; similarly, if there is a request for the object of the verb, look forward. But there is no parsing of the entire text into constituents. All FRUMP wants is a good summary of the main points; everything else is disregarded.

All of these operations proceed from the top down. The only time FRUMP studies the text from the bottom up is at the beginning, when it decides what script to use. This is done by assigning to each script a key request – a much more sophisticated approach than the use of key words. For instance, the Vehicle Accident script is activated when the following information is found in the text: some kind of vehicle strikes some physical object in some location. The script contains three more requests: one for the number killed, one for the number wounded, and one for the cause of the accident. On the basis of this script, a UPI wire from December 1978 was summarized as follows: "A vehicle accident occurred in Colorado. A plane hit the ground. 1 person died." (Actually, the output of FRUMP is a conceptual dependency representation, which then is turned into either English, Chinese, or Spanish.)

FRUMP, then, really works, and that is as unusual for an AI program as it is for a linguistic theory or a psychological model. It is of course far from perfect. Though it could do much better if it were given more scripts (it has 48 now), obviously not all newspaper stories are stylized enough to be handled by this approach. Even when FRUMP summarizes a story correctly it may miss the point, as in fact happened with the Colorado plane crash cited above. That private planes crash with the loss of a few lives is hardly news in the Rocky Mountains. The news bulletin summarized, however, reported that an airliner had crashed into a mountain, and the news was not that one was killed but that 21 survived! Some work on text analysis remains to be done, even after FRUMP.

In general, however, the summaries that FRUMP produces are very much like what human readers would produce for the same texts. Each reader would produce a somewhat idiosyncratic summary, but the commonality between readers would undoubtedly be very close to FRUMP's summary. This points to an important difference between FRUMP's comprehension processes and the real thing. It is a quite reasonable hypothesis that people summarize in ways not unlike FRUMP. People, however, are of course much more flexible, because they have available vastly more knowledge sources to control their processing, and are not restricted to fuzzy scripts. And there appears to be another, more essential difference. The comprehension of real readers or listeners comprises not only the global operations on which summaries are based but also more local processes. Not even when skimming rapidly do readers manage to concentrate entirely on the important global text properties and exclude unnecessary detail.[12] Human comprehension is not nearly as top-down as FRUMP's. It is much more text-driven, as is implied by the regular sweep of eye movements during reading. For a model that combines global abstraction processes with local comprehension processes, I shall turn to my own work and that of my collaborators.

1.3 A psychological process model of text comprehension

Our work appears woefully incomplete after looking at FRUMP. But then it does a few things FRUMP was never meant to do. An AI program and a psychological model have different goals, of course. The main difference is probably that from the very beginning we have built into our model certain capacity limitations reflecting the state of our knowledge about human cognitive processes. Second, we want to set up a model that can be tested by conventional experimental methods.

  Thus, in some ways, we demand a lot more from our theory. In other ways, we have to pay a price for the stringent requirements of simulation and testability. We have chosen to pay our price in the following way. We analyze the problem into semi-independent modules, and then concentrate our work on some of these, excluding others completely from consideration and bypassing them in some ad hoc, intuitive way. These components are only provisionally excluded. We hope eventually to be able to deal with them too or, even better, to effect some convergence among the various current approaches to comprehension, so that we can use the work of others to plug the holes in our model.

  The model[13] distinguishes between sentence-by-sentence and phrase-by-phrase comprehension processes, and global, gist-oriented processes: the micro- and macroprocesses. The microprocesses are:

  ▶ a parser – which turns the verbal text into an intermediate semantic representation, in the form of a proposition list;
  ▶ a coherence graph generator – which builds a coherent network from the proposition list;
  ▶ an inferencer – which fills in propositions missing from the network; and

▶ a fact organizer – which determines the facts represented by the input propositions on the basis of world knowledge.

The macroprocesses consist of two interacting modules:

▶ the macro-generators – which serve to reduce the input propositions to their gist, and

▶ a control structure – which guides the application of the macro-operators.

Of these components, we have a running computer program for the coherence graph generator, and have performed extensive experimental tests of the implications of this component of the model for free recall of prose paragraphs and their readability. We are now working on the fact organizer, which we hope eventually to bring to a similar level of formalization. We do not have an inferencer, nor do we plan to work on it: our model merely says when an inference must occur, and constrains some of its properties; the problem of how it is to be generated we leave to others. Similarly, we do not have a parser at present. A text must be hand-coded into a proposition list. This is done in a reasonably principled but non-algorithmic way. The arguments for the particular propositional representation we use have been stated.[14] Bypassing the parser in such a way is not unheard of (FRUMP's immediate predecessor, SAM, worked the same way, except that it had to be fed a conceptual dependency representation rather than a proposition list), but it is certainly a major weakness in the theory. Some initial steps to deal directly with the input text have recently been taken.[15]

The components of the theory dealing with the macroprocesses are more completely worked out, although they have not yet been formalized in a computer program. We also have lots of experimental results in that area. Another part of the theory deals with the production of texts – either through a reproduction of processing traces retained in memory or by a reconstruction of plausible inferences on the basis of incomplete memory traces. This is achieved through the inversion of the macro-operators, again under the guidance of a control schema.

To show what this sort of theory can and cannot do, let us take an example from Kozminsky, Kintsch, and Bourne,[16] involving a task in information analysis. Consider either an intelligence or stock market analyst who wades through numerous texts each day, most of which are of no use whatever, looking for those few, elusive bits of information that bear on his current interests.

• What characterizes his performance?

• How can we make it more efficient?

We are working on a project that we hope will produce some answers to these questions. Here I am concerned with only one aspect of the analyst's performance: his memory for the texts he has read.

- How does our model simulate the analyst's reading task?
- How are its recall predictions derived?
- How accurate are the predictions?

Consider the following laboratory task. Subjects read a stock market report on a certain company, evaluate it in various ways, and decide whether to buy the company's stock. They then receive feedback about the correctness of their decision. In some trials, more or less unexpectedly, they are also asked to recall what they have just read. The market, of course, is rigged, and the reports the subjects read, although they look much like real stock market reports, have been carefully and systematically constructed. Each report contains information on six categories relevant to the market: sales, earnings, dividends, capitalization, growth, and general economic factors. If the information is positive in two of these categories (as determined from the ratings of previous subjects), a decision to buy is indicated; otherwise subjects should not buy the stock. The two relevant categories were arbitrarily selected to be relevant by the experimenter. The same two categories were relevant for all stocks. Through repeated experience the subjects slowly learn which categories are being taken as criteria, and begin making their decisions accordingly.

The actual sequence of events in each trial is as follows: the subject reads a new market report, evaluates it on each of the six critical dimensions, selects the two dimensions thought to be decision-relevant, and makes a decision.

In spite of all the simplifications we have introduced, this is a complicated task. For present purposes, however, we are interested only in some fairly specific questions:

- What is learned in this task?
- How does it affect recall of the texts?

The Kintsch and van Dijk model has a ready answer for both of these questions, and the recall data will give us an idea of how adequate this answer is.

According to the theory, subjects in this task induce a decision schema, which then controls both the decisions they make and the information they recall from the texts. This schema contains six slots, one corresponding to each of the textual categories mentioned above, which are to be filled with an evaluation of each category based on the current input text. In addition, two of these categories are designated as decision-relevant, so that a buy-decision is made if and only if both of these categories are perceived as positive. This same schema, according to the theory, also controls the process of text comprehension itself, and hence determines what subjects can recall.

One of the paragraphs used in the experiment reads as follows:

> The company has skipped the dividend again this year, advancing cash problems as the cause. Furthermore, banks have refused to renew the credit line without representation on the board of directors. However, recent strengthening in the monthly composite of leading indicators provides an appearance of a better underlying tone to the economy, and company sales could reach $420-$440 million, up 25% from the last fiscal year. But, considering the higher prospective costs, earnings can fall in the range of $6.00 to $7.00 per share next year rather than the previously estimated $7.00-$8.00. Thus, we anticipate a period of slower growth next year, between 3 and 4% per annum.

In this task the relevant categories were Growth and Earnings, information about which is contained in the last two sentences of the paragraph. The process of comprehending this paragraph, according to the model, is as follows. The subject reads the paragraph in cycles, each cycle corresponding to a sentence except when a sentence is too long, in which case an input cycle is terminated at the first phrase boundary after some fixed number of words. In the present case, this number was estimated as 21 words, by analogy with some earlier results obtained by Kintsch and van Dijk. Thus, each of the first two sentences is processed as a unit, and the third sentence is broken into two separate cycles, with a break just before the "and." Table 1 shows how the model "comprehends" the second half of that sentence (that is, the fourth processing cycle in this paragraph). The input that the model receives at that point consists of seven propositions that express the meaning of "...and company sales could reach $420-$440 million, up 25% from the last fiscal year."

The conventions used here are those of Kintsch.[17] Each proposition is thought of as a meaning unit consisting of a predicate (written first) and one or more arguments, depending on the semantic cases associated with the predicate; the arguments are concepts or other propositions. The model constructs a *coherence graph* from the input propositions; that is, it checks whether the propositions are related by common arguments. If not, it requires that some bridging inference be made in order to establish coherence. Only referential coherence is considered at this point, in order to keep the operation of the model simple and objective.

Table 1.
Analysis of a text fragment: I.

		Theory	Predictions	Recall (%)
	:			
	:			
	BREAK AFTER 21 WORDS			
24	(AND, P26)	S	16	15
25	(COMPANY, SALES)	S	16	0
26	(COULD, SALES, P27)	S	16	8
27	(REACH, SALES, $420M)	SS	29	46
28	(UP, SALES, 25%)	SSM	60	62
29	(FROM, P28, LAST-YEAR)	S	16	15
28	(FISCAL, LAST-YEAR)	S	16	8
	SENTENCE			

MACRO:
Cue word "SALES"
selects P28

```
              25
            /
    27  <------- 26 ------- 24
            \
             28 ----- 29 ----- 30
```

This is, of course, no more than an approximation to textual coherence;[18] eventually a more intelligent model will have to be constructed. But for the moment, this approximation appears to be a robust and usable one.

The coherence graph for our example is shown at the bottom of Table 1. P27 is selected to head the graph, as the first substantive proposition containing a concept directly related to the schema ("sales"). P25, 26, and 28 are connected to it via the common argument SALES; P24 is connected to P26, and P28 is the superordinate for P29, which in turn functions as a superordinate for P30 because of the structure of argument overlap in this proposition list. Thus, each input proposition is processed once in the course of constructing this coherence graph, and is represented in the theory by the application of the Storage Operator S. Two propositions, P27 and P28, are selected for retention in a short-term memory buffer, so that they might form a bridge from one cycle to the next one. Thus, these propositions receive some extra processing, symbolized by a second application of the S-operator.[19]

Finally, we need to consider the macroprocesses. Remember that the subject, as part of the experimental task, must evaluate the paragraph with respect to each of the six critical stock market dimensions. Thus he must select an evaluation-relevant statement from the text for each dimension or, if no relevant statement is present, he must infer an evaluation. In the present case, the key word "sales" causes P28 to be selected as the most evaluation-relevant statement, and hence as a macroproposition for this paragraph. Formally, this corresponds to an application of the macro-operator **M**. In the theory, **S** and **M** are stochastic operators – predictions that a proposition thus operated on will be reproduced on the recall test. Before we consider how well these predictions fit the data, however, we shall continue our example a little further.

Consider the next sentence in the sample paragraph. It also is too long; hence the last phrase ("rather than...") is chopped off, and the first part of the sentence is processed alone. As Table 2 shows, this part contains nine propositions. None of these relate to the two propositions carried over in the buffer from the last processing cycle; hence a new graph is started (with a bridging inference, probably something as vague as "this is still about the same company"). Again a key word is present, this time "earnings." It determines the choice of a superordinate for the coherence graph, as well as the application of the macro-operator **M**. However, since P37, which contains the key word "earnings," is dominated by a sentence connective ("rather-than," P39), the latter replaces P37 as the head of the graph. The actual construction of the graph then proceeds strictly on the basis of argument overlap, as in Table 1. The two top propositions in the graph are selected for the buffer, and we proceed to the next cycle. The input now consists of Propositions P40-42, which can be annexed to the propositions retained in the short-term buffer as shown at the bottom of Table 2.

In P42, furthermore, we have another macroproposition. The macropropositions for this text segment (P37 and 42, connected by P39), are treated differently from the sales proposition in Table 1: the Earnings category is decision-relevant, and hence we not only form macropropositions, as for all six categories (the operator **M**), but also use these propositions in making a decision (the operator **D**), further strengthening their memory traces.

The three operators – **S** for micropropositions, **M** for macropropositions, and **D** for decision-relevant macropropositions – represent the memorial effects of the various processing operations

Table 2.
Analysis of a text fragment: II

:
:

Sentence	Theory	Predic-tions	Recall (%)
31 (BUT, P32)	S	16	14
32 (CONSIDERING, P33, P36)	S	16	25
33 (HIGHER, COST)	S	16	25
34 (SHIPMENT, COST)	S	16	25
35 (PROSPECTIVE, COST)	S	16	0
36 (CAN, P37)	S	16	8
37 (RANGE, EARNINGS, $6-7PSH)	SSMD	79	83
38 (NEXT-YEAR, P36)	S	16	0
39 (RATHER-THAN, P37, P42)	SSSM	82	83
BREAK AFTER 21 WORDS			
40 (PREVIOUSLY, P41)	S	16	25
41 (ESTIMATED, P42)	S	16	50
42 (RANGE, EARNINGS, $7-8PSH)	SSMD	79	83
SENTENCE			

:
:

MACRO:
Cue-word "EARNINGS"
selects P37, P42.
Add P39.

hypothesized by the model: corresponding to the operator **M** there is a probability p that the processing of a microproposition results in a memory trace that can be reproduced at the time of the recall test, and similarly there are probabilities m and d for the macro-operators **M** and **D**. Thus the model has three stochastic parameters, which can be estimated by conventional statistical methods.

We now fit the model predictions to the observed pattern of recall in the experiment, as in Tables 1 and 2. For each proposition in the text, we determine how many of our subjects managed to recall it; we then adjust the model's parameters in such a way that the resulting predictions come as close as possible to the pattern of results.

Table 3.
Goodness of fit of the model for four experimental texts

Text	X^2	df	p	m	d	r	r^2
A	46.51	36	0.30	0.86	0.68	0.81	0.66
B	18.54	20	0.22	0.44	0.00	0.84	0.71
C	22.75	21	0.27	0.80	0.00	0.87	0.76
D	27.94	19	0.16	0.70	0.31	0.83	0.69
	115.74	96	0.24	0.70	0.25	0.84	0.71

As is obvious from the tables, data and predictions correspond reasonably well. Indeed, if measured by conventional statistical criteria, the fit of the model is quite satisfactory, as Table 3 shows. The deviations of the predictions from the data, as measured by a chi-square goodness-of-fit test, are not statistically significant for any of the four paragraphs for which we obtained recall data. The average correlation between the recall data and predictions is a respectable 0.84. Thus, the model fits the recall data about as well as can be expected.[20]

Besides the three stochastic parameters, the model has two structural parameters, which have not been considered in the estimation process so far:

▶ the maximum input size – that is, the number of words in a sentence beyond which the model breaks up a long sentence; and

▶ the number of propositions held over in the short-term buffer from one processing cycle to the next.

Because there were not enough recall observations to estimate these parameters on the basis of the present data, we used estimates that appeared to be reasonable from previous work:[21] the buffer capacity was assumed to be two propositions, and the maximum number of words per cycle was held at 21. Obviously these are not the best possible estimates, but little could be gained by more sophisticated estimates here, given the overall level of fit shown in Table 3. We take the good fit of the model, obtained here and in the studies just cited, as an indication that at least in some general way we are on the right track.

Unquestionably, the model is quite incomplete: to mention only the most obvious gaps, we have to work with a propositional representation of the text rather than with the text itself, and we have no knowledge base from which to derive inferences. Also there are oversimplifications (for example, the coherence graph analysis relies on a very crude definition of coherence), some inelegances, and some residual vagueness (the macro-operations are not yet formalized enough to be embodied in a computer algorithm, as we have done for other parts of the model). Nevertheless, I think that we have here a workable framework for a model of text comprehension and recall.

The lacunae in this model correspond to strong points in the two approaches discussed earlier. Perhaps the psycholinguistic approach to sentence parsing, as represented in Section 1.1, can be developed and formalized to the point of a parsing program that could serve as the front end for the present model! An approach to parsing with reference to semantic, syntactic, and pragmatic heuristics, as suggested by Clark and Clark, is certainly compatible with the general orientation of the present model. Similarly, our macroprocesses are not very different from the way FRUMP summarizes newspaper stories (Section 1.2). FRUMP's fuzzy script, as used here, is a control schema; it is triggered by "key requests," in a manner not unlike the formation of the macrostructure in the examples in Tables 1 and 2. The main difference is that whereas FRUMP is narrow and strongly top-down controlled, and is focused exclusively on newspaper reports, here we want to design a more general model, with provisions for bottom-up processes in addition to the top-down ones and for considering a wide variety of schemata – not just fuzzy scripts and the conventions of news reports. We pay for this generality, in that the present model is not as well worked out and formalized as FRUMP. But at the level of principles, which is what we as psychologists are most interested in, the two approaches appear highly compatible: FRUMP is a special case of macroprocesses.

Thus, what appeared so different – the surface-structure-oriented psycholinguistics, the working artificial intelligence program, and the psychological process model – may stand in a relationship that is more complementary than competitive or contradictory. Of course these approaches differ in goals as well as in methods, but there is also the possibility of some convergence. In the next section, I investigate how these three approaches compare on some of the general issues that divide the field. If we think that a convergence to some "cognitive science" is possible and desirable, then we need first of all to take careful stock of the current situation – of our real and imaginary differences – so that the emergent cognitive science can be based on more than benevolent misunderstandings of one another.

2. Issues in Cognitive Science

2.1 Beyond the sentence

One real difference between Clark and Clark and the other two approaches discussed above lies in the unit of analysis. Linguists had sold the psycholinguists the idea that the study of language was all about sentences. This idea was widely and uncritically accepted, so that in 1974 Johnson-Laird could write in an article in the *Annual Review* that "The fundamental problem in psycholinguistics is simple to formulate: What happens when we understand sentences?" Far fewer people would agree with this assessment today than when it was made.

As psychologists discover prose paragraphs, conversations, lectures, and stories, they are becoming disillusioned with what linguistics has to offer them. If much or most of the experimental work that so faithfully followed the twists and turns of linguistic theory was a waste of time, then why bother with linguistics any more? Johnson-Laird titled one of his 1977 papers "Psycholinguistics without Linguistics."[22]

This, I think, is a deplorable and dangerous development. People who study language can save themselves much grief if they listen to what experts in other disciplines have to say; but they should listen to the linguists who deal with phenomena relevant to their work. If you are interested in text comprehension, the standard syntactic theory is of very little help: it simply does not deal with the same phenomena. But that does not imply that all of linguistics can be safely disregarded. Much of the work in AI today is on theorem proving, which is irrelevant to psychology, but no one suggests that therefore all of AI is irrelevant to psychology. We should avoid such generalizations. Just as researchers in speech perception cannot or should not do without phonology, some issues in psycholinguistics must be based on syntactic theory. The psychological work on text comprehension, on the other hand, has its foundation in textlinguistics. In the past, textlinguistics received much less attention from linguists than phonology or syntax, but today it is an active and burgeoning field,[23] well suited to an interdisciplinary approach. Indeed, if one looks at de Beaugrande's textbook, or van Dijk's programmatic statement on textlinguistics at the First Cognitive Science Meeting held in San Diego in 1979,[24] it is clear that progress in textlinguistics will depend just as much on developments within cognitive psychology and AI as on developments within linguistics itself.

Traditionally, the data of linguistics have been, apart from phonological observations, isolated sentences illustrating various syntactic or semantic phenomena. Textlinguists argue for a new data base.

▶ How do people initiate conversations?

▶ What is better left unsaid in a text?

▶ At what point will omissions destroy coherence?

▶ What are the major constituents of a narrative?

▶ What are the beliefs, knowledge, and expectations that are shared in a communication?

What textlinguistics has to say with respect to such questions is of direct relevance to psychologists interested in how people use language. One might, of course, object that these are the wrong questions – that a science properly proceeds from the simple to the complex, and that the inclusion of human knowledge and belief systems makes the task of linguistics hopelessly complex. I don't think this objection has merit: what is in question is not simply complexity, but a different subject matter. The problems posed by the analysis of sentences out of context are exceedingly complex, as a glance into the current or past philosophic and linguistic literature shows. Much of that complexity is simply irrelevant for text studies. This does not mean that these ancient problems are solved, but that we need not solve them for our purposes. I have tried to argue this point in my 1974 book, using some well known sentence ambiguities as my examples. I think it is an important point: Although texts have their own set of complexities, taking the whole text into consideration may make our task simpler in the long run.

2.2 The meaning of meaning

> The poem, then, must be thought of as an event in time. It is not an object or an ideal entity.
>
> Rosenblatt: *The Reader, the Text, the Poem*[25]

Logicians, semanticists, and to some extent, linguists are often scandalized when they look at some of the propositional representations of texts psychologists and computer scientists use today. In what way, do they ask, do such formalisms represent the "meaning" of a text? They are neither complete, nor explicit, nor unambiguous; they are very "surfacy" – a long way from a system that is precise and logical, preferably with reference to semantic elements. If it takes a Montague grammar to represent meaning, then let's face up to the complexities and do it right, they would say.

True, what we are doing is far from a precise, logical representation of "the meaning" of a text. We attempt nothing like this. The position taken here with respect to the meaning of meaning is an entirely psychological one. We are not concerned with abstract entities called "meanings," as Frege said philosophers must be. Meaning, for the psychologist, is in the mind.

Our model wants to describe what happens when a comprehender constructs the meaning of some text. It starts out with some very superficial low-level representation – the proposition list – and then, through various operations, successively refines that representation: it builds a coherent structure, identifies the facts represented in that structure, selects the relevant facts, and builds a macrostructure from them. The meaning of the text, for a particular comprehension episode, is the end result of this process. For readers alike in their training and goals, this end result will be approximately the same. But readers with different backgrounds or motivations can construct different meanings from the same text, for meaning is always the result of an interaction between comprehender and text.

In philosophy, literary criticism, and education, many objections have been raised against this psychological, constructivist position. Mostly, these were based on the failure of constructivist arguments to specify adequately what sorts of processes are involved in constructing meaning from a text. If meaning is a construction, how can one talk about meaning without knowing what these constructions are? We still don't have a complete theory of comprehension but, as I tried to show above, several components of such a theory have been worked out at least to some extent, and the outlines of a complete theory are beginning to emerge. In the future, the constructivist position will have to be taken more seriously.

But if representations carry a lesser burden than the whole meaning of a text, what exactly is their function in models of text comprehension?

2.3 Representations

In a sentence a word is put together tentatively, as an automobile accident
is represented with puppets in a Parisian court of law.
Wittgenstein: *Notebooks*[26]

Formally, a representation can be considered as some function of a
stimulus that encodes it internally. Performance is obtained by
operating on the internal representation with another function, the
output function. The problem is that both the representation itself
and the encoding and output functions must be inferred from the
observable stimuli and responses. Nevertheless, we like to infer
internal representations because we believe that the scientifically
interesting regularities reside at that level, rather than in the behavior itself. The representations that I am concerned with here deal
with the meaning of texts.

I shall briefly review a few of the current proposals for representing the meaning of texts, and then attempt to compare and evaluate
them. First we have to consider imagery versus propositional
representations. Let me start with a few remarks on the age-old
imagery controversy.

How do we represent images? One answer is, by means of propositions, much like linguistic information. For instance, Winston has
shown how a simple scene can be represented as a propositional
network.[27] This approach can become psychologically very
sophisticated,[28] but it will never satisfy imagery theorists, from
Titchner to Koffka, to Arnheim, and to Paivio. Imagery theorists
demand of a representation some properties that they do not find in
propositional representations. The trouble is that it is difficult to
specify a precise alternative. The photographs-in-the-head theory
will not work.[29] Instead, images have to be generic (something that
Bishop Berkeley already claimed was impossible) and selective,
focusing on some features and leaving many others unclear; they
are also supposed to be abstract in some sense, more like metaphors
than pictures.

Such an imagery representation is said to offer manifold advantages. First, it avoids the untenable equation of thought with
language (propositional representations are of course conceptual,
too, but they openly betray their linguistic parentage). More significant is the claim that imagery – as an analogic, isomorphic representation – is more suitable for the description of human thought
processes than are nonisomorphic propositional systems.[30] This may
indeed be the case for some types of thinking. There are claims
that one must distinguish between analytic and intuitive thinking,[31]

the latter being mostly neglected today, perhaps because our notions about propositional representations bias us against it. Further, imagery appears to be ideally suited for parallel processing, whereas words demand sequential processing.[32] But consider my earlier description of the Kintsch and van Dijk model of text comprehension: are the macro-operations necessarily sequential? Reading obviously contains some sequential processes, but if we consider the higher-level processes in reading, many of those could be in fact performed in parallel, in spite of the verbal input and the propositional representation. Indeed, many models of memory that are basically propositional or featural assume parallel processing.[33].

Whatever the final fate of imagery representations will be, it is clear that right now propositional representations are much better worked out. I want to compare some examples of propositional representations currently used in text comprehension work. First, I shall discuss the system that I have been using for some time. In Kintsch 1974,[34] the sentence "Mary gives Fred a book" is represented as:

(GIVE, AGENT: Mary, RECEIVER: Fred, OBJECT: book)

The arguments of the proposition are classified according to their semantic case relationships, but in actual practice it is usually superfluous to include cases – mostly they are obvious, but in more complex propositions (for example, sentence connectives as predicates), no generally accepted classifications exist, nor would they be very helpful if they did.

In Schank's conceptual dependency representation,[35] the same sentence would look like

Clearly, the same information is represented here as before (the double arrow indicates an ACT relationship), though the representation is slightly more explicit: Mary is shown as both a source and an agent. More important is the change from GIVE to PTRANS (physical transfer). The concepts that enter into the propositions in Kintsch[34] are complex semantic entities; Schank, on the other hand, analyzes concepts into semantic primitives, an example of which is PTRANS. Others have taken the decomposition much farther than Schank. For Norman and Rumelhart, "transfer" does not appear very elementary at all; instead, they decompose it into the network shown below:[36]

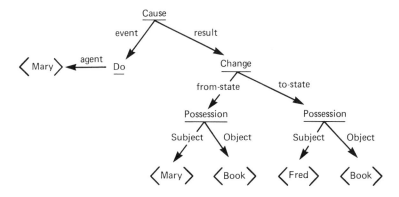

Much more of what we know about "give" is represented here, and therefore one might prefer this semantic element representation. Things are not that simple, however, because Kintsch associates with the concept "give" a meaning postulate that contains the same information.[37] Such a meaning postulate states that "give" implies

(CAUSE, (DO, AGENT), (CHANGE,
    (POSSESS, AGENT, OBJECT), (POSSESS, RECEIVER, OBJECT))).

The point I am trying to make is that everything that can be represented in one system can also be dealt with in either of the other two considered here. The differences are not in *what* is represented, but in *how*: a representation implies something about the processing model that is most suitable for it. Let us look at the three representations discussed above from that standpoint. (There are, of course, several more, similar proposals for propositional representations, but I can neglect them here because they would not affect my argument.)

What criteria might help us to compare and evaluate proposals for semantic representations? There are two positions on this point. Anderson claims that they are in principle indistinguishable, and presents a formal nonidentifiability proof.[38] Like many others, however, I have problems with his arguments.[39] In the most general terms, Anderson's point is that there is always more than one way of describing a set of data. This is a widely acknowledged truth. But there are other criteria for choosing among theories, such as Chomsky's "explanatory adequacy".[40] There are good and bad identifiability proofs. A good one was Greeno and Steiner's demonstration in 1964 that no choice between the then current Markov models of learning was possible on the basis of certain kinds of experimental data.[41] The models in question were all psychologically motivated, serious efforts at explanation, and it was of critical importance to know that the kind of experiments people were doing then could not possibly discriminate among them.

I am much less sanguine about another famous nonidentifiability theorem, Townsend's proof of the equivalence of serial and parallel processes.[42] Sure, one can construct a mimicking parallel model for any serial device, and vice versa; but, as Townsend points out, the mimicking model can easily become bizarre for any but the simplest situation. In one case, a well motivated serial processing model is described, which can be mimicked by a parallel model – if we permit the latter to be clairvoyant. I don't find it difficult to decide which is the better model.

The situation may be similar when we go to Anderson's proof for the nonidentifiability of representations. Only representation-process pairs can be tested; representations alone cannot be. If there are no constraints on the process function, any representation will do, because one can always adjust the process to ensure that the same input-output mapping is maintained. This is a bit like Chomsky's proof of the insufficiency of finite-state devices for a theory of language: it would be important for us if there were sentences of infinite length, or humans whose processing capacities are arbitrarily complex.

If representations are not in principle undecidable, what sort of criteria might help to distinguish among them? Most obvious is the amount of semantic decomposition that is implied: a Norman and Rumelhart or Schank parser would routinely decompose complex semantic concepts into their elements.[43] Others[44] have argued that automatic decomposition is psychologically implausible and introduces unnecessary complexity. We know people chunk information in memory all the time, and operate with these chunks as units. Why should they not do so with language material? And what, anyway, is the real list of primitives? In principle, this is an empirical issue, though decisive experimental results are hard to come by. Nevertheless, it appears likely that this issue will be decided in the near future on the basis of empirical results, and most likely against representations that require automatic decomposition.[45]

Other criteria have been suggested from time to time. Norman and Rumelhart, as well as Schank, stress invariance under paraphrase as a highly desirable property of a semantic representation. Others[46] have cautioned against too strict an interpretation of this criterion. It appears desirable because it guarantees a certain efficiency of inference processes, but how are we to determine when two expressions really have "the same meaning"? Does "Mary gives Fred a book" have the same meaning as "Fred takes a book from Mary"? We may be buying ourselves a lot of trouble if we take this criterion as seriously as Norman and Rumelhart want us to.

Finally, there is the criterion of completeness, as used for instance by Anderson.[47] But again more harm than good may come from a strict insistence on completeness. The predicate calculus, for instance, is quite incomplete in that you can't represent in it even the simplest paragraph of a real language text. Yet it is extremely useful for certain purposes. Indeed, most of the semantic representations under discussion here are not at all complete. In a review of Kintsch 1974, Anderson points out that a straightforward use of the system there described would miss the difference between "All philosophers read some books" and "Some books are read by all philosophers."[48] Therefore, the system does not account for an important phenomenon, scope of quantification. Anderson is quite right: the way that system handles quantification is extremely primitive and trivial. As another example, consider one of Wexler's complaints about Anderson 1977, that what Anderson's theory ACT has to say about opacity of reference is inadequate in view of the literature in philosophy and linguistics.[49]

Of course he is right, too, and one could collect many more such examples. But both criticisms are beside the point. Anyone interested in logic or formal semantics would be foolish to use the representational systems considered here; there are much better, very well developed alternatives for those purposes. Logic, semantics, linguistics are specialized knowledge areas, as well as myriad others, which have developed their own representational systems and conventions, known to the experts in that field. Psychologists are interested in representing natural, naive thinking; the fact that our representational systems are incomplete with respect to many domains of expertise, from quantum physics to semantics, is not an indictment of such systems. People are able to do a great many things, and a system that completely represents human thought in all its complexity is neither feasible nor necessary.

Theories of text comprehension must be representation-process pairs. Only as pairs are they subject to empirical test. Nevertheless, the pairing of process models and representation cannot be arbitrary. The representation must be suited to a specific task. Different tasks will require different representations, but it is not meaningless to say that for some specific purpose one representation is better than another.

2.4 The competence–performance distinction

> All data that the grammar cannot treat are shunted off into the domain of "performance" and are excluded from consideration as nonissues.
>
> de Beaugrande: *Text, Discourse, and Process*[23]

A recent statement of Chomsky's notion of competence can be found in Dresher and Horstein:[50] "A study of competence abstracts away from the whole question of performance which deals with how language is processed in real time, why speakers say what they say, how language is used in various social groups, how it is used to communicate, etc." The notion has not been without its detractors, as for instance de Beaugrande:[51] "A language used without all that knowledge could be called competent only by a bizarre perversion of the whole notion in its commonsense usage."

Everything I have said here about representation implies a rejection of the distinction between competence and performance. If a cognitive theory is a representation-process pair, then it makes no sense to isolate competence. One can take note of a theory of competence as an intellectual achievement, but it is hard to discover the relevance of such a theory to the kinds of problem of interest here. A rejection of the competence-performance distinction, however, does not imply a rejection of linguistics; although linguistics-as-the-study-of-competence may be irrelevant for our purposes, much of linguistics is needed as a basis for cognitive science, for example, textlinguistics.[52]

Refusing to draw a distinction between competence and performance along the lines Chomsky has suggested does not mean that all versions of a competence-performance distinction must be rejected. Both van Dijk and de Beaugrande advocate a distinction between textual competence and language performance. Textual competence is a much broader concept than Chomsky's, close to the everyday sense of the term – what real people can do in real situations, as distinguished from what they actually do. A distinction of that type is, in one way or another, a component of almost every psychological theory: it parallels the distinction between learning (or "habit strength") and performance in Hull:[53] not everything learned is immediately expressed behaviorally, except under the appropriate motivational conditions.

2.5 Modularity and the evaluation of theories

> There is no conservation law requiring the description to be as cumbersome as the object described.
>
> Simon: *The Science of the Artificial*[54]

The issue here is whether a cognitive theory must permit interactions among all of its elements, or whether such a theory can be designed with nearly independent components. The former approach is exemplified by Rumelhart's theory of reading comprehension,[55] or Anderson's ACT;[56] the Kintsch and van Dijk model[57] favors the modular approach, for reasons that I shall sketch here.

Simon[58] has stated the case for a modular approach so well that I shall merely remind you of his main points, and then indicate their relevance to the sticky problem of how to evaluate theories of complex systems.

Because complex systems are often hierarchical, they can be described at various levels. The cell may be a convenient unit of analysis for some purposes, but the analysis may shift to larger units, or downward to the protein molecule, or even to the amino acid constituents of the molecules. A book is composed of chapters, which are divided into sections (or episodes, depending on the nature of the book); we can further distinguish paragraphs, sentences within them, clauses and phrases, and finally words. Even these must be further decomposed for certain purposes. Descriptions at one level may be approximately independent of the other levels in the short run. The long-term dependencies involve levels in an aggregate way only. Concretely, in the Kintsch and van Dijk model the coherence graph generator operates independently from the macro-operators in each cycle, though at certain points it needs some input from them. However, in accepting such an input (in order to know what to put at the head of the graph that is to be constructed) the coherence graph generator needs to know only the current result of the macro-operations, and is quite independent of how this was obtained. Simon calls such a system "nearly decomposable."

According to Simon, the time required for the evolution of a complex system depends crucially on the number of stable intermediary forms it evolves. Similarly, in complex problem-solving tasks, the availability of partial results that signal recognizable progress greatly increases the chances of success. Modularity also increases the likelihood that a theory can be evaluated empirically, for very much the same reasons.

How can one evaluate the complex theories in present-day cognitive science? There appear to be three major possibilities:

- ▶ to base an evaluation on intuition,
- ▶ to take the writing of a successful computer program as evidence in support of a theory, or
- ▶ to proceed by the old-fashioned method of observation and experiment.

Here, I think, we come to what may be the most important contribution that psychologists can make to cognitive science: our experimental methods may play an indispensable role in the evaluation of theories, for the first two methods by themselves are insufficient. The objections that many authors have made against equating a simulation program with a theory – and considering the simulation as a proof for the the theory – appear to be cogent.[59] Scientific theories are supposed to yield general principles. A running program does not guarantee us these principles; it may run (or not run) for numerous extraneous reasons. This is, however, not to question the utility of simulation programs: computer programs are today a major formalism for theories in cognitive science. But in order to evaluate a psychological theory, we need more than a running program.

A similarly critical position is indicated with respect to intuition, including linguistic intuition. Intuitions are indispensable as data, and hence as a source for theories, but they cannot validate a theory. Experimental psychologists have a complex attitude vis-à-vis the role that intuition plays in their science. Not too long ago, it was dogma that the report of a thoughtful, trained observer must be rejected as mere intuition. (At the same time the average opinion of 30 bored sophomores was accepted as "data".) Today, some psychologists go a long way toward accepting intuitive plausibility as a substitute for experimental test of a theory.[60] To me it appears crucial to keep apart the questions where good theories come from and how they are to be evaluated. Intuition plays a significant role in the former, but is irrelevant to the latter.

Theories, then, are verified by observation, especially by the kind of systematic observation we call experiment. The problem is, of

course, that theories of complex phenomena are often so loosely
stated that no clear-cut experimental predictions are possible. That
brings us back to the modularity issue. It may not be possible to
test a whole theory, but its semi-independent components may
prove much more tractable in this respect. For instance, we have
today a lot of information about perception and memory from
which we can construct components of more complex cognitive
theories. Thus if we incorporate a memory buffer into some complex theory,[61] we know about what its properties will be, so that
there is at least one element in the theory we don't have to worry
about when we evaluate it. Similarly, if we build in notions about
chunking in working memory, or about encoding specificity in
retrieval, we know enough to take these components for granted.
This, then, may help in isolating those parts of the theory that are
most in need of empirical validation. To test the whole theory at
once may not be productive, because some element of it will always
be wrong, and if we have to redesign the whole system every time,
we shall very likely get nowhere. In a nearly decomposable system,
the chances for evaluation are much better. The trick is, of course,
to design experiments in such a way that they provide reasonably
independent tests of the separate components of a model. Thus, we
have tried in Miller and Kintsch[62] to investigate the microprocesses
of the Kintsch and van Dijk model, independently of macroprocesses. Within limits, this sort of approach appears feasible.

If theories must be modular in order to be experimentally testable,
what are the modules to be? As usual, there are no recipes for how
to do good science; presumably, time and success will tell which
parsings of the problem were the good ones. In psycholinguistics
the traditional parsing split along the lines syntax-semantics-pragmatics. In this respect, it is interesting that both of the comprehension models I have outlined here – FRUMP and the Kintsch and van
Dijk model – fail to adhere to this distinction. Kintsch and van
Dijk is highly modular, but the basic distinction is between local
and global processes; syntax is simply beyond the scope of the
theory, but nothing like a semantics-pragmatics distinction occurs.
Do different tasks (for example, comprehension models vs. linguistics and philosophy) require different decompositions?

3. Applications

The last issue I want to consider here concerns applications. This
may not be an issue for AI, which is basically applications-oriented,

and I don't know about linguistics, but experimental psychology has traditionally emphasized its pure science character. Boring even rewrote the history of experimental psychology to remove any applied spots from it.[63] The motives for this interest in purity are honorable: too often have grandiose promises been made on the basis of half-baked ideas.

Nevertheless, the ivory tower atmosphere has not become experimental psychology very well. We have often picked up on an interesting, significant problem, which within a few generations of experiments spawns a highly inbred literature, the arguments becoming more and more baroque, until eventually everybody loses interest.

A case in point is the semantic memory research of the last decade. It started with a significant question, concerning the structure of human knowledge, and a promising experimental procedure, the reaction time paradigm of Collins and Quillian.[64] But soon the procedure became an end in itself, and the original question was replaced by narrowly conceived, sterile subproblems. I have tried elsewhere to put together the details of this unpleasant story;[65] unfortunately other examples are not hard to come by. I would like to suggest that such developments would be less likely if experimental psychologists were in closer contact with applied problems. Anyone working on a real-world problem, say from an AI perspective, could not possibly take the semantic memory work in psychology seriously in the long run, simply because the arguments were about issues that did not seem to matter all that much for the applied purpose. If psychologists had been interested in some practical problems, semantic memory research might not have been conceived as narrowly as it was.

What sorts of applications might there be for cognitive psychology? I shall mention two projects with which I have been associated. On the first, readability, we have done considerable work; the second one is in the planning stages.

Readability is an important practical problem. Almost everybody has trouble matching the difficulty of a text with the abilities of those who are supposed to read it — whether it is an insurance policy, an income tax form, a high school science text, or a navy training manual. Traditional approaches measure some superficial text properties, mostly sentence length and word frequency, and combine them by means of some readability formula that is supposed to predict ease of comprehension. These methods are widely used, but what can be achieved with them is strictly limited.[66] It is useless to try to measure readability as one would measure the

height of a tree. Readability is not a property of a text but a result
of a reader-text interaction. Claims of this sort have been made
before, but one needs a model of reading comprehension to give
them substance. With the Kintsch and van Dijk model, for instance, we have been able to show that the readability of a given
text may differ greatly according to the reader. And we have been
able to show why this is so, what exactly are the stumbling blocks
in reading, which may range from macro- to micro-operations. In a
recent study with relatively short paragraphs,[67] we found that the
number of bridging inferences necessary to construct a coherent
text base, and the number of memory searches for concepts no
longer readily available, were the most important predictors of
readability. Our predictions were quite good, with multiple correlations all above 0.80. Work like this may eventually have two practical outcomes:

- It might provide diagnostic procedures that determine why
  certain people have comprehension problems, and
- It may give us a better understanding of how to write texts that
  people with limited abilities will be able to read.

My second example of an application is about adjunct questions.[68]
Intuitively, it would seem that directing the reader's comprehension
processes by means of some well placed questions during the course
of reading ought to facilitate comprehension. But years of empirical research had yielded somewhat disappointing results. Perhaps
one cannot predict the effect that some question will have on a
reader, unless one has a fairly precise idea of what that reader is
actually doing. Questions that would supply bridging inferences, or
reinstate the right context at a particular point in a text, may very
well help the reader. But, to ask those questions, a reasonably
accurate model is required! On the other hand, questions that simply duplicate processes that are already part of comprehension may
have little effect. And with such a model one can also construct
questions that interfere with the normal comprehension process. In
general, research on the effect of adjunct questions has paid little
attention to the nature of the questions asked and their exact role
in the comprehension process. Indeed, without some theoretical
understanding, how could it?

Applications like this are interesting not only because they may
eventually yield some useful results but also because they keep our
theoretical enterprise focused on the big issues, so that it will perhaps be less likely to become only an end in itself.

4. Conclusions

The psychology of language is today an active, fruitful field of research. One merely needs to take a look at the numerous journal articles, books, and monographs that have been published in this field during the last years; there can be no doubt that we have learned a great deal from all that work. Many researchers have contributed to the effort, which from the very beginning has been interdisciplinary. I have tried here to analyze the role psychology has played in this interdisciplinary enterprise, concentrating entirely on the work done in text comprehension in the Colorado laboratory. Obviously that is not more than a small fraction of current research, and not necessarily a representative one. I hope, however, that the advantages of being concrete and specific will outweigh the danger of parochialism. At least for this small segment of current psychological research on language, I have tried to show precisely what its position is with respect to some typical alternative approaches and to some of the familiar issues that characterize this field of investigation, some of which have a venerable tradition in philosophy and linguistics.

The primary concern in this analysis has been the prospect for a confluence of research from the various disciplines – that is, the possibility for a new cognitive science. There are, of course, many differences between the approaches of linguistics, artificial intelligence, and psychology. Obviously the goals and methods of these disciplines are not the same. More seriously, the criteria for the evaluation of theories and observations that are used by researchers in these areas also differ – a fact that poses numerous problems of communication across the boundaries between disciplines. There can be no question that large areas of linguistics, artificial intelligence, and psychology have simply nothing to offer to each other, and will undoubtedly continue their separate existence, with no more than an occasional glance across boundaries. As I have tried to show, however, there are subareas of psychology, linguistics, and artificial intelligence that could profitably develop a more intimate relationship. Their methods and results appear to be complementary, and, at least for the problem of text comprehension, it may very well be that progress ultimately presupposes the kind of joining of forces that is envisioned by the idea of a cognitive science.

REFERENCES

1. H. Rubenstein and M. Alvorn, "Psycholinguistics." *Annual Review of Psychology* 11 (1960): 291-322.
    S. Fillenbaum, "Experimental Psycholinguistics." *Annual Review of Psychology* 25 (1974): 135-160.

2. For some recent reviews, see
    W. Kintsch, "Comprehension and Memory of Text." In *Handbook of Learning and Cognitive Processes, VI,* W.K. Estes, ed. Hillsdale, NJ: Lawrence Erlbaum Associates, 1978.
    J. H. Danks and S. Glucksberg, "Experimental Psycholinguistics." *Annual Review of Psychology* 31 (1980): 391-417.

3. H. H. Clark and E. V. Clark, *Psychology of Language.* New York: Harcourt, Brace, Jovanovich, 1977.

4. G. DeJong, "Skimming Stories in Real Time: An Experiment in Integrated Understanding." Research Report 158. New Haven, CT: Department of Computer Science, Yale University, 1979. Also published in *Strategies for Natural Language Processing,* W. Lehnert and M.H. Ringle, eds. Hillsdale, NJ: Erlbaum, 1982.

5. W. Kintsch and T. A. van Dijk, "Towards a Model of Text Comprehension and Production." *Psychological Review* 85 (1978): 363-394.

6. J.A. Fodor, T.G. Bever, and M. F. Garrett, *The Psychology of Language.* New York: McGraw-Hill, 1974.

7. Clark and Clark, op. cit.

8. T.G. Bever, "The Cognitive Basis for Linguistic Structures." In *Cognition and the Development of Language,* J.R. Hayes, ed. New York: Wiley, 1970.

9. G. DeJong, "Skimming Newspaper Stories by Computer." Research Report 104. New Haven, CT: Department of Computer Science, Yale University, 1977.

10. DeJong, "Skimming Newspaper Stories," p. 2, and
    R.C. Schank, "Understanding Paragraphs." Technical Report. Castagnola, Switzerland: Instituto per gli studi semantici e cognitivi, 1974.

11. R.C. Schank and R.P. Abelson, *Scripts, Plans, Goals, and Understanding.* Hillsdale, NJ: Lawrence Erlbaum Associates, 1977.

12. M. Masson, "Cognitive Process in Skimming Stories." *Journal of Experimental Psychology: Learning, Memory, and Cognition* 8 (1982): 400-417.

13. For example, Kintsch and van Dijk, op. cit., and
    W. Kintsch and D. Vipond. "Reading Comprehension and Readability in Educational Practice and Psychological Theory." In *Perspectives on Memory Research,* L.G. Nilsson, ed. Hillsdale, NJ: Lawrence Erlbaum Associates, 1979.
    W. Kintsch, "On Modeling Comprehension." *Educational Psychologist* 14 (1979): 3-14.
    W. Kintsch, "Levels of Processing Language Materials." In *Levels of Processing in Human Memory,* L.S. Cermak and F.I.M. Craik, eds. Hillsdale, NJ: Lawrence Erlbaum Associates, 1979.

J.R. Miller and W. Kintsch, "Readability and Recall of Short Prose Paragraphs: A Theoretical Analysis." *Journal of Experimental Psychology: Human Learning and Memory* 6 (1980): 335-354.

14. W. Kintsch, *The Representation of Meaning in Memory.* Hillsdale, NJ: Lawrence Erlbaum Associates, 1974.

15. Miller and Kintsch, op. cit.

16. E. Kozminsky, W. Kintsch, and L. E. Bourne, Jr., "Decision Making with Texts: Information Analysis and Schema Acquisition." *Journal of Experimental Psychology, General* 110 (1981): 362-380.

17. Kintsch, *The Representation of Meaning in Memory.*

18. T.A. van Dijk, *Text and Context.* London: Longman, 1977.

19. The details of this process are not of primary concern here, but see Kintsch and van Dijk, op. cit.

20. For similar results, see Kintsch and van Dijk, op. cit., Miller and Kintsch, op. cit., and
G.J. Spilich, G.T. Vesonder, H.L. Chies, and J.F. Voss, "Textual Processing of Domain Related Information for Individuals with High and Low Domain Knowledge." *Journal of Verbal Learning and Verbal Behavior* 18 (1979): 275-290.

21. Kintsch and van Dijk, op. cit.; Spilich et al., op. cit.; Miller and Kintsch, op. cit.

22. P.N. Johnson-Laird, "Psycholinguistics without Linguistics." In *Tutorial Essays in Psychology,* N.S. Sutherland, ed. Hillsdale, NJ: Lawrence Erlbaum Associates, 1977.

23. See, for example, R. de Beaugrande, *Text, Discourse, and Process.* Norwood, NJ: Ablex, 1980.

24. T.A. van Dijk, "From Text Grammar to Interdisciplinary Discourse Studies." Paper presented at the La Jolla Conference on Cognitive Science, 1979.

25. L.M. Rosenblatt, *The Reader, the Text, the Poem.* Carbondale: Southern Illinois University Press, 1978.

26. L. Wittgenstein, *Notebooks 1914-16.* Oxford: Oxford University Press, 1961.

27. P.H. Winston, *Artificial Intelligence.* Reading, MA: Addison-Wesley, 1977.

28. D. Kieras, "Beyond Pictures and Words: Alternative Information Processing Models for Imagery Effects in Verbal Memory." *Psychological Bulletin* 85 (1978): 532-554.

29. Z.W. Pylyshyn, "What the Mind's Eye Tells the Mind's Brain: A Critique of Mental Imagery." *Psychological Bulletin* 80 (1973) 1-24.

30. For example, R. Arnheim, *Visual Thinking.* Berkeley, CA: University of California Press, 1971.

31. For example, K.R. Hammond, "The Unification of Psychological Decision Theory and Social Judgment Theory." Technical Report. Boulder, CO: Institute of Behavioral Science, University of Colorado, 1979.

32. G.E. Lessing, "Laokoon oder Uber die Grenzen der Malerei und Poesie." In *Lessings Werke, 5.* Leipzig: Goschen, 1887.

A. Paivio, *Imagery and Verbal Processes*. New York: Holt, Rinehart and Winston, 1971.

33. See my discussion in "Levels of Processing Language Materials," loc. cit.

34. Kintsch, *The Representation of Meaning in Memory*.

35. R.C. Schank, "Conceptual Dependency: A Theory of Natural Language Understanding." *Cognitive Psychology* 3 (1972): 552-631.

36. D.A. Norman and D.E. Rumelhart, *Explorations in Cognition*. San Francisco: Freeman, 1975.   .

37. Kintsch, *The Representation of Meaning in Memory*.

38. J.R. Anderson, *Language, Memory and Thought*. Hillsdale, NJ: Lawrence Erlbaum Associates, 1976.

39. Z.W. Pylyshyn, "Validating Computational Models." *Psychological Review* 86 (1979): 383-394.
    F. Hayes-Roth, "Distinguishing Theories of Representation." Distinguishing Theories of Representation. *Psychological Review* 86 (1979): 376-382.
    J.M. Keenan and R.E. Moore, "Memory for Images of Concealed Objects." *Journal of Experimental Psychology: Human Learning and Memory* 8 (1979): 374-385.

40. N. Chomsky, *Current Issues in Linguistic Theory*. The Hague: Mouton and Co., 1964.

41. J.G. Greeno and T.E. Steiner, "Markovian Processes with Identifiable States: General Considerations and Applications to All-or-None Learning." *Psychometrika* 29 (1964): 309-333.

42. J.T. Townsend, "Issues and Models Concerning the Processing of a Finite Number of Inputs." In *Human Information Processing: Tutorial in Performance and Cognition,* B.H. Kantowitz, ed. Hillsdale, NJ: Lawrence Erlbaum Associates, 1974

43. Norman and Rumelhart, op. cit.; Schank, "Cognitive Dependency."

44. Anderson, op. cit.; Kintsch, *The Representation of Meaning in Memory*.

45. Precisely such data have recently been reported, with the predicted outcome, in J.A. Fodor, M.F. Garrett, E.C.T. Walker, and C.H. Parkes, "Against Definitions." *Cognition* 8 (1980): 263-367.

46. For example, Anderson, op. cit.

47. Ibid.

48. Ibid.

49. K. Wexler, "A Review of John Anderson's Language, Memory and Thought." *Cognition* 6 (1978): 327-352.

50. B.E. Dresher and N. Hornstein, "On Some Supposed Contributions of Artificial Intelligence to the Scientific Study of Language." *Cognition* 4 (1976) 321-398.

51. de Beaugrande, op. cit.

52. T.A. van Dijk, *Some Aspects of Text Grammar*. The Hague: Mouton and Co., 1972.
    de Beaugrande, op. cit.

53. C.L. Hull, *Principles of Behavior.* New York: Appleton Century Crofts, 1943.

54. H.A. Simon, *The Science of the Artificial.* Cambridge, MA: MIT Press, 1969.

55. D.E. Rumelhart, "Toward an Interactive Model of Reading." In *Attention and Performance,* S. Dornic, ed. Hillsdale, NJ: Lawrence Erlbaum Associates, 1977.

56. Anderson, op. cit.

57. Kintsch and van Dijk, op. cit.

58. Simon, op. cit.

59. Dresher and Hornstein, op. cit.; Anderson, op. cit.

60. See Wexler's criticism of ACT in this respect, op. cit.

61. As in Kintsch and van Dijk, op. cit., or
     M.E. Atwood and P.G. Polson, "A Process Model for Water-jug Problems."
     Cognitive Psychology 8 (1976): 191-216.

62. Miller and Kintsch, op. cit.

63. E.G. Boring, *A History of Experimental Psychology.* New York: Appleton Century Crofts, 1950.

64. A.M. Collins and M.R. Quillian, "Retrieval from Semantic Memory." *Journal of Verbal Learning and Verbal Behavior* 8 (1969): 240-247.

65. W. Kintsch, "Semantic Memory." In *Attention and Performance, VIII,* R.S. Nickerson, ed. Hillsdale, NJ: Lawrence Erlbaum Associates, 1980.

66. For a review, see Kintsch and Vipond, op. cit.

67. Miller and Kintsch, op. cit.

68. Kintsch, "On Modelling Comprehension," op. cit.

TOWARD AN ABSTRACT PERFORMANCE GRAMMAR

Charles E. Osgood

In this chapter I give a sketch of a general theory of sentence understanding and sentence production.[1] This theory is a theory of language *performance* and so, to distinguish it from linguistic competence grammars, I will refer to it as an *abstract performance grammar* (APG). In contrast to the "mini-theories" popular in current psycholinguistics, the APG is an attempt to develop a *comprehensive* theory of language understanding and production. This theory is a multi-level, componential approach strongly rooted in the non-linguistic cognitive system. Some of the basic assumptions of the theory are that:

▶ The "deep" cognitive system is essentially semantic in nature, with syntax involved solely in transformations between this structured semantic system and the surface forms of sentences produced and received.

▶ The structures developed and utilized in prelinguistic cognizing determine the basic ("natural") cognitive structures underlying sentence understanding and creating.

▶ The more surface forms of sentential inputs and outputs correspond to these "natural" structures, the more easily will they be processed.

▶ This "deep" cognitive system is shared by both linguistic and non-linguistic (perceptual) information-processing channels, which continue to interact throughout adult communicative activities.

▶ Sentencing (comprehending and producing) in ordinary communication is always context-dependent, influenced probabilistically by linguistic (conversational, discourse) and non-linguistic (situational, social) factors.

▶ The only way to extract what is universal in human communicative behavior from what is unique to particular languages and cultures is via cross-linguistic and cross-cultural studies utilizing demonstrably comparable methods.

After some orientation, I present the structural and functional principles of APG – as presently conceived – along with some commentary and some evidence on the predictive adequacy of the theory.

1. By Way of Orientation

1.1 What is a language?

To begin I offer a set of defining criteria, both for anything being *a language* and for something being *a humanoid language* – along with a set of non-defining, but universal, characteristics of the latter. Then I tackle the hoary question of how human languages may have originated, and conclude with my own naturalness theory of language origins – both in the human species and in the developing individual.

If *anything* is to be called "a language," it must satisfy at least the following six criteria:

- ▶ **non-random recurrency** – production of identifiably different and non-randomly recurrent physical forms in some communication channel;
- ▶ **reciprocality** – these forms being producible by the same organisms that received them;
- ▶ **pragmatics** – use of these forms resulting in non-random dependencies between the forms and the behaviors of the organisms that employ them;
- ▶ **semantics** – use of these forms following non-random rules of reference to events in other channels;
- ▶ **syntactics** – use of these forms following non-random rules of combination with other forms in the same channel; and
- ▶ **combinatorial productivity** – the users of the forms being capable of producing indefinitely long and potentially infinite numbers of novel combinations that satisfy the first five criteria.

Applying these criteria to communications by other, non-human animals, I conclude that both the bee (innately) and the ape (via human training) can be said to "have" a language, albeit limited in what they can talk about (the bee) and how complicated it is (the ape).

If something is to be called "a natural humanoid language" (beyond meeting the criteria for *anything* being a language), it must satisfy the following STRUCTURAL criteria:

- ▶ use of the **vocal–auditory channel**; thus displaying
- ▶ **non–directional transmission but directional perception** and
- ▶ **evanescence in time of the forms**; and hence requiring
- ▶ **information integration over time,** but also providing
- ▶ **prompt feedback** to senders of their own messages[2]

and the following FUNCTIONAL criteria:

- ▶ **arbitrariness of form/meaning relations** (as the general rule);

▶ **discreteness** (rather than continuousness) **of form-shifts signaling differences in meaning** (as the general rule);
▶ **hierarchical organization** (into levels of units-within-units);
▶ **componential organization** (larger numbers of units at each higher level being exhaustively analysable into smaller numbers of units at each next lower level); and
▶ **transferral-via-learning to other members of the species** (both generationally over time and geographically over space).

As to non-defining, but apparently universal, characteristics of human languages, I would argue that if we encountered a humanoid language (as defined above) whose speakers

▶ didn't **propositionalize** (producing sentences like "a robin is a bird" or "the moon is made of green cheese") and thus could have no science, or
▶ didn't **prevaricate** (tell lies, be deceptive, or deliberately produce meaningless sentences like "colorless green ideas sleep furiously") and thus could have neither fiction nor poetry, or
▶ displayed no **reflexiveness** (never gave definitions of words or produce performative sentences like "I christen thee 'the Jimmy Carter'" for some future nuclear aircraft carrier) and thus could have no dictionaries, philosophies, linguistics, or even puns,

that language would still have to be classified as a *human-type* language.

However, there are some interesting characteristics of human languages, based on language performance principles, that I would also claim to be non-defining at all levels of units:

▶ **selection and combination rules are statistical rather than absolute** – at the phonemic level, selection of those differences in sound that will make a difference in meaning and, at the syntactic level, selection of that subset of possible "re-write" rules that will be employed;
▶ **progressive differentiation varies statistically across languages** – for example, progressive differentiation of color terms cross-linguistically, as Berlin and Kay have demonstrated;[3]
▶ **a least effort principle** – as Zipf claimed many years ago,[4] the higher the usage-frequency of forms, the shorter their length, the smaller their number, and the larger their range of alternative senses;
▶ **affective polarity and the Pollyanna principle** – as Greenberg has demonstrated,[5] it is statistically universal that positive members of pairs are distinguished from negative members (by marking of the negatives and by priority of the positives both in development and in message form-sequencing), and Pollyannaism is

demonstrated by the greater diversification, more frequent use, and easier processing of the affectively positive forms.

1.2 Things and words

A capsule life-history of behaviorism – from single-stage (Skinnerian) through two-stage mediational (Hullian/Tolmanian) models – leads into my own, more complex, three-level, and semantically componential model. The three levels – on both the comprehension and production sides of the behavioral coin – are these:
- most peripherally, sensory and motor **projection systems;**
- more centrally, sensory and motor **integration systems;** and,
- most centrally, the **representational** (meaningful) **system**
  (significances in comprehending and intentions in producing).
These central representational processes are structured sets of bipolar mediational components (that is, semantic features). The remainder of this section emphasizes the "intimate parallelism" of cognitive processing in non-linguistic (perceptual/motor) and linguistic channels.

1.2.1 A capsule life–history of behaviorism

As an aid in exposition, I will use the notion of a Little Black Egg (see Figure 1), considering this more appropriate for biological entities than the notion of a Little Black Box. The evolution of behaviorism can be viewed as increments in the number and complexity of mechanism that are put *into* the Egg. In revulsion against the "junkshop theorizing" of the late nineteenth century, Watson, Weiss, and Kantor – and later Skinner – went to the other extreme and claimed *that there was nothing whatsoever inside the Little Black Egg that was the proper business of an objective behaviorist!* However, since even the most adamant Skinnerian would admit that it is not external stimuli and overt movement themselves that are associated in nervous systems, such single-stage behaviorism should be termed $\dot{s} \rightarrow \dot{r}$ psychology – thus associations between what I call *icons* and *motons* at the **projection level** (Roman I in Figure 1) of my Little Black Egg. Rats replaced humans as subjects, or humans were limited to rat-level performance.

But even at the "rat level," replicable phenomena appeared that were impossible for a single-stage theory to handle – for example, semantic generalization and semantic satiation, both embarrassing for a theory that dismisses meaning as a "mentalistic ghost." Classic two-stage behaviorism – exemplified by the theorizing of Hull

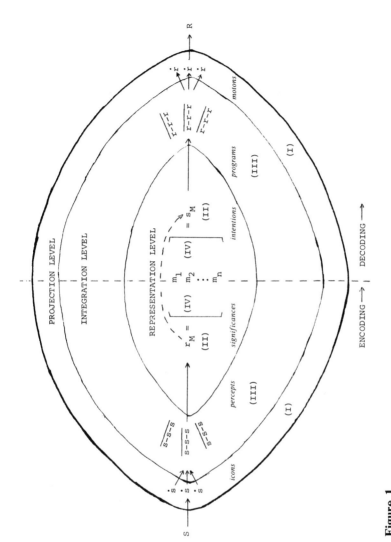

Figure 1
Evolution of the Little Black Egg of behaviorism.

and Tolman[6] – put a mediating "replica" of the peripheral $\dot{s} \rightarrow \dot{r}$ relation back into the Egg at the most central **representational level** (Roman II in my *historical* sequencing). For Hull, clinging to his behaviorist moorings, this mediation process was an implicit response (r_M) producing a distinctive stimulus (s_M); for Tolman, anticipating a theory of meaning, this same process was a "sign-significate expectancy." What both had done, in effect, was to break the S-to-R relation into two, *separately manipulatable,* associations, $S \rightarrow r_M$ and $s_M \rightarrow R$, thereby greatly amplifying the power of behavior theory.

By the mid 1950s I had become convinced that there were two gross insufficiencies with the two-stage models of Hull and Tolman. One was the incapability of handling the phenomena of *perceptual organization* (so amply documented in the literature of Gestalt psychology). The other was the incapability of handling the phenomena of *behavioral organization* (the central programming of complex behavior skills, as so forcefully argued by Lashley in his 1951 Hixon Symposium address[7]). So, I proposed an **integration level** of processing (Roman III's) *between* the projection and representational levels, on both the sensory (encoding) and motor (decoding) sides of the equation.

Whereas sensory *icons* and motor *motons* are essentially isomorphic relations between surface stimulations/behaviors and corresponding sensory and motor projection cortical areas, the proposed *percepts* and *programs* at the **integration level** may be innately determined, but are mainly acquired through experience – the learning principle being that the greater the frequency with which icons ($\dot{s}, \dot{s}, \dot{s}$) or motons ($\dot{r}, \dot{r}, \dot{r}$) have co-occurred in input or output experience, the greater the tendency for their post-projectional ($\overline{s - s - s}$) or pre-projectional ($\overline{r - r - r}$) correlates to activate each other centrally as percepts or programs respectively. In effect, *redundancies* in either sensory input or motor output will come to be reflected in evocative or predictive *integrations* in the nervous system.

1.2.2 The componential nature of representational mediators

You will note that there is a Level IV at the very center of my Little Black Egg, with a vertical array [m_1, m_2, ..., m_n] that is at once the componential meanings of *perceptual inputs* (their *significances,* r_M) and of *behavioral outputs* (their *intentions,* s_M). Just as the phonemes and sememes of linguistic theory are compo-

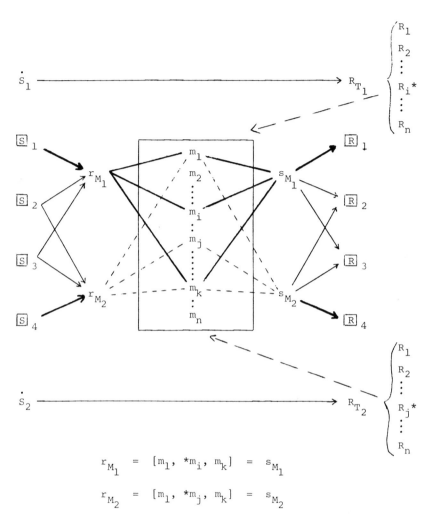

$$r_{M_1} = [m_1, *m_i, m_k] = s_{M_1}$$

$$r_{M_2} = [m_1, *m_j, m_k] = s_{M_2}$$

Figure 2
The componential nature of representational mediation processes.

nential in nature, being exhaustively analysable into sets of *distinctive features,* so in my APG_O it is postulated that global mediation processes (r_M's) are exhaustively analysable into sets of distinctive mediator components (r_m's). Figure 2 illustrates a crucial implication of this postulation: *a shift in a single component can completely shift the total meaning and hence behavioral function.* Thus, shifting from the m_i of r_{M_1} to the m_j of r_{M_2} changes the significances of signs S_1 versus S_4, and hence the intentions expressed by behaviors R_1 versus R_4. This figure also illustrates two other implications:

▶ Signs and behaviors associated with the same global mediation process will be *functionally equivalent* (for example, signs 1, 2, and 3 with r_{M_1} as their significance and behaviors 1, 2, and 3 with s_{M_1} as their intention).
▶ Signs and behaviors associated with different and incompatible global mediation processes will necessarily be *ambiguous* as to their significance in comprehending and as to their intention in expressing (here signs 2 and 3 and behaviors 2 and 3).

1.2.3 The intimate parallelism of non–linguistic and linguistic cognizing

There are two very general principles of my version of neobehaviorism that apply equivalently to cognitive processing in both perceptual-motor and linguistic channels:

▶ the "emic" principle – applying where the percepts and the programs for expression are variable but the significances and intentions are constant;
▶ the "ambiguity" principle – applying where significances and intentions are variable but the percepts that activate them and the programs for expressing them happen to be the same.

The "emic" principle. By virtue of the fact that both things and organisms are mobile with respect to each other, it follows that the distal signs of things will be variable through many stimulus dimensions. Thus MOTHER FACE will vary in retinal-image size as a function of distance, and in brightness and hue as functions of the time of day (illustrated by signs 1 through 4 in Figure 3). Yet, since the signifying relation ($\dot{S} \rightarrow R_T$) remains constant (mother eventually cuddles child), there will in theory be an extension of a *common* mediation process ($r_M \rightarrow s_M$, the "mother meaning") across the class of signs (the heavy *convergent* lines) – hence these will be percept differences that do *not* make a difference in meaning. In the psychology of perception, this common significance is the *constancy phenomenon,* of course, but the same paradigm applies to *synonymy* and *paraphrase* in language.

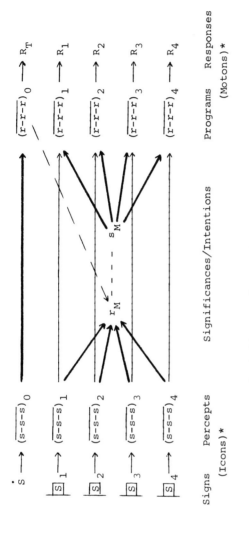

Figure 3
The "emic" principle in behavior theory.

Looking now at the heavy *divergent* arrows, it can be seen that we also have a situation where intentions are constant but the expressive programs are variable – *and* we face the issue of *control and decision* in neobehaviorism. Let signs 1 through 4 represent the perceptual signs of a desired APPLE object at decreasing distances and the responses 1 through 4 the appropriate apple-acquiring responses. The varying retinal sizes provide the controls and the responses selected are the decisions. Thus for sign 1 (APPLE over on a table), we have an R_1 of "locomoting toward," for sign 2 (APPLE near arm's reach) an R_2 of "reaching for and grasping," for sign 3 (APPLE at crooked arm's distance) an R_3 of "inspecting for edibleness," and for sign 4 (APPLE approaching toward face) an R_4 of "mouth opening and biting." Thus there is a *syntax of behaving* just as there is a syntax of talking – for the child to make biting, then grasping, then reaching responses (all in thin air) before he approaches the distant apple would be just as "ungrammatical" as it would have been for Caesar to announce "Vici, vidi, veni!"

The "ambiguity" principle. Whereas the signs discussed under the "emic" principle are *unambiguous* – one significance-intention mediation process having high probability for all signs and other alternatives having negligible probability – here we have the converse situation. A single sign (either perceptual or linguistic, as suggested in Figure 4) is variably associated with a divergent set of significances and (as also suggested in the figure) the variable set of intentions may also be associated with the same expression. On the input side of the behavioral equation, this is the condition for perceptual as well as linguistic *homonomy* – the familiar ambiguous figures like the Necker Cube in perception and the polysemy of many words in language, as in "he went to the BANK" and "the SHOOTING of the hunters was terrible." On the output side, the perceptual combination – for example, of TIGHT-LIPPED SMILE with SHAKING OF FISTED HAND – may be ambiguous as to being an intent to threaten *or* to express satisfaction with a completed task. Linguistically, "He was a Colt last year, but now he's a Bear" is entirely mind-boggling (to a non-sportsoholic, at least), and the intention behind "Can you open the window?" – as to being a request or an inquiry as to the listener's competence – is equally ambiguous.

Given the ubiquity of ambiguity for signs in both linguistic and perceptual channels, why aren't we hopelessly ambiguated most of the time? As suggested by S_X and S_Z in Figure 4, potentially ambiguous signs are nearly always *disambiguated* by other contextual

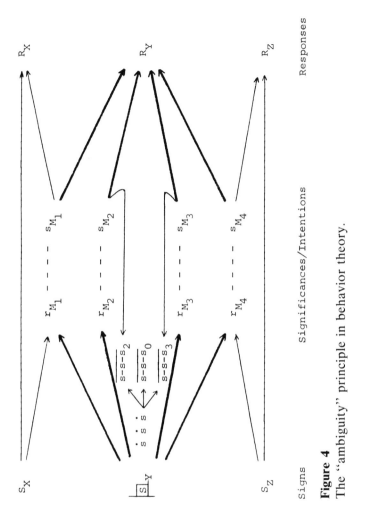

Figure 4
The "ambiguity" principle in behavior theory.

signs – which may be either perceptual or linguistic in their relations to the signs and responses in question:
▶ **linguistic/linguistic**
  "He **rowed** to the bank.   The shooting of the hunters **by the
  natives** was terrible."
▶ **perceptual/linguistic**
  When my friend exclaims "Duck!" in a barnyard, I'm likely to
  look around for the bird, but when passing a busy sandlot base-
  ball field, I'm more likely to "duck" my head!
▶ **linguistic/perceptual**
  As is notoriously the case on television, the faces of people in a
  shouting mob can be modulated from "violent" to "sincerely
  determined" by the linguistic commentary.
▶ **perceptual/perceptual**
  The tight-lipped smile plus shaking fist of the boxer will shift
  from "threatening" when the fight is perceived as about to start
  to "prideful satisfaction" when it has just been won.

2. Structure and Meaning in Cognizing

In a well-known paper,[8] W.C. Watt argues that the deep *mental
grammar* (MG) cannot be equated with any linguistic *competence
grammar,* but rather must be equated with an *abstract performance
grammar* (APG).   But since he is quite vague about how this APG is
to be characterized, we are left with MG = APG = ?, a most unsatisfactory state of affairs!   Here I attempt to reduce the "empti-
ness" symbolized by the ?.   The Structural (S) and Functional (F)
notions I offer *all* apply solely to the most central representational
level of the Little Black Egg (Figure 1).

2.1 Structure of the representational level

At least the following "mechanisms" – by which I mean structures
capable of certain functions by as yet unspecifiable means in the
central nervous system – must be postulated:
• a LEXICON (LEX),
• an OPERATOR (OPR),
• a BUFFER (BUF), and
• a MEMORY (MEM).
All of these are kinds of "memory," but of very different sorts, as
will be seen.   Figure 5 provides a sketch of this "structuring" of the
representational level.   While outlining the structural notions relating to each of the "mechanisms," I repeatedly refer you to this

figure. For each postulated "mechanism" – LEX, OPR, BUF, and MEM, in that order – I move from grosser to finer structural notions.

The LEXICON. The LEXICON is a semantic encoding and decoding mechanism, transforming *analogically coded percepts* (perceptual and linguistic signs) into *digitally coded significances* (meanings) in comprehending and then transforming this same information, now intentions, into *analogically coded programs* for behaving (linguistically or otherwise) in expressing. Note that I use – appropriately, I think – *encoding* for putting information *into* the semantic code and *decoding* for taking information *out of* the semantic code. Thus LEX is a "process" rather than a "storage" type of memory – relating signs (percepts) to semantic-feature sets – and can be used at a very fast clip, "wiping itself clean" after each transducing operation by transferring its information elsewhere. More finely, then, the *code strips,* transferred "upward" to the LEXICON in comprehending or "downward" to the motor programming level in expressing, are the semantic representations of *entities* (later NPs) and *relations* (later VPs) in cognizing (for example, THAT NASTY DOG / IS CHASING AFTER / MY LITTLE KITTEN). And, most finely, in the LEXICON semantic features are ordered "left-to-right" according to the over-all frequency with which they differentiate meanings of signs, both perceptual and linguistic – this being a reflection of basic frequency/latency relations in the nervous system. Since all "higher" mechanisms operate on outputs from LEX, this same ordering must hold throughout the representational system.

That *word-like* linguistic percepts are the "natural" units for LEX in its transducing operations is strongly implied by the findings of Osgood and Hoosain.[9] Tachistoscopic recognition thresholds were compared for various sets of materials and the following significant results were obtained:

- When *non-word morphemes* were compared with *words* containing these morphemes (for example, *ment* versus *mental,* the former being both shorter and of higher usage frequency), words had significantly lower recognition thresholds.
- When *multisyllabic non-words* were compared with *multisyllabic words* of the same length (for example, *famness* versus *dashing,* with usage-frequency clearly favoring the non-words), again words had significantly lower thresholds.
- When more word-like *nominal compounds* were compared with nonsense compounds (for example, *looking glass* and *stock market* versus *motion glass* and *shade market*), again with usage-

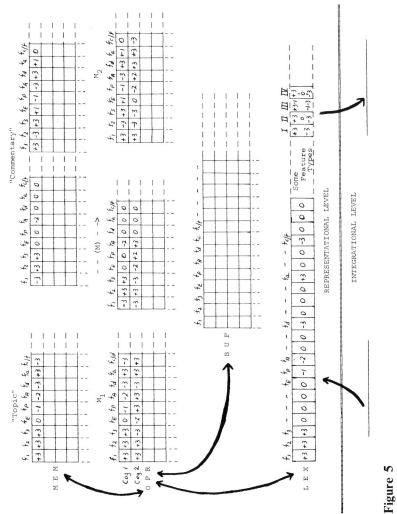

Figure 5

Structure of the representational level – four "mechanisms".

frequencies of included words controlled), nominal compounds had significantly lower recognition thresholds.

We attribute this higher salience of words and word-like units to facilitative *feedback* from the representational level to the perceptual integration level.

The OPERATOR. Grossly, the OPERATOR is a *tripartite mechanism* that gives *cognitive structure* to functionally related sets of semantic outputs from the LEXICON (in "fresh cognizing") or from the MEMORY (in "re-cognizing"); the OPERATOR is where the *dynamic interactions* among such sets occur (to be detailed later in the discussion of functional notions), and, I assume, is the locus of conscious awareness. The OPERATOR is also a very short-term process memory (like LEX), holding the semantic information only while the postulated cognitive interactions occur, and then outputting it either to MEM (in comprehending) or to LEX (in expressing). More finely, the three components of the OPERATOR are the complete semantic representations as simplex cognitions of a pair of entities, M_1 and M_2, and the signed and directed action or stative relation, $-(m) \rightarrow$, between them. The symbol M simply stands for "meaning." A further structural notion here is that all complex cognitions, involving multiple but related perceived actions or states (later conjoined clauses in sentencing), are analyzed by the OPERATOR into concatenations of simplex cognitions, represented in parallel in its three components ("vertically," as shown in Figure 5). In comprehending, then, "the ball the boy hit broke the window" is paraphrased analytically as "the boy hit a ball" (and then) "the ball broke the window." More of this anon, under functional notions.

My postulation of a tripartite structure of simplex cognitions (rather than the bipartite structure of Chomskyan TGG) follows Greenberg's argument that this structure is necessary for the demonstration of grammatical universals[10] – as well as my own intuitions about "naturalness" in prelinguistic cognizing. The OPERATOR diagrammed here is for English, a subject-verb-object language (SVO), a type accounting for about 60% of world languages, but it could equally well be for SOV (about 30%) or even VSO. Even if VSO accounts for only 10% of the world's languages, the existence of languages of this form would seem to refute Chomsky's postulation of a bipartite (NP + VP) structure, since the V and O constitutes of the VP are separated – but as far as I am aware, he has never dealt with this problem.

The BUFFER. The BUFFER is a *temporary* information-holding mechanism, receiving from the OPERATOR constituent code strips found to be *unnaturally ordered* and returning this information to OPERATOR as soon as the displaced constituents have been "naturalized" in the OPERATOR. BUF is thus a storage-type memory, but very short-term and fading rapidly. Given the many transformations in sentences produced and received, some such mechanism is essential for any performance theory. In effect, then, such OPERATOR – BUFFER interactions constitute the *transformational syntax* of the APG. More finely, the BUFFER is structured ("vertically") as a "pushdown" storage for displaced constituents of simplex cognitions or for all constituents of whole cognitions unnaturally ordered in conjoined complexes. As will be seen in the discussion of the functional notions, such a pushdown storage mechanism is postulated to guarantee the restoration of the natural ordering of cognitions.

The MEMORY. The MEMORY is a mechanism for *long-term* storage of processed cognitions inputted from the OPERATOR, and it is organized both in terms of the tripartite structure of the OPERATOR and of the feature-ordering structure of the LEXICON. More finely, the MEMORY is structured "horizontally" in terms of the semantic representations of the topics of processed cognitions (the M_1's), each with its associated commentary, the semantic representations of the relation ($-(M) \rightarrow$'s) and the relateds (M_2's) of the same cognitions. Most finely, the MEMORY is organized "vertically" by topics (M_1's) from maximum positiveness of the ordered semantic features ($+ + + \ldots +$) to maximum negativeness ($- - - \ldots -$). As a cognitive psychologist, I find it inconceivable that there could be an alphabetized "encyclopedia" somewhere in the brain. However, the "vertical" organization postulated here does guarantee that semantically related topics having the same higher-order, entailed features (for example, "robin," "sparrow," and "hawk" all entailing superordinate "bird-meaning") will be close in scanning.

The postulated organization of MEM with respect to the M_1's of cognitions has a very strong implication: that the topics of sentences (as well as the actors and figures of perceptual events and states) will be retrieved from MEM more quickly than the associated commentaries (or the recipients and grounds of perceptual cognitions). This is not unlike "network" models,[11] on the one hand, and the set-theoretic models,[12] on the other. Too, while the MEMORY in this APG is quite literally a semantic memory (with respect to semantic feature code strips), it is also a store of knowledge of the world (by virtue of the propositional character of the whole cognitions stored, hence a "memory for ideas"). Finally, let me emphasize that "above" the LEXICON all processing at the representational level of this APG consists of operations on organized sets of semantic features. As will be seen, this implies that all *syntactic* distribution and orderings must be given a *semantic* base.

2.2 Meaning at the representational level: three functions of the LEXICON

The three most "primitive" functional notions of the APG apply to the form-meaning relations that the LEXICONs of the users of languages must acquire if the transducing functions of this mechanism are to be developed – and they all derive from a componential elaboration of Hullian two-stage behaviorism.

- F I is a global *sign-learning* paradigm,
- F II is a finer *feature-learning* paradigm, and
- F III is a *frequency/recency* principle governing the accessibility of semantic features.

F I, a sign-learning paradigm: When a percept that does not elicit a predictable pattern of behavior (for example, SIGHT OF COOKIE) is repeatedly paired with a percept that does (for example, EATING COOKIE), the former will become a sign of the latter by virtue of becoming associated with a mediation process $[r_M \rightarrow s_M]$ in the LEXICON that represents the behavior produced by the significate and thereby mediates behaviors appropriate to the significate. Keep in mind that r_M is a summary symbol for a *set* of mediator components. This principle, relating to the development of what might well be called "behavioral competence," suggests how, bit by bit, a child acquires knowledge about his world.

F II, a feature-learning paradigm: To the extent that differences in percepts are associated with reciprocally antagonistic differences in behavior, the central representations of these differences ($^+r_{m_i}$ versus $^-r_{m_i}$ in the LEXICON will become the bipolar semantic features that distinguish the significances of percepts. This principle suggests how a child acquires awareness of what differences make a difference (for example, are "emic") – and, bit by bit, more knowledge, first about his world and later about his language.

F III, a frequency/recency principle:

a. The greater the overall frequency with which mediator components ($^\pm r_{m_i}$ = semantic features) have been elicited in the LEXICON by signs, the shorter will be the latencies of their evocation.

b. The more recent the prior elicitation of sets of related components (r_M code strips), the more available such sets will be for
re-elicitation.
c. Massed repetition of related sets of mediator components will
result in reduced availability.

The latency notion (a) derives directly from the habit-strength
principle of Hullian (and most other) behavior theories. It is the
functional basis for the order-of-scanning structural characteristic
of the LEXICON – and the "scanning" is therefore not spatial (as
the word implies metaphorically) but rather temporal, in terms of
the finely differentiated speeds of component reactions. Interestingly, since all higher-order features are entailed in the code strips for
exemplars, the taxonomic tree structures of lexicons can be derived
from this principle. The facilitating effect (b) of recently activated
meanings (code strips) on subsequent elicitation would underlie
what is called "topicality" in discourse. The inhibitory effect of
massed elicitation of particular meanings (c) is well documented, of
course, in the extensive literature on what is appropriately termed
"semantic satiation" – such effects presumably being a basis for
redundancy deletions and paraphrasings in ordinary language.

3. Naturalness in Cognizing and Sentencing

This is the focal section of my Abstract Performance Grammar.
Starting with the axiomatic notion that the basic cognitive structures which interpret sentences received and initiate sentences
produced are established in prelinguistic experience, it arrives at the
empirically testable hypothesis that *the more closely sentences correspond in their surface structures to these prelinguistically based cognitive structures, the earlier they will be understood and produced by
children and the more easily they will be processed by adults.* Functional notion IV is concerned with naturalness of ordering constituents within simplex sentences (and within the clauses of complex
sentences), F V deals with naturalness in ordering word-forms
within constituents, and F VI treats naturalness in the ordering of
simplex clauses within complex, conjoined sentences. In all these
cases, natural ordering is the order that corresponds to the order in
which the subunits at each level are (in theory) cognized in prelinguistic experience.

3.1 F IV: naturalness in ordering the constituents of simplexes[13]

Donning the booties of very early babyhood, three primitive, perception-based, semantic distinctions are postulated: *substantivity, directionality,* and *stativity*. This leads to a *semantic* characterization of the most basic *syntax* (SNP/VP/ONP) of simplex sentences.

In this section, the strong claim about the universality of "SVO" structuring in prelinguistic cognizing is critically evaluated against the existential facts of SOV and VSO languages. Finally, relevant cross-language linguistic and experimental evidence on bitransitive sentencings is offered.

A semantic characterization of the syntax of simple sentences. We all begin separate existences in a state much like that of prenatal experience – near-complete amorphousness – but soon three very primitive meaningful distinctions develop:[14]

▶ *Substantivity* – distinguishing +substantive entities from ⁻substantive relations, and later generalizing to NPs versus VPs – is the most basic. Entities may be either redundantly experienced contoured things like MOMMY FACE or uncontoured things like CEILING. Also, relations are *not* directly perceptible, but must be inferred from changes-of-state of entities.

▶ *Directionality* is the distinguishing of +salient figures of states and sources of actions from ⁻salient grounds of states and recipients of actions – presumably on the basis of innate gestalt-like predispositions.

▶ *Stativity* is the distinguishing of +stative, stable figure/ground relations from ⁻stative, unstable actions, including change-of-state relations. One suspects that, given an infant's motoric capacities, stable stative relations develop somewhat earlier than unstable action relations.

What is proposed here, of course, is a *semantic* characterization of the most fundamental *syntactic* distinctions made by linguists in defining the constituent structures of simple sentences – which is essential for an APG that operates entirely on semantic information inputted from the LEXICON. Thus we have two basic types of simplex cognitions:

• *stative* [FIGURE/STATE/GROUND], and
• *action* [SOURCE/ACTION/RECIPIENT].

CAT / IS ON / PILLOW and CAT / JUMPED ON / PILLOW are naturally ordered stative and action *perceptual* cognitions. Compare the naturalness in later sentencings of stative "the cat is on the pillow by the window" and action "the cat jumped on the pillow for the toy mouse" with the jarring unnaturalness of stative "the window is by the pillow under the cat" and action "for the toy mouse the pillow was jumped on by the cat." Yet neither of the latter sentences is in any way ungrammatical, and both, under appropriate motivational conditions, could be produced by speakers.

Why are there any SOV or VSO languages? We must raise this question because this naturalness principle asserts that prelinguistic cognizing will be *universally* SVO, and thus would seem to predict both that non-SVO languages would be somewhat more difficult to process and that children acquiring them should display strong SVO tendencies initially – for neither of which is there any evidence. However, note that

▶ the distribution of human languages is 60% SVO, 30% SOV, and only about 10% VSO;

▶ although there have been many spontaneous historical shifts from SOV to SVO types, there are apparently no recorded shifts in the reverse direction (in the absence of occupation and cultural dominance);

▶ VSO languages are found mainly in small, isolated groups.

It appears that S-before-O is a universal ordering principle, thus fitting the ±directionality features above. It should also be noted that entities (Ss and Os) are *directly perceptible,* while relations, stative or action, *must be inferred* from the stability versus instability of the perceived contingencies among the perceptible things. It would appear that, whereas the dominant SVO-ers have opted for *one* naturalness principle (locating the inferred relations in the "relational" place), the SOV-ers have opted for *another,* highlighting the perceptible entities over the only-later-to-be inferred relations. The fact that VSO-ers *reverse* the latter principle may explain their rarity!

Some relevant evidence on bitransitive constructions. Sentences that involve three entities (NPs) but only one relation (VP) put pressure on a theory that postulates an underlying tripartite structure for simplexes: *either* the meaning of a third entity must be "absorbed" into one of the postulated three components, *or* it must be demonstrated that the three-entity sentence type is in reality the *fusion* of two ordinary simplex cognitions – which is difficult to do if only one relation (VP) is involved. To put oneself back in the booties of early childhood again, it seems intuitively clear that

• when a prelinguistic child perceptually cognizes BIG BROTHER GIVE BALL TO BIG SISTER, the *ball-object* is cognitively "embedded" in the act of transferring, and therefore

• the *recipient,* the so-called indirect object, is in fact the *real* direct object – contrary to the claims of traditional grammarians. This was the thrust of a paper by Osgood and Tanz; a concise summary of their findings follows.[15]

Cross-language linguistic evidence: One prediction – based on the dative, D, being the "real" independent ONP constituent – was that D would be more frequently marked than the VP-embedded object; this was supported by a consistent ratio of 2:1. A second prediction was that, if the O is marked in unitransitive sentences but not in bitransitive sentences, then the same marker will be used for D in bitransitives; this was upheld for the thirteen languages that met these conditions in a sample of 106. A third prediction was that O is more likely to be incorporated in verbs than D; this was strongly upheld in the data of Sapir, for American Indian languages, and Chao, for Chinese.[16]

Experimental psycholinguistic evidence: Osgood and Tanz report three experiments testing the hypothesis that, in the processing of bitransitive sentences presented to subjects in *either* basic SVOD or transform SVDO, *the O will be more tightly bound to the V than the D.* In Experiment I, given the SNP of sentences as cues and the subject correctly recalling the V, the conditional probability of *also recalling the O was significantly greater* than that of also recalling the D. In Experiment II, given *both* SNP and V as cues, there were *significantly more correct recalls* of whole SVOD sentences than of SVDO. And in Experiment III, using a probe-association method (where either the V was used as a cue for O versus D as associates, or vice versa) and prior presentation of several sentences, Vs as probes produced more Os than Ds *and* Vs were given *as responses* to Os as probes more often than to Ds as probes – both directions at ratios of about 2:1.

3.2 F V: naturalness of word–ordering within the constituents of simplexes

Here we consider the rather complex interactions between the LEXICON and the OPERATOR in the processing of within-constituent information in both comprehending and producing sentences. Whereas LEX functions on a "word-like" basis (as we have already seen), and therefore must reflect *language-specific* rules for word-ordering within constituents, OPR functions on a "whole-constituent" basis (fusing semantic information from LEX), and therefore can reflect *language universals* in cognizing and sentencing. So the problems for APG theory become, in essence, these:

1. Since, in the process of *comprehending* sentences, an individual's LEXICON segments the more or less continuous flow of incoming percept information into the meanings of word-like units and

transmits these code-strips sequentially "upward," how does his OPERATOR come to segment this flow and assign it to the "whole-constituents" on which it must "operate" (the M_1, $-(M) \rightarrow$, M_2 components)?

2. Since, in the process of *producing* sentences, a speaker's OPERATOR transmits "whole-constituent" semantic information sequentially "downward" into LEX for expression, how does his LEXICON now extract feature subsets corresponding to word-like units and order the transmission of these units to the motor integration level for utterance programs?

LEX/OPR functions in comprehending versus expressing. In the process of comprehension, LEX encodes word-like forms (free morphemes like "a" versus "the," wordbound morphemes like "unintentionally," and nominal compounds like "stumbling block") into their semantic feature codes and transmits these "upward," the OPERATOR, utilizing language-specific cues that signal the boundaries of NP and VP constituents, assigns this information sequentially to its three components (at this point, regardless of the appropriateness of assignments to M_1, $-(M) \rightarrow$, and M_2). All languages provide surface cues for the boundaries of constituents. For example, in English, the cues for NP *initial* are often articles and quantifiers ("a," "the," "some," "many," etc.) and for NP *terminal* are often the nominal heads ("ball," "man," "mountain," etc.) The cues are sometimes ambiguous, of course, as in "ship sails today." Since the surface cues are language-specific, they must be learned by the developing OPERATORs of individuals acquiring their own particular languages – and I must confess that I haven't considered the nature of such learning.

In the process of speaking, the OPERATOR sequentially transmits "downward" the semantic code-strips for whole constituents; to avoid utter confusion, LEX cannot "accept" any subsequent code-strip until it is again empty ("featureless"). From each complex constituent feature-strip, LEX

- *extracts* sequentially subsets that constitute the meanings for word-forms in its language and that together exhaust the semantic information of the constituent.
- *outputs* these feature-sets to the motor integration level, where the appropriate programs for speaking are successively activated.

The output ordering for LEX within each constituent is that which this mechanism has acquired in comprehension – and again I have no ideas about this learning – but there is ample psycholinguistic evidence, at all levels of language processing, for developmental priority of comprehension over production.

Naturalness in ordering within constituents. All of these notions assume that what I call naturalness in constituent ordering for each language type will be guaranteed by the LEXICON → OPERATOR → LEXICON interactions. In particular, it is assumed that within each component OPERATORs "scan" features in the order of their criticality:

- for *affective* E-P-A features prior to *denotative* features – by virtue of their primitive survival value (the good-bad, strong-weak, and fast-slow of things);
- for denotative features characterizing *entities* (later NPs), *substantive* (identifying) prior to *modulating* (qualifying) features;
- for denotative features characterizing *relations* (later VPs), similarly, *nature-specifying* (identifying) features prior to *modulating* (adverbial) features.

This clearly implies that an OPERATOR should process

- N-followed-by-A orderings in M_1 and M_2 components more rapidly than A-followed-by-N orderings,
- V-followed-by-AV ordering of the $-(M)→$ component more rapidly than AV-followed-by-V ordering – that is, ordering with identifying information before modulating information.

Most relevantly, Greenberg informs us that, for NPs, languages that confirm the prediction outnumber languages that do not by about 2 to 1; unfortunately he has nothing to say about VP orderings.[17]

3.3 F VI: Naturalness in ordering the clauses of complexes.

The basic assumption here is that in both comprehending and expressing complex sentences with conjoined clauses **the natural order of processing by the OPERATOR is always that corresponding to the order in which the states and/or events referred to in the clauses are typically cognized in prelinguistic experience.** Given the orderly nature of the physical world, perceptual experiences (of adults as well as prelinguistic children) are almost always in their natural order – thus perceiving MOMMY GET UNDRESSED *(and then)* MOMMY GET IN BED, or DADDY DROP GLASS *(and so then)* GLASS SHATTER IN PIECES. However, all known languages provide means by which speakers can move clauses about to satisfy their momentary interests. But still, given the prelinguistic base for cognizing, disordered (by speakers) complexes must be restored to natural ordering in processing by listeners if they are to be comprehended.

Naturalness of clause ordering in English. A variety of types of complexes can be ordered simultaneously in terms
- of increasing semantic complexity of their modes of conjoining, and
- of increasing syntactic complexity of their ordering.

The simple junction mode is coded $^+$congruent (and_1 with its adverbial derivatives like "while") or $^-$congruent (but_1 with adverbial derivatives like "although"), and either clause order is natural. The simple sequence mode adds a $^\pm$sequence feature to congruence (and_2 (then) versus but_2 (then) and adverbials like "before/after" versus "yet/although,") and clause ordering can be either natural or unnatural: for example, natural "Mommy got undressed before she went to bed" versus unnatural "Mommy went to bed after she got undressed.". For the sequential cause mode, a $^\pm$cause feature is added to congruence (and_3 (so) versus but_3 (still) and adverbials like "because" and "although," and again orders can be natural ("because it was raining on the golf course John got wet") or unnatural ("John got wet because it was raining on the golf course."). As is indicated by numeral subscripts on the *and*s and *but*s, these most basic and earliest acquired conjoiners are polysemous, shifting sense with the mode of conjoining.

Ordering with respect to syntactic complexity increases as follows.
- ▶ Underlying *and/but* conjoiners are also the most constrained. They must be centered between the clauses, and the clauses must be naturally ordered. (Witness the "mind-boggling-ness" of "!And Mommy went to bed she got undressed" as well as "!Mommy went to bed and got undressed.")
- ▶ Centered adverbials that maintain natural order should be somewhat less difficult than
- ▶ Preposed adverbials that also maintain natural order. ("The road was slippery so the car skidded" is somewhat easier than "Because the road was icy the car skidded.")
- ▶ Centered adverbials that require unnatural order ("Papa put on his street clothes after he took a shower.") should be much more difficult, and
- ▶ Preposed adverbials that require require unnatural order ("Before Papa put on his street clothes he took a shower.") should be the most difficult.

Considerable research on the processing of complexes by both adults and children is now available, and the results are generally consistent with these expectations. Clark and Clark, using only "before" versus "after," report that naturally ordered preposed and centered complexes were recalled better than unnaturally ordered ones.[18] E. Clark found that in a comprehension task – simply acting out heard sentences with toys – young children acted out naturally ordered sentences ("after" preposed and "before" centered) with only 8% errors as compared with 58% errors (pure chance) for unnaturally ordered sentences ("before" preposed and "after" centered). In a study comprehension by Dutch children of two-clause sentences conjoined by "omdat" (because), it was reported that correct acting out increases with age from three to seven; only the youngest children tend to act out *as given* the unnaturally ordered sentences (with "omdat" centered).[20] At our Center for Comparative Psycholinguistics, Linda Hunter is piloting an extension of this design to other modalities for cross-language replication.

Unambiguous signaling of naturalness. In English, basic "and"s and "but"s can only be centered, and the clauses must be in natural order. In the simple junction mode, since the events are contemporaneous, there is no natural order to be signaled. For all other modes of conjoining,

- all adverbials that can *only* be centered must also signal natural order unambiguously, but
- for all other adverbials in sequence, cause, sequential cause, and intention modes that can be *either* centered or preposed, the combined cues of the FORM ("after," "before," "because," "although," etc.) along with its LOCUS (centered versus preposed) provide completely unambiguous signals of naturalness versus unnaturalness of clause ordering.

For just one example, (preposed) "because John poisoned his mother-in-law he was executed" is naturally ordered, whereas (centered) "John was executed because he poisoned his mother-in-law" is unnaturally ordered (effect before cause). Shifting the contents of the clauses without shifting adverbial locus results in "mind-boggling" products, here both "!because John was executed he poisoned his mother-in-law" and "!John poisoned his mother-in-law because he was executed."

Is such unambiguous signaling of naturalness versus unnaturalness in clause ordering unique to English? A native speaker of Kannada (an SOV language spoken in Bangalore, India) has made a parallel analysis of such signaling, as well as less detailed analyses of Israeli Hebrew, Mexican Spanish, Turkish, Japanese, and Chinese.[21] The evidence strongly suggests that such unambiguous signaling is indeed a language universal. Since what is being signaled here is naturalness rather than grammaticality – although my !-marked sentences are "mind-boggling," we know of nothing in TGG that would tag them as ungrammatical – and since naturalness signaling is surely a part of linguistic competence (*sans* awareness, as is usually the case), it would seem to have serious implications for the explanatory adequacy of any extant linguistic competence theory.

4. Production and Comprehension of Unnaturally Ordered Sentences

We now move into a domain of central concern to linguists as well as psycholinguists – the dynamics of producing and comprehending sentences that are transformations from base structures (in TGG terms) or from naturally ordered sentences (in APG terms). Here we must distinguish between the "natural" salience with which Section 3 (functional notions F IV, V, and VI) was concerned and the "unnatural" salience that speakers impose to express their own momentary motivational states. (Incidentally, I miss in the linguistics literature any concern about just *why* speakers ever produce sentencings other than those generated directly from the deep structures.) Needless to say, such shenanigans by speakers put pressure on listeners if they are to comprehend.

4.1 Production of unnatural transformed sentencings

Three salience variables affecting speakers.
- ▶ *Vividness.* This is intrinsic to the intensity of semantic feature codings of words or whole constituents. Examples would be "a VAMPIRE the maid dusting the hallway saw" (word salience) and "RUNNING LIKE MAD John fled from the bar" (VP constituent salience).
- ▶ *Motivation-of-speaker.* Extrinsic to feature codings, this is attributed by the speaker because of his focus (personal involvement, interest, etc.). It can lead a concerned speaker, for example, to passivize – "the KEY was taken by somebody!"
- ▶ *Topicality.* This is due to the relatively greater availability of reverberating code-strips representing information recently processed. Thus, having just perceptually cognized my poodle, Pierre, rushing to the window, growling at A BIG BLACK DOG on the lawn, I'm more likely to say to my house guest "that ugly mutt belongs to the Smiths down the street" than to say "the Smiths down the street own that ugly mutt."

Cooperation and competition between "natural" and "unnatural" salience principle. Compare the following sentential variations on the same theme:

- "The boy tossed the FRISBEE to his dog" (cooperation, since SV$\underline{O}$D is the natural bitransitive order (see pp. 166-167 for evidence).
- "The boy tossed his SAINT BERNARD the ball" (competition, since SVD$\underline{O}$ is the unnatural bitransitive order).

Experimental results reported by Osgood and Bock[22] generally confirm predictions about retaining versus shifting structures in recall with a variety (dative, genitive, passive, etc.) of transformational types. Also relevant to speaker motivations is what Cooper and Ross[23] refer to as the "me first" principle — for example, spatial deixis ("we hunted HERE and there" / * ... "there and here"), temporal deixis ("I think of him NOW and then" / * ... "then and now"), and even "WASPness" ("they played COWBOYS and Indians" / * ... "Indians and cowboys"!

Processing unnaturally ordered sentencing by speakers. Functional notion VIII-I is so complex that only the gist of it can be given here.

▶ Since in his own listening behavior the speaker-to-be must always naturalize perceptual and linguistic inputs in order to comprehend and store them in his MEMORY, he must start his productions with naturally ordered cognitions in his OPERATOR.

▶ Assuming that salience dynamics are operating on him, if overt expression of the salient information leaves the rest in OPR in natural order, no BUFfing is required. (For example, if starting from natural "I will have a martini," our motivated speaker first says "a martini...," the remaining "I will have" is simply expressed.)

▶ But if expression of the salient information leaves the rest in unnatural order, the unnaturally ordered constituents are BUFfed, the rest of what is in OPR is expressed, and then the information in BUF is expressed as returned to OPR. (For example, if, starting from natural "everyone admires Napoleon," salient "Napoleon" is expressed, leaving "everyone admires," the leftward "everyone" is BUFfed, features for the remaining "admires" are expressed — but, given the shift to ⁻Directionality of the relation, as the passive "is admired by" — and then "everyone" is expressed as returned from BUF.)

These two simple examples, topicalization (or "clefting") and passivization, must suffice here. However, a wide variety of transforms of increasing complexity can be similarly analyzed — including, for *simplexes,* AV preposing, subject-verb (auxiliary) inversion, PP-phrase preposing, particle movement, dative movement, and possessive reversal; and, for *complexes,* simple sequence, simple cause, and sequential cause complexes conjoined by adverbials, complexes involving relative clauses (SNP-, ONP-, and PP-phrases), and a variety of commentative complexes (for example, "it is obvious that Peter Pan was a fairy"). What is important about the APG analyses is this: a relatively small number of LEX → OPR → BUF → LEX rules, governing the effects of salience dynamics and the cognitive processes that "compensate" for them, serve to account for the production of a relatively large and diverse number of transformations. The same assertion applies to the comprehension of transformations by listeners – to which I now turn.

4.2 Comprehension of unnatural transformed sentencings

Salience-motivated unnatural sentencings by speakers put pressures on listeners if they are to comprehend – and speakers can't lighten the load by expressing certain information before "naturalizing" the whole. The same transform types analyzed for speaker production can be analyzed for listener comprehension – and comparative processing difficulties can be directly assessed by counting the OPR/BUF interactions involved. Following a brief discussion of Functional Notion VII, which specifies detection of unnaturalness by the listener's OPERATOR, a comparative analysis of the production and comprehension of the two simple transforms illustrated above is offered.

Detection of unnaturalness by the OPERATOR. Unnaturalness in sentence production and the comprehension of sentences are, in a sense, mirror images of each other. However, although the speaker's OPR must detect and adjust for unnaturalness in constituents remaining after motivated expression of salient information (as in the production of "Napoleon is admired by everyone" example above), the processing load on the listener's OPR for naturalizing transformed sentences is generally much greater. In essence, F VII states:

▶ that OPR scans the semantic code-strips in its three components (constituents) in terms of their behavioral criticality –
- primitive survival-value affective features prior to denotative, and
- substantive entity- and relation-identifying features before modulating (adjectival and adverbial) features.

▶ that OPR checks the component code-strips of simplexes (including the simplex clauses of complexes) for Naturalness within, and Compatibility between, constituents on the basic Substantivity, Directionality, and Stativity "syntactic-semantic" features (see F IV, pp. 164-165) to guarantee, for example,

- that the M_1's and M_2's are +substantive, with the former +directional and the latter ⁻directional,
- that the $-(M)\rightarrow$'s are ⁻substantive as well as +directional, and
- that either +stative or ⁻stative (action) relations involve compatible entities.

▶ that OPR checks for naturalness in the clause sequencing of complex sentences (see F VI, pp. 169-172). Whenever unnaturalness is detected, interactions with the BUFFER are initiated, and if naturalness cannot be restored, the child is just plain "mind-boggled".

Processing unnaturally ordered sentences by listeners. Very briefly again, the gist of F VIII-II is as follows.

▶ Only when speaker disordering has occurred is any listener reordering required; and there is no guarantee that the listener will be successful.

▶ When the listener's OPERATOR has detected cues for disordering of simplexes, a first cycle of OPR/BUF interactions is initiated and if – after "leftward" shift of remainders in OPR and the return of feature code-strips from BUF to the now empty slots – there are still cures for unnaturalness, a second cycle is initiated. (My linguist research assistant and I were unable to come up with any transformations in English requiring more than two cycles.)

▶ Details the OPR/BUF interactions required for processing disordered simplexes.

▶ Details the OPR/BUF interactions required for processing complexes. Any disordered simplex clause must be naturalized before continuing the processing of complexes. If the subsequent clause should naturally be the initial clause (for example, in "John was executed because he poisoned his mother-in-law)," then the entire prior clause, as received, must be transferred "right-to-left" to the push-down, temporary BUFFER-type memory.

Now let's compare the APG analyses of producing and comprehending the two relatively simple topicalization and passivization examples used earlier:

PRODUCTION BY SPEAKER

Topicalization: I will have a martini => A martini I will have

(1) Given SPKR MOT, EXP "A martini" → [I / will have / ϕ]

(2) EXP remainder, "I will have"

Passivization: Everyone admires Napoleon => Napoleon is admired by everyone

(1) EXP the SPKR-salient "Napoleon" →
     [everyone / admires / φ]

(2) Avoiding ungrammaticality ("everyone" in the Relation slot), BUF "everyone" → [φ / admires / φ]

(3) EXP unnaturally-directed Relation, "is admired by"

(4) As returned from BUF, EXP "everyone"

COMPREHENSION BY LISTENER

Topicalization: A martini I (=SPKR) will have => SPKR will have a martini

(1) Since "I" is unnatural for the –(M)→ slot, BUF "a martini" → "a martini" in BUF

(2) Shift remaining constituents "leftward" →
     [SPKR / will have / φ]

(3) Returning "a martini" from BUF to empty M_2 slot → [SPKR / will have / a martini]

Passivation: Napoleon is admired by everyone => Everyone admires Napoleon

(1) Since "is admired by" is an unnaturally directed relation, BUF "Napoleon" → "Napoleon" in BUF

(2) "Leftward" shift yields → [is admired by / everyone / φ]

(3) Since "is admired by" is unnatural as M_1, BUF it → "is admired by / Napoleon" in BUF (top-to-bottom)

(4) "Leftward" shift of "everyone" yields →
     [everyone / φ / φ]

(5) On return of "is admired by" from BUF, given $^+$directional coding (M_1) of "everyone," OPR shifts it to "admires" ($^+$directional relation)

(6) Return of "Napoleon" from BUF → [everyone / admires / Napoleon]

Although the same number of steps (three) are involved in both topicalizations, comprehension requires one OPR/BUF transfer but production does not. For passivization, production involves only four steps and one OPR/BUF interaction, while comprehension involves six steps and two OPR/BUF interactions. Across all types of transformation, comprehension generally (though not always) involves more processing difficulty than production, as measured by both the number of OPR/BUF transfers and the length of storage (while decaying) of information in the BUFFER, thus we can set up a hierarchy of predicted levels of processing difficulty across our entire gamut of natural versus unnatural (transform) types, which can then be studied experimentally.

Finally, let us relate the APG analysis of natural versus unnatural sentence production and comprehension to some of the most relevant literature in the field.

▶ *Center-embedding: the greatest cognizing complexity?*
George Miller has presented a classic example: "The race that the car that the people whom the obviously not very well dressed man called sold won was held last summer." Using much simpler, single-embedding examples, we can show
- that the embedded clauses must always be prior in cognizing (even if held up in production),
- that both the double-function of NPs (ONP-to-SNP) and the processing complexity of center-embeddings can be handled within the APG rules for production and comprehension.

▶ *Yngve's "depth hypothesis" versus the OPERATOR/BUFFER interactions of this APG.*
Analysis leads me to conclude
- that, although similar in purpose, the two mechanisms generate very different predictions about processing difficulty, and
- that in many cases the "depth hypothesis" predictions fail to fit ordinary intuitions about processing complexity.

5. Conclusion

In this chapter I have only been able to give a bare outline of my APG. However, I hope that I have been able to show
▶ that is is possible to provide a general account of sentence understanding and sentence production based on the underlying non-linguistic system, and

▶ that such a theory can deal with many specific aspects of language performance not treated in other current approaches.

REFERENCES

1. I should emphasize that, for reasons of space in a multi-author volume, the APG presented here will be a "bare bones" version, with citation of empirical evidence limited mainly (but not exclusively) to research by myself and my associates (including many students) and with practically no attempt to relate this theory to other psycholinguistic models. For a more elaborate presentation, the reader is referred to

   C.E. Osgood. *Lectures on Language Performance.* New York: Springer-Verlag, 1980.

2. Thus the sign languages of the deaf would be *unnatural* humanoid languages — while clearly satisfying the criteria for *anything* being a language (above) and the *functional* criteria for something being a humanoid language (below).

3. B. Berlin and P. Kay, *Basic Color Terms: Their Universality and Evolution.* Berkeley, CA: University of California Press, 1969.

4. G.K. Zipf, *Human Behavior and the Principle of Least Effort.* Cambridge, MA: Addison-Wesley, 1949.

5. J.H. Greenberg, "Language Universals." In *Current Trends in Linguistics: III. Theoretical Foundation,* T.A. Sebeok, ed. The Hague: Mouton, 1966.

6. C.L. Hull, "Knowledge and Purpose as Habit Mechanism." *Psychological Review* 37 (1930): 511-525.

   C.L. Hull, *Principles of Behavior: An Introduction to Behavior Theory.* New York: Appleton-Century-Crofts, 1943.

   E.C. Tolman, "Determiners of Behavior at a Choice-Point." *Psychological Review* 45 (1938): 1-41.

   E.C. Tolman, "Cognitive Maps in Rats and Men." *Psychological Review* 55 (1948): 189-208.

7. K.S. Lashley, "The Problem of Serial Order in Behavior." In *Cerebral Mechanisms in Behavior: The Hixon Symposium,* L.A. Jeffress, ed. New York: Wiley, 1951.

8. W.C. Watt, "On Two Hypotheses Concerning Psycholinguistics." In *Cognition and the Development of Language,* J.R. Hayes, ed. New York: Wiley, 1970.

9. C.E. Osgood and R. Hoosain, 1974. "Salience of the Word as a Unit in the Perception of Language." *Perception & Psychophysics* 15 (1974): 168-192.

10. J.H. Greenberg, "Some Universals of Grammar with Particular Reference to the Order of Meaningful Elements." In *Universals of Language,* J.H. Greenberg, ed. Cambridge, MA: M.I.T. Press, 1963.

11. For example, J.R. Anderson and G.H. Bower, *Human Associative Memory.* Washington, D.C.: Winston, 1973.

12. For example, E.E. Smith, E.J. Shoben, and L.J. Rips, "Structure and Process in Semantic Memory: a Feature Model for Semantic Decisions." *Psychological Review* 81 (1974): 214-241.

13. Full, formal statements of all functional notions of this APG are given in an appendix to my *Lectures on Language Performance,* op. cit. The statements given here are highlights for communicating the major ideas.

14. See T.G.R. Bower, *Development in Infancy* [San Francisco, CA: W.H. Freeman, 1974.], and elsewhere.

15. C.E. Osgood and C. Tanz, "Will the Real Object in Bitransitive Sentences Please Stand Up?" In *Linguistic Studies in Honor of Joseph Greenberg,* A. Juilland, ed. Saratoga, CA: Anma Libri, 1977.

16. E. Sapir, "Noun Incorporation in American Languages." *American Anthropologist* 13 (1911): 250-282.
    Y.R. Chao, *A Reference Grammar of Spoken Chinese.* Berkeley, CA: University of California Press, 1968.

17. Greenberg, "Some Universals of Grammar," op. cit.

18. H.H. Clark and E.V. Clark, "Semantic Distinctions and and Memory for Complex Sentences." *Quarterly Journal of Experimental Psychology* 20 (1968): 129-138.

19. E.V. Clark, "On the Acquisition of the Meaning of *Before* and *After.*" *Journal of Verbal Learning and Verbal Behavior* 10 (1971): 266-275.

20. G.B. Flores d'Arcais, "The Perception of Complex Sentences." In *Studies in the Perception of Language,* W.J.M. Levelt and G.B. Flores d'Arcais, eds. New York: John Wiley and Sons, 1978.
    G.B. Flores d'Arcais, "The Acquisition of the Subordinating Construction in Children's Language." In *Recent Advances in the Psychology of Language: Language Development and Mother-Child Interaction,* R.N. Campbell and P.T. Smith, eds. New York: Plenum Press, 1978.

21. S. N. Sridhar, unpublished manuscript.

22. C.E. Osgood and J.K. Bock, "Salience and Sentencing: Some Production Principles." In *Sentence Production: Developments in Research and Theory,* S. Rosenberg, ed. Hillsdale, NJ: Erlbaum, 1977.

23. W.E. Cooper and J.R. Ross, "World Order." In *Papers from the Parasession on Functionalism,* R.E. Grossman, L.J. San, and T.J. Vance, eds. Chicago: Chicago Linguistic Society, 1975.

UPGRADING A MIND

David Premack

Once the chimpanzee has been exposed to language training, it can solve certain kinds of problems that it cannot solve otherwise. Specifically, it can solve problems on a conceptual rather than a sensory basis. For example, while the normal chimpanzee can match, say, half an apple with half an apple, or 3/4th cylinder of water with 3/4th cylinder of water, it is only after it has been language trained that it can match, say, 3/4th an apple with 3/4th a cylinder of water, that is, match equivalent proportions of objects that do *not* look alike. Similarly, the normal chimpanzee can readily match like *objects,* say, A to A (rather than B), but it cannot match like *relations,* say, AA to BB (rather than CD). However, after it has been language trained, it can not only match sameness to sameness (AA to BB) but also difference to difference (AB to CD). The change from sensory to conceptual level responding that language training appears to induce in the chimpanzee thus resembles a developmental transition that normal children are thought to undergo in the "natural" course of things – though, of course, whether the two changes are genuinely comparable is one of several ontogenetic questions that will not be answered in a day.

A serendipitous comparison between two groups of animals trained in the laboratory in the past 10 years suggests that language-, and nonlanguage-, trained chimpanzees differ. What makes the suggestion strong is that the effect is specific. Language training does not enhance all mental abilities but only those of the kind indicated. There are other tasks, also of a rather specific kind, on which the language-trained and nonlanguage-trained animals cannot be differentiated. In fact, with respect to the latter set of tasks, neither group of animals can easily be differentiated from a normal child. In brief, the chimpanzees exposed to language training are not generally superior but superior only on a specific kind of task. On other tasks, they perform no better than do non-language-trained animals, and on these tasks both groups are difficult to distinguish from normal children.

In this paper I characterize the two sets of tasks, the one that is and the one that is not affected by the language training, and propose some hypotheses as to why the training should have such an effect. We begin by characterizing the language training itself. If we are to understand the effect this special experience appears to have on the ape, we need a good account of the experience itself. Language training is hardly a homogeneous entity. Ultimately, in order to identify the causal factors, we shall have to divide the training into its many parts, and this decomposition is a major preoccupation of the experiment in progress. But at this point, we need a simple description of the procedure, starting with an account of the animals themselves.

The animals that form the basis of the comparison are seven African-born apes, all of which were received in the laboratory as infants and reared in close contact with human trainers. Sarah, Peony, and Elizabeth were exposed to language training; Bert, Luvy, Jessie, and Sadie were not. Although the latter were not language trained, they were given as many hours of intensive training as the other group – indeed more, for on the whole they were received in the laboratory at an earlier age. Their experience included many forms of match to sample, reasoning tasks, conservation, map reading, and the like. Sarah, who has been in the laboratory over 20 years at the time of writing, received both the language training and the tasks given the nonlanguage-trained animals, whereas Peony and Elizabeth (the other two language-trained animals) received a narrower training more nearly confined to language. It is not possible to equate the animals for intelligence in any strict sense, though both on the basis of test results and qualitative impressions one would single out Sarah and Jessie as bright, Peony and Luvy as dull. There is thus a bright and dull animal in both groups; more important, as we shall see later, a dull but language-trained animal passed tests that a bright but nonlanguage-trained animal failed.

Does the language training instill language? This is a question that I could reasonably bypass here, for it has no essential bearing on our present questions, viz., in what way(s) is the chimpanzee changed by the training? What in the training accounts for the change? The language question is so insistent, however, that I will address it briefly before returning to the main content of the paper.

Picture, if you will, advocates of both the positive and negative views, the one confidently asserting, "Yes, the chimpanzee does acquire language," the other, "No, he does not acquire language." Each time, as devil's advocate, we shall remind the claimant of the dissenting evidence. For example, starting with the positive claimant, we shall remind him of Ann Fowler's data[1] concerning the systematic deletion of children as young as two-and-a-half. Sometimes a child will say such things as, "Daddy come home," at other time, "Come home." The child may say, "Where Mommy go?" at other times, "Where go?" Notice, these are observed deletions, not inferred ones. We have both forms of the sentence and can observe that a word has been omitted from one of the forms of the sentence.

Does the child delete just any word, or is there something distinctive about the words the child treats in this fashion? Are they words with particular kinds of meaning? Words that appear in a particular position in the sentence? Or words that have been in the child's lexicon for so long a time that the child feels comfortable ignoring them? It turns out that none of these hypotheses is correct: the words the child deletes are, in fact, the subject of the sentence.

To characterize the child's performance, we must, in some sense, credit the child with a knowledge of what a sentence is – for the concept of subject is defined by (or presupposes) the concept of sentence. Of course, we do not mean that the child's access to this distinction is such that he could operate on it. For example, we do not suppose that the child could sort his own productions into two piles of sentences – one in which the subject was deleted and one in which the subject remained. Nevertheless, the child's ability to delete the subject, on a systematic basis, requires us to credit him with some knowledge of the structure of a sentence. The chimpanzee, in contrast, does not exhibit any performances along this line. While we find evidence for semantic distinctions (distinctions in the meaning of words), syntactic distinctions of the kind shown by the human child do not appear to be within the capacity of the chimpanzee.

The child's performance is interesting because, while syntactic distinctions are almost always connected to semantic ones, the child's deletion strategy is not. It is based on purely syntactic considerations: the subject alone is deleted. Further, the evidence for deletion is detected at a time when the child is young, and the grammatical system weak – so weak that the sentences consist of no more than three or four words. As a rule, in order to find evidence of syntactic knowledge, we have to reply on the human adult who is already using a strong grammatical system. If, however, the only evidence we had for grammatical sensitivity were supplied by the human adult, we would hardly be surprised by the lack of it in the chimpanzee. After all, even the most avid proponents for language in the ape never suppose that the ape would be capable of human grammar. But, the evidence we have makes it clear that even the brightest ape can acquire not even so much as the weak grammatical system exhibited by very young children.

Faced with this argument, the positive claimant is likely to retreat to words, that is, to admit that "Of course, apes do not have sentences, but they do have words." This claim suffers from "unclarity". Ironically, given the complexity of sentence relative to word, we are in a better position to define sentence than word. Until we can state clearly what a word is, the claim that apes have them is necessarily somewhat empty. Will they still have "them" when we are better able to say what a word is, or will possession prove to depend on unclarity?

We are not at a total loss, however, as to what a word is. Consider two fundamental things that are done with words, and whether they are done not only with human words but also with the chimpanzee's plastic words. A word is first of all an information retrieval device, enabling one to reinstate the information that one has stored about a particular item. This is the basis for the traditional "displacement" claim made for language, for example, that one should be able to talk about, say, giraffes in the absence of giraffes. Of course, if one's representation of giraffe is inadequate, the word "giraffe" will be of little service. But if, on the contrary, one has in memory a well-formed representation of giraffe – in the limiting case, a representation equal to what one can perceive of an actual giraffe – then the word giraffe should serve to retrieve this representation, and one should be able to say as much about giraffes in their absence as in their presence. On this analysis, to decide whether or not apes have words, even in this most preliminary sense, one must measure at least two things. First, the quality of the internal representation that the ape has for those items that are to be named, and secondly, in the event that the ape proves to have nontrivial representation, how much of the stored information can be retrieved by the words that name the items.

Tests we made some years ago[2] of these two issues gave highly positive results on both counts. First, apes formed impressively complete representations of eight different fruits in their diet, and second, they were decidedly able to retrieve this information with the plastic words that had been taught them as names of the fruit.

With that much established, we were encouraged to turn to another fundamental property of a word. In humans, words do not serve only to retrieve information; on the contrary, words are an essential part of the information that is to be retrieved. Consider, for example, how the eight fruits used in the first test series are likely to be represented in human memory. Do the representations consist exclusively of sensory images ("pictures," tastes, smells, and the like) or do they consist also of discursive information, phrases such

as "apple is a sweet red fruit," "mostly eaten raw though sometimes cooked (especially by grandmothers)," "can be stored over
winter," "outstanding varieties grown in the northwest," and so on?
To say that human representations are discursive is to say that in
humans words define words and are a part of the information to be
retrieved. Do words also play this role in the ape? Do the plastic
words make their way into the chimpanzee's mind, becoming a part
of the information stored there, so that in the ape as in the human
words define words?

As a first step toward answering this question, we concealed the
color of various fruit by painting them white, and then, using a
match-to-sample format, required the animals to match the fruit to
a patch of color. For instance, we gave the animals a white apple
and a white banana, along with a red patch. The three animals
tested in this way – Sarah, Peony, and Elizabeth – performed well:
an average of about 80% correct. Next, we made a slight change,
painting the fruit a color other than white, for example, blue, and
found that this slight change produced an appreciable decrement;
performance declined to an average of about 67% correct. And
when the two fruits were not only painted a non-veridical color but
each was painted a different color, performance in all three animals
fell to chance.[3]

Why should the animal succeed when the fruit are white, but fail
when, say, the apple and banana are blue and orange, respectively?
The answer could lie in the animal's representation of the fruit.
Suppose the ape's representation has no discursive component but
is exclusively imaginal. This would impose limits on its use, limits
compatible with the possibility that the animal can imagine the
color of the painted fruit, while at the same time perceiving white –
but cannot imagine the color of the painted fruit while at the same
time perceiving two different colors (indeed, perceiving even one
color other than white already strains the system).

We need now to make exactly the same tests with humans. If the
present interpretation is correct, humans should have little difficulty. Since the human representation of fruit is discursive as well as
imaginal, a person need not solve the test by imagining one color
while at the same time perceiving others. The human could look at
the, say, blue apple and imagine its real color, "translate" the
imagined color into the word ("red") and match the word to, say,
the phrase "apple is a small red fruit." If humans succeed where
the apes have failed, we will have already distinguished ape words
from human ones. I say "already" because certainly the two properties – information retrieval and form of the information stored –

are preliminary features of words. Human words must have many characteristics, which very much need to be clarified, though we may not need to take them into account to differentiate human from ape words. Simple first-order properties may distinguish between human and ape words. In summary, apes not only do not have sentences, in all likelihood they do not even have words, in the sense of human words.

Turn now to the negative claimant, the individual who confidently asserts, "Of course, language training does not instill language in the ape." We tell him quite a different story, starting with the reminder that by language one does not mean human language. By language, one means a non-iconic representational system that can be used to carry out two basic functions: reference and truth claims. Since truth claims presuppose reference and are the stronger function of the two, let us direct our attention to them.

For our purposes the correspondence theory of truth will be sufficient, and we need not consider coherence theory or other alternatives. The essential component of the correspondence view of truth is straightforward, and tests for this component can be equally straightforward. We present the individual with a condition, say, a red card on a green one, along with a set of linguistic strings; or we present a string, say, "red is on green," along with a set of conditions. The individual's task is to map the one kind of item onto the other, string onto condition, and/or vice versa. If he can do so, he has the capacity to make truth claims (for the language and conditions in question, of course). Will the individual who passes such a test spontaneously make truth claims? One cannot say, for the test in question establishes only that there is the cognitive capacity for truth claims. It says nothing about a disposition to use the capacity.

As we shall see in what lies ahead, the language-trained ape can put simple strings of plastic words into conformity with simple conditions, and thus carry out the most critical function of a non-iconic representational system. In that quite explicit sense, language training does teach apes language. There are, therefore, quite different, yet equally warranted, answers to the question: Does language training teach the ape language?

A further point of interest is that the truth claim use of a representational system does not depend specifically on human syntax, phonology, or any other aspect of human language. Far simpler systems than the human one can be used for this purpose, indeed, systems so simple they can be acquired by the ape.

Why then do we not find such systems in nature? The practical value to a species of making truth claims would seem incontrovertible: there is no higher form of communication, or at least none that has been invented. Given that the chimpanzee has the cognitive capacity for making truth claims, why then do we not find apes in the wild making truth claims commensurate with their cognitive competence: simple "sentences" used to describe simple conditions? Why, rather than finding intermediate systems, do we find no systems at all and hence no truth claims of any kind? The absence of intermediate representational systems may result more from socio-motivational factors than from strictly cognitive ones. We find evidence of social attribution in the ape, evidence that it attributes to others intention, belief and possibly other states of mind,[4] but we also find sharp limitations on the ape's competence. Although it has been customary to tout the ape's social intelligence (for example, to note that apes touch and appease one another in "sensitive" ways), when we desist from clinical impression and actually measure the ape's social competence, we find that its social intelligence is below that of a four-year-old child.[5] For instance, even the four-year-old child can distinguish the content of his own mind from that of another's mind. The ape and the three-and-one-half-year-old child, in contrast, fail tests that impose this requirement; the beliefs they attribute to others are the same as their own beliefs. The human would appear to be the only species whose social competence is of a sufficient quality to support truth claims. In holding both himself and others responsible for producing sentences that conform to the conditions they describe, the human is substantially more peculiar than one might consider. In any case, this is not an obligation that chimpanzees impose either on themselves or on others.

1. Language Training

In language training the animal was given a string of elements representing simple propositions, such as "apple is red," "blue is on yellow," "round shape of apple," and so on. The strings increased in complexity over the course of training, including, for example, "apple is red – same – red color of apple," "red on yellow, if – then, Sarah take chocolate," and "Sarah take apple in red dish, banana in blue dish." Whether the strings were simple or complex, they all represented n-term (usually two-term) relations. This is transparent in simple cases – for example, when "shape of" is the relation and "round" and "apple" the arguments – but was equally

the case with the longer strings – for example, when "if – then" is
the relation and the simple constructions "red on yellow" and
"Sarah take chocolate" are the arguments.

In all cases, the animal was taught by a procedure akin to sentence completion. With few exceptions, the training strings always
had one incomplete slot, marked by an interrogative particle; all the
"words" in the string were known to the animal from prior experience. Thus, when the new word taught was the *relation,* both
arguments in the string were already known; for example, "color
of" was introduced at a time when words such as "red" and
"apple" were known, so the animal could be given "red? apple" –
in effect, what is the relation between red and apple? – and could
answer "red color of apple." Conversely, when the new word was
one of the *arguments,* the relation and the other argument were
known; for example, "brown" was introduced by the instruction
"brown color of chocolate," given at a time when both "color of"
and "chocolate" were known from earlier experience.
(Incidentally, the last case shows that in order to acquire a new
"word" the animal need not actually insert the "word" but can
benefit merely by "reading" it in the string.)

The animal was trained to perform the same operation on all
incomplete strings; remove the interrogative particle, replace it with
the correct word, and thereby complete the string. A moment's
reflection will show that this constitutes a method for interrogation.
The incomplete string represents a question – questions being
nothing more than incomplete constructions whose complete form is
recognizable – and the animal's choice of "word" represents an
answer, one that completes the construction. Children taught the
written language of the apes could be questioned in the same manner. A child could be asked, for instance, "Billy is X years old," to
which Billy could reply, replacing the X with, say, four, "Billy is
four years old." The advantages of such interrogation are that the
child need not remember the question and that it is not necessary to
transform the question in order to answer it; a single word suffices
as an answer. (This interrogative procedure has proved effective
not only with apes but with pathological human populations as well
– children with various kinds of language deficiency[6] and globally
aphasic adults.[7])

The whole procedure can be described as having three basic
forms: the individual was required either
1. to identify the relation that a pair of arguments instantiated,
2. to identify the argument needed to complete a relation-argument
   pair (in a two-term relation), or

3. to answer yes/no questions about simple relational propositions. The training was basically an exercise in the use of relations. That a chimpanzee could be interrogated in this fashion surprised us; very little in the behavior of the wild ape suggests the possibility. Yet, when the animal is interrogated about four hours a day for a period of 18 months, as Sarah was, it is not excessively surprising that the procedure should have some appreciable effect. And the effect is not just a temporary one but in all likelihood permanent – for the tests that follow were given in the last five years, at least six years after the language training ended.

2. Tests that Differentiate

2.1. Analogies

In an analogy, the individual is given two pairs of items arranged in a specific pattern, for example A/A' and B/B', and is required to judge whether the relation between them is same or different. Or the individual can be given an incomplete analogy, for example A/A' same B/?, and be required to complete the analogy by choosing among alternatives. Sarah can do analogies in both formats.[8] Unfortunately, she is the only language-trained animal we were able to test on analogy, the other two language-trained chimpanzees having been replaced to make room for infant chimpanzees.

Sarah's success with analogies, though impressive, is predictable: individuals that can make same/different judgments should be successful at analogies. We have only to rewrite the same/different judgment to see that it is itself an analogy – for example, $apple_1/apple_2$:$elephant_1/elephant_2$ – one that differs from the standard analogy only in being restricted to the relation of *sameness* and *difference*. The standard analogy, in contrast, is not so restricted and can concern any relation. Some of the more interesting analogical relations Sarah passed were the functional ones of *opening* and *marking,* namely,

can opener/can:same:key/lock

paintbrush/painted surface:same:pencil/marked paper

Can the nonlanguage-trained animals do analogies? It was desirable to answer this question, yet not possible to do so in the usual way because the animals lacked the words "same" and "different." Fortunately, a simple revision of the match-to-sample procedure provided a test that preserved the logic of the analogy while not requiring any words. To make the revision we had only to substitute pairs of items for the usual single item. Rather than offer X as the sample with X and Y as alternatives, we could offer XX as sample with YY and CD as alternatives, or XY as the sample with CD and BB as alternatives. We tested Sarah, the four nonlanguage-trained animals, and children from about three-and-one-half to six years of age on these nonverbal analogies or double-item matching tests.

The first series consisted of 12 trials, six of the XX-YY variety (same-same) and six of the XY-CD (different-different), in a random order. Common items – toys, hardware, and the like – were the stimuli. Because each trial was unique, making each trial a transfer test, differential feedback was given. Sarah was right on all 12 trials. The nonlanguage-trained animals responded at a chance level, showing no progress over 15 additional sessions. This failure is in keeping with the earlier failure of these animals to acquire the plastic words "same" and "different." After more than 900 training trials, none of them showed any progress. The failure of the nonlanguage-trained animals contrasts with the success of Peony and Elizabeth, both of whom were taught these words at the same age as the nonlanguage-trained juveniles.

The children had appreciably more difficulty with the nonverbal analogies than Sarah did. Children below about four years of age failed both the XX-YY and the XY-CD type of problems; by about four-and-one-half they passed XX-YY but still failed XY-CD; and they may have to be as old as six before passing both types of problems.[9] The children may have done poorly because they did not come to the test with the benefit of Sarah's extensive background in match to sample and analogies; in any case, their failure was not permanent. Even three-and-one-half-year-olds succeeded when given additional training, thus differing from the nonlanguage-trained animals, whose failure was "permanent."

2.2. Proportions

The test of proportions also strikingly differentiated Sarah from the nonlanguage-trained juveniles. Two quite different kinds of objects were used in these tests, spherical fruits in one case and glass cylinders in the other. The fruits (apple, grapefruit, potato) were either left intact or cut vertically into quarters, halves, or three-quarter pieces. The glass cylinder was either filled completely with tinted water or filled to the 1/4, 1/2, or 3/4 level. To accommodate the nonlanguage-trained animals, the tests were given in a match-to-sample format. At first, the fruits and cylinders were separated and tested in independent series. Each animal was given, say, 1/4 apple as the sample, with 1/4 and 3/4 apple as alternatives, each of the proportions being used equally often as the sample and as both correct and incorrect alternatives. Comparable tests were given with the glass cylinders. Both Sarah and the juveniles passed these tests.

Next, the two kinds of objects were combined, the cylinder always being used as sample, the fruit as alternative. For example, the animal was given a 1/2-filled cylinder as sample, a 1/2 apple and 3/4 apple as alternatives. Each of the four proportions was used equally often as the sample and as correct and incorrect alternatives. In addition, all the fruit alternatives were equated for size. On this series, Sarah and the four juveniles parted company. All the young animals failed the tests, whereas Sarah passed from the beginning. Each of the first eight trials was unique, and Sarah was right on all of them (p < .01).[10]

The test items in the first series (a fruit in one case and a cylinder in the other) could be represented in the imaginal code, and the correct alternatives could be matched to the sample on the basis of similarity. This approach would not work in the second series, however, for a 1/4 potato is no more similar to a 1/4-filled cylinder than is 3/4 potato, and so on. Now it is not the given parts of the stimuli that must be represented, but the given part relative to the whole, for example, the given part of the apple (x) relative to the whole apple (X), the filled part of the cylinder (y) relative to the completely filled cylinder (Y). The proportions, part-whole relations or relative areas (how we designate them does not seem to matter) are clearly relations and must be represented in the abstract code. Matching 1/4 apple to a 1/4-filled cylinder, as Sarah did, is tantamount to judging that, for example,

$$\frac{1/4 \text{ apple}}{1/4 \text{ cylinder}} : \text{same} : \frac{3/4 \text{ apple}}{3/4 \text{ cylinder}} .$$

Could Sarah pass this test? We have not yet used proportions as arguments in the analogical format, but from Sarah's success on the match-to-sample test with proportions and her performance on other analogies, I predict that she could.

2.3. Action

A test very different from those we have so far considered deals with the idea of action or causality. This test also distinguishes between the two groups of animals; this time not only Sarah versus the nonlanguage-trained animals but all three language-trained animals versus the others. In a classical physical action, an individual operates on an object (for example, an apple), changing either its state (for example, cutting it), its location, or both, typically with the use of an instrument (for example, a knife). This suggests that an action could be represented by a three-element sequence:

▶ an object in its initial state,
▶ an instrument capable of changing the object, and
▶ the object in a terminal state.

For instance, the action of cutting could be represented by the sequence: apple, knife, cut apple; that of marking by the sequence: paper, pencil, marked paper; that of wetting by the sequence: sponge, water, wet sponge; and so on.

Does the chimpanzee have the idea of action in the sense that it would recognize the above sequences as representations of action? Would it complete the sequences appropriately, if given them in various incomplete forms? To answer this question, we used specifically the actions of cutting, marking, and wetting, for these were actions with which all animals had abundant experience. They were presented to the animals in the sequences described. We did not present a complete sequence, however, but one that was incomplete, either in the terminal state of the object or in the instrument. For instance, the animal received either the incomplete sequence: apple, knife, blank; or apple, blank, cut apple. Along with the incomplete test sequence, the animal received a set of three alternatives appropriate to the test sequence: for example, cut apple, cut orange, pierced apple (as by a nail), in the first case; cutting instrument, writing instrument, container of water, in the second case. The animal was required to select the correct alternative and place it in the designated position in the sequence.

All three language-trained animals passed both versions of the test in the first session consisting of 12 trials.[11] The object-implement pairs were unique on each trial, so the animal could not have passed by memorizing correct answers from the differential feedback that was given. In contrast, all four nonlanguage-trained animals failed both versions of the test. Moreover, they continued to fail even though given eight replications of the same 12 object-implement pairs. In other words, the language-trained animals passed (though they could not have done so on the basis of associative learning); whereas the nonlanguage-trained animals did not pass (though in principle they could have done so on the basis of associative learning). This would seem to say that associative learning has little to do with performance on this test. Sarah was tested when several years older than the other animals, but Peony and Elizabeth and the four nonlanguage-trained animals were the same age when given the test.

Appreciably stronger forms of the test,[12] examining two other aspects of action or causality, have been given to Sarah. One of these concerns the fact that action has a temporal order; cause precedes effect, even as the initial state of the object precedes the terminal or transformed one. The simple tests above do not establish explicitly whether or not the animal maps the temporal order of action onto the spatial order of the test sequence or even reads the sequence in a fixed order. To determine whether or not Sarah was capable of using order, we first familiarized her with three new actions, each one the reverse of one of those on which she had been tested. Thus, she was familiarized with joining (putting together with tape), drying, and erasing, leaving her with the pairs: cut-join, wet-dry, mark-erase.

Next, we taught Sarah to read the test sequences from left to right by giving her sequences consisting of the same items in the opposite order – for example, paper, blank, marked paper; and the reverse: marked paper, blank, paper – along with three alternatives: container of water, pencil, and eraser. In the first case, it is pencil that changes paper into marked paper, whereas in the second case, it is eraser that changes marked paper into clear paper (water being irrelevant in both cases). After being trained with 12 different examples of this kind, she was given a transfer test with nondifferential feedback on 60 novel pairs. She was right on 40 of the 60, which, with three alternatives, is highly significant (p < .001 binomial test). Additional tests have established other aspects of Sarah's competence with these sequences. For example, she was given sequences in which the same terminal state – such as paper that was marked, wet, and cut – was reached from different initial states. She was required to sort the instruments into two piles – those that were needed to make the change, and those that were not. She succeeded nicely, demonstrating that she could compute the difference between two states of an object and identify the instrument(s) needed to produce the transition.[13]

Even in their simplest version, these tests are not as simple as they seem. In order for the sequence to be seen as standing for action, the animal must read or interpret the sequence in a particular way, since it can be given indeterminately many readings. Apple, cut apple, can be read as: red-red, one-two, fruit-fruit, and so on; it need not be read as asking, How do I get from here to there? or, With what instrument do I make this change?

To claim that the animal can read the sequence so as to discover a particular question is another way of saying that the animal can represent the sequence not only in the imaginal code but also in the abstract one. For, above all, an action is a relation – a dynamic one (in contrast to static ones such as proportion and the like) – between an agent, an instrument, and an object. In addition, the transfer performance of the successful animals demonstrates that the representation is abstract. The animal did not select correct items only for sequences they had experienced, or even for sequences that were new but canonical; they also solved anomalous sequences in which objects were operated upon in "peculiar" ways, for example, ping-pong balls severed, pieces of apple written on, or paper dunked in water.

The above examples, starting with analogies and concluding with action, do not exhaust the possibilities among tasks that distinguish between the language-trained and the nonlanguage-trained animals. But to add others would not help clarify the nature of the tasks that benefit from language training. We would do better now to turn in the opposite direction, to tasks that do not benefit from language training.

3. Tests that Do Not Differentiate

3.1 "Natural reasoning"

Whenever the question of reasoning is raised with regard to nonhuman animals, we encounter essentially the same test. Since we cannot talk to animals about, say, the mortality of man (or the fact that Socrates was a man) and see what conclusions they may draw from this combination of propositions, we instead show them things we know they want, such as food. The food is not simply there for the taking, however; on the contrary, to get the food the animal must "reason," for example, put sticks together to overcome the distance between itself and the food,[14] or take an indirect route that will circumvent a barrier.[15] Reasoning tasks for animals thus have two characteristics: the information is given the animal perceptually instead of verbally, and the problem tends to be spatial – a distance or a barrier must be overcome.

We have been testing both children and chimpanzees on variations of problems of this general kind, and though the work with the children is incomplete, the major surprise that has already arisen is the difficulty in distinguishing between the children and the chimpanzees.[16] By chimpanzees I now mean the language-trained as well as nonlanguage-trained ones, for on these tests Sarah, the four language-trained animals, and the young children perform in a comparable manner.

In a representative example of a spatial reasoning task, two widely separated containers are pointed out to an individual in a room or field and he is show that, say, an apple is put in one container and a banana in the other. He is then temporarily removed from the room or field and when brought back, he finds an individual standing midway between the two containers eating either an apple or a banana. After this individual leaves, the subject is released to choose one container or the other. Surprisingly, many children in a three-and-one-half- to four-year-old range fail on this problem — they go to one container as often as to the other. By about four-and-one-half years of age, they perform as well as the chimpanzees (the nonlanguage-trained ones and Sarah). For example, Sadie, the oldest juvenile, performed correctly on the first trial, Bert and Jessie performed at chance, whereas Luvy went consistently to the wrong container. Within 10 trials, however, all four juveniles were performing correctly. The performance of four- to five-year-old children was very comparable.

To solve this problem, one must remember the location of the fruit and make the "similarity assumption," that is, that the fruit one sees being eaten is the fruit that was hidden. Control procedures show that most of the failures come not from the memory factor but from the "similarity assumption." At this time I cannot do justice to factors that lead an individual to make this assumption. Obviously the assumption is not always warranted; logically, it may never be warranted. We can even make the assumption grossly unwarranted (for example, arrange for the fruit to be eaten so quickly after being hidden that it could not possibly be the fruit that was hidden).

In another test, items of the same kind are placed in each of two containers with the child or ape watching at a short distance. Then the subject is shown, say, that we add an item to one of the containers. When the subject is released and allowed to go to only one container, each responds correctly. With that base condition established, we then introduce two test conditions. Rather than show the subject that we actually added an item to one of the containers, we allow him to infer this by observing an individual walking either toward or away from one of the containers. That is, we allow the subject to watch an individual walk from the starting point halfway to one of the containers on some trials, and from the halfway point back to the starting point on other trials. These inference conditions are combined not only with the base condition in which we visibly add to a container, but also (in other blocks of trials) with conditions in which we visibly subtract from a container, or take an item from one container and put it in another, and so on. Both the young children (three-and-one-half to five) and the nonlanguage-trained chimpanzees (Sarah cannot easily be tested on this series because of her caged condition) tend to do better on forward than on backward extrapolation.

In a third series of tests the animal is required to combine information based on inference with that based on perception. In the first part of a two-step experiment the trainer shows the animal that he has only one piece of food in his hand, places the animal behind a blind, and then disappears into the field. In a moment he reappears to show the animal that he is now empty-handed. Next the animal is taken into the field (to the container in which the trainer placed the food) and is allowed to observe the removal of the food. The animal is then returned to the starting point and released. Typically, after this demonstration the animal does not go into the field at all, but sits behind the blind grooming itself or gazing into space. This is not merely indolence; only a small change in the procedure produces a quite different outcome. The procedure is kept the same, except that at the start the trainer shows the animal that he has two pieces of fruit in his hand, not one; now the animal does not linger at the starting point but goes directly to the container that was not emptied in its presence. The only point in testing children on this series would be to see whether they would do less well than the apes; they could not do better.

To be sure, comparable performance by different species does not guarantee that a comparable underlying process is involved. I anticipate that as we come to understand reasoning better we will find differences between the two species. They are certain to be more subtle, however, than the gross differences we already find when contrasting children with nonlanguage-trained apes on tests that require judgments about the relation between relations, for on most tests of this kind normal three-and-one-half- to four-year-old children perform as Sarah does. For example, they pass the action tests,[17] the proportions tests, and the same/different judgment (and indeed they may do so when appreciably younger — we have simply not tested them at an earlier age). On the whole, then, the three-and-one-half- to four-year-old children perform as well as Sarah does, and both are markedly superior to the nonlanguage-trained ape. In light of these easily detected differences, the absence of differences in natural reasoning is interesting.

3.2. Relations between relations

The difference between the language- and nonlanguage-trained animal has to do with the ability to compute an equivalence on grounds deeper than mere appearance. In matching half an apple to half an apple, both Sarah and the nonlanguage-trained apes could react merely to appearance or physical similarity. But when Sarah matched half an apple to half a tube of water, the equivalence could no longer be based on appearance.

This distinction applies also to the comparison between the standard matching test and the double-item matching test. In the standard test, A can be matched to A on the basis of appearance, but in the double-item test, AA does not look like BB, at least not in the simple sense that A looks like A.

To explicate the difference between the single- and double-item matching tests, let us first define an element. An element is any item that is perceived as a whole, whether it be a red dot, a giraffe, or the city of Paris; a relation is then two or more elements that, when presented together, are still parsed as elements (rather than being perceived as an emergent of some kind). The relation between A and A, as in a standard matching test, is a relation between elements; whereas the relation between AA and BB is a relation between relations. Recognizing the identity between elements is evidently simpler than recognizing the identity between two physically different exemplars of the same relation.

4. The Contribution of Language Training

Why should language training enable the chimpanzee to deal with relations between relations? The answer may lie in the truth claim. A truth claim, as we have already noted, depends on the ability to map sentences onto conditions, or vice versa. The direct test for this ability is to present a linguistic string (or a condition) along with a set of conditions (or strings) and require the individual to select the corresponding item. But this ability can be demonstrated in other ways, such as by the yes/no question. The animal is shown some simple condition, such as a red card on a green one, and is then asked in its plastic words "?red on green." Sarah successfully answered questions of this kind, removing the interrogative particle, and substituting the word "yes" or "no."

In answering yes/no questions, Sarah judged the agreement between a condition and a discursive representation of the condition, an ordered-string of plastic words. It does not matter that the conditions and strings were simple; the essential nature of a truth claim does not hinge on a level of complexity. The condition and the string describing the condition are both relations; hence, in answering yes/no questions, one judges the relation between relations, the same kind of judgment one makes in the double-item matching test.

Notice that the yes/no question is our only unqualified example of an equivalence or agreement that is in no way based on appearance or physical similarity. Even the agreement between AA and BB, in the double-item matching test, though more complex than that between A and A, can be viewed as a higher-order kind of similarity. After all, different exemplars of the same relation do instantiate the same invariant, one that can be given a physical description, however complex. But, the agreement between sentences and conditions is not of this kind. The invariants that we use in describing sentences will not reappear in the conditions that are described by the sentences.

In emphasizing the language-trained animal's ability to compute equivalence on a conceptual rather than a physical basis, and thus to go beyond similarity, I may inadvertently have suggested that similarity is a primitive criterion, widely used among all species. In fact, similarity appears to go beyond the reach of most species. Although only perhaps two species can go beyond similarity – the human and the specially-trained ape – few can reach even to similarity. Indeed, most species appear limited to associating one item with another on the basis of temporal and/or spatial factors; they do not associate items on the basis of their similarity. I know of only one exception to this claim, a study by Rescorla and Gillan[18] indicating greater second-order conditioning in pigeons when CS 1 and 2 are similar, though the authors themselves doubt that the advantage is truly based on similarity. They note that exposure to a stimulus of one kind may prime the animal for that kind of an event, giving a temporal advantage to the next occurrence of the same kind of event.

Let us consider that similarity can be used by a system at different levels. The stimulus generalization that may be a part of all conditioning is perhaps the most primitive use of similarity. Even one-celled animals condition, and, so far as I know, show stimulus generalization; there may be no conditioning without stimulus generalization. What may constitute a higher level of use is the kind of effect tested by the Rescorla-Gillan experiment, viz., the effect of similarity on the rate of formation of an association. Let us suppose that similarity between stimuli genuinely enhances the formation of an association between them. If so, this higher level of use may not be found in one-celled organisms, or even many-celled invertebrates, though it would be found in all vertebrates.

A still higher level of use is the one found in match to sample where similarity provides the basis for matching one item with another. This level of use is seen unequivocally in primates, especially apes and humans, where it can be demonstrated in the most straightforward way, by the transfer that these individuals show from one problem to another. The evidence in nonprimates such as pigeons and rats, in contrast, is equivocal, and depends on exotic multi-stage transfer designs whose interpretation is controversial. I have not given up the possibility that what appears to be a matching level of use of similarity in the nonprimate can be explained in terms of a lower level of use.

Some recent experiments point up the contrast between the robust use of the matching criterion in primates, and the hardly detectable use of this criterion in nonprimates. Let us start by comparing 18-month-old human and chimpanzee infants on their first (and subsequent) match-to-sample tests. David Oden, Paula Durlach, Roger Thompson, and I trained these subjects using only two items, a cup and a lock. Training consisted of only four kinds of trials: the cup and lock (counterbalanced for position) were always the alternatives, while the cup was the sample on half the trials, and the lock on the other half.

The children reached criterion in about eight trials, the apes in about 800.[19] The child's quick success on matching is no surprise. Children do spontaneous matching of both a temporal and a spatial kind, and in fact by 18 months they have begun to do simple one-to-one correspondence.[20] For children, match to sample is thus merely a new or standardized version of an idea that occurs to them spontaneously. In contrast, the chimpanzee shows no spontaneous spatial sorting, indeed very little temporal sorting, and never gets to one-to-one correspondence; for the chimpanzee match to sample is virtually a new idea, not merely a new form of an old idea.

After the two species reached criterion, we gave them transfer tests, presenting the same new items to both of them. The new items included metallic things like the cups and locks, and nonmetallic things, swatches of cloth in one case, foods in another. The results could not have been more simple: for all items in both species, transfer was perfect.

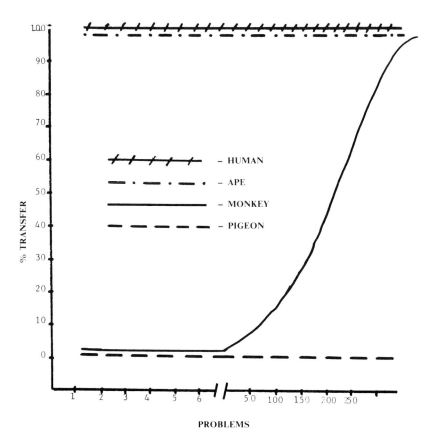

Figure 1

A comparison of the transfer results of four species.

Note: More recent data suggest that this figure underestimates the capacity of the monkey and pigeon. With improved training procedures, the pigeon does show some degree of transfer[21] – though substantially less than that shown by the monkey – and the monkey shows transfer earlier than this figure indicates.[22] These more recent data are compatible with suggestions I made earlier:[23]

In Figure 1 I have compared the transfer results of four species: humans, chimpanzees, monkeys, and pigeons (not because these comparisons are recommended by evolutionary theory, but because these are the species for which even some data are available). Amount of transfer is plotted as a function of the number of problems on which the animal was trained to criterion. Both the ape and child are at 100% from problem one, indicating that after reaching criterion on a single problem, they show 100% transfer on new problems. The monkey, in contrast, shows no transfer after being trained on one problem, or even five or ten problems, but gradually over the course of training on many problems reaches a high level of transfer. Pigeons show no transfer, no matter how many problems they are trained on.

The pigeon data are based on extensive extrapolation, for I can find no case of an impressively stubborn trainer who continued the pigeon's training beyond five or ten problems. The monkey data, too, are troubled, though for other reasons. The monkey is trained on so many problems before showing transfer that it is difficult to separate generalization from transfer. Is the monkey really showing transfer, or simply generalizing on the basis of similarity from old cases? If a monkey trained on, say, hard-thick-colored objects showed as much transfer to soft-thin-uncolored objects as to new hard-thick-colored ones, we could defend the claim of transfer; but no such data appear to be available. We do not face this problem in interpreting the child or chimpanzee data, for the amount of transfer they showed did not vary with the similarity between the training and test items, but was perfect for all test items.

After matching A to A, both child and ape perfectly matched X to X. Given their success on this, why are they unable to match AA to XX? Surely, A no more resembles X than AA resembles XX, in fact, less so. However, the matching of elements is not the equivalent of the matching of relations. And construing an element abstractly does not make of it a relation. We can use the customary abstraction hierarchy to characterize what an individual learns when doing simple match to sample. When trained to match, say, red to red, the individual need learn no more than that – match red to red. He may, however, take a step up the hierarchy and learn in addition match colors, that is, any color with any other color. He may continue up the hierarchy and thus learn, again in addition rather than in exclusion to the more concrete conditions, match properties, for example, shape with shape, size with size, etc. As a possible further step, he may match objects, not only properties, provided of course that he distinguishes objects from properties, that is, structures his perceptual space as we have.

Now, both the young child and the nonlanguage-trained ape obviously construed the matching abstractly, and moved as high on the hierarchy as possible. After matching cup to cup (and lock to lock), they perfectly matched pieces of cloth, foods, and other metallic objects; they matched every object we tried. Nevertheless, neither the nonlanguage-trained ape nor the 18-month-old child can match AA to XX; not at all, not even a little bit. Both the child and the ape can, however, match AA to AA as opposed to BC, just as they can match A to A as opposed to B − thus showing that the difficulty of double-item matching does not lie in the sheer number or complexity of the items. If we allow a little overstatement, we can characterize the nonlanguage-trained ape (and young child) as follows: this creature can match all elements no matter how complex they may be, but cannot match any relations no matter how simple they may be.

The logician tells us that a relation is merely a special kind of property, not one of objects, as in the standard case, but one of an ordered N-tuple of items. This view of a relation suggests that an individual who is able to match properties should also be able to match relations, less well or quickly perhaps − the one kind of property being more complex than the other − but to some degree at least. The data do not comply with this view, however. The nonlanguage-trained ape can match properties, somewhat less accurately than objects, but it cannot match relations at all.

From a processing point of view, rather than a logical one, what is the difference between relations, properties, and objects? What special demands are made by the processing of relations that are not made by the processing of objects or properties? We might approach this question from two directions, by complicating the single-item matching case, on the one hand, and attempting to simplify the double-item matching case, on the other. If we could get the difficulty of the two cases to coincide, we would then have more understanding of both of them; at the very least we could translate one kind of case into the other.

Unfortunately, we have no simplicity metric for relations, one that says, for example, the relation of *larger than* is simpler than *sameness,* or *sameness* simpler than *inside,* etc., though there is nothing that prevents us from following our intuitions. Indeed, we are advised to try several relations, for as things stand we do not know whether all relations are processed in the same way. If an individual can process one relation, can he process all others?

Conversely, if he fails to process one, will he fail to process all others? We are making such tests now, starting with *larger than* and some other cases. However, we are not encouraged to suppose that we can simplify the double-item case. Formal simplicity metrics for relations concern either the number of terms in the relation, for example, larger than (a two-term relation) versus giving (a three-term relation), or the number of items in a term, for example, A same A (single-item terms) versus A+B+C (three-item terms). And the relations the animals have already failed are all of the simplest kind, that is, two-term relations whose terms consist of single items.

Although simplifying the relational case may not be possible, we can readily do the opposite, complicate the simple case. In fact, there are too many ways in which to increase the difficulty of single-item-matching – most of which would have no theoretical interest at all. For example, we might increase the difficulty of the standard matching problem either by increasing the number of alternatives, or making the alternatives unusually small. But this would be of no interest, for there is not the remotest chance that what accounts for the difficulty in these cases is comparable to what accounts for the difficulty in the matching of one relation to another. We must do more than merely increase the difficulty of single-item matching; we must increase the difficulty in a theoretically-relevant way.

Suppose we increase the difficulty of the standard matching problem by *transforming* the matching alternative. For instance, we rotate the correct alternative, reduce or enlarge it, remove some part of it, etc. – so that, to recognize the identity between the sample and the matching alternative, the individual must now apply an appropriate transform. Is this process – of undoing a transformation – comparable to the process that underlies recognizing the identity between two physically different examples of the same relation? One might think so on the grounds that in both cases the individual must extract an invariant, the invariant being that which is shared by the transformed and untransformed element in the one case, and by the two exemplars of the same relation in the other.

Pilot results do not sustain this argument, however. For the two cases that David Oden and I have tried – 90 degree rotation, and 50% reduction in area – the four infant chimpanzees tested so far showed only a momentary reduction. Perhaps other transformations will have a more drastic effect, though if they do it now seems doubtful that they will produce the total failure that holds for the matching of relations. In other words, in the nonlanguage-trained chimpanzee perceptual transformations may produce no effect, a temporary decrement, or even perhaps a permanently reduced level of performance, but not the chance level of responding that these individuals show in matching one relation to another.

Evidently, there is no analogy between transformed and untransformed elements, on the one hand, and physically different exemplars of a relation, on the other – the processes involved in recognizing the two kinds of equivalences are not comparable. If this negative conclusion is sustained by further work, how shall we interpret it? I would take it to suggest that the process the language-trained animal uses in making a truth claim – for example, in answering a yes/no question – is analogous to the process it uses in matching one relation to another. Now, of course, they need not be analogous; we have already seen that relations can be matched on the basis of a physical invariant, for example, one case of sameness is like another case of sameness at some physical level. Whereas a linguistic string and the condition it describes are not physically alike, at any level of description. Nevertheless, suppose that language training (as I have described it here) is one procedure – one of several, perhaps – that has the effect of enabling the chimpanzee to match one relation with another. This would suggest that, even though in principle one relation can be matched with another on a physical or sensory basis, in fact they are not so matched. Rather, the two relations are matched in a way that is comparable to the way in which a condition is matched to a discursive representation of the condition.

Thus are we brought by tedious steps to a conclusion that is not surprising: we need an account of the process by which one makes a truth claim, that is, computes the equivalence between a condition and a discursive representation of the condition. The only surprise is that we may be helped in getting this account by a nonhuman species.[24]

REFERENCES

1. Ann Fowler. Personal communication.

2. D. Premack. *Intelligence in Ape and Man*. Hillsdale, NJ: Lawrence Erlbaum Associates, 1976.

3. D. Premack. Unpublished data.

4. D. Premack and G. Woodruff. "Analysis of Causal Action in Chimpanzees." (In preparation.)

5. D. Premack and A.J. Premack. *The Mind of an Ape*. New York: W.W. Norton and Co., 1983.

D. Premack. "Determinants of Culture: Pedagogy, Esthetics, Consciousness." Cambridge, MA: Harvard University Press (in preparation).

6. For example, J. F. Carrier. "Application of Functional Analysis and Non-Speech Response Mode to Teaching Language. Kansas Center for Research in Mental Retardation and Human Development, Parsons: Report No. 7, 1973.
R.F. Deich and P.M. Hodges. "Learning from Sarah." *Human Behavior* (May 1975): 40-42.
J. De Villiers and J.M. Naughton. "Teaching a Symbol Language to Autistic Children." *Journal of Consulting and Clinical Psychology* 42 (1974): 111-117.
J. Hughes. "Acquisition of a Nonvocal Language by Aphasic Children." *Cognition* 3 (1975): 41-55.

7. A. Velettri-Glass, M. Gazzaniga, and D. Premack. "Artificial Language Training in Global Aphasics." *Neuropsychologia* 11 (1973): 95-103.

8. D.J. Gillan, D. Premack, and G. Woodruff. "Reasoning in the Chimpanzee. 1. Analogical Reasoning." *Journal of Experimental Psychology: Animal Behavior Processes* 7 (1981): 1-17.

9. D. Premack and M. McClure. "Nonverbal Analogies in Children and Chimpanzee." (In preparation.)

10. G. Woodruff and D. Premack. "Primitive Mathematical Concepts in the Chimpanzee: Proportionality and Numerosity." *Nature* 293 (1981): 568-570.

11, Premack, *Intelligence in Ape and Man*. op. cit.

12. Premack and Woodruff, in preparation a.

13. Premack and Woodruff, in preparation a.

14. W. Köhler. *The Mentality of Apes*. New York: Liveright, 1925.

15. N.R.F. Maier. "Reasoning in White Rats." *Comparative Psychology Monographs* 6 (1929): 1-93.
E.C. Tolman. *Purposive Behavior in Animals and Men*. New York: Appleton-Century, 1932.

16. M. McClure, D.J. Gillan, G. Woodruff, R. Thompson, and D. Premack. "Comparison of 'Natural Reasoning' in Children and Chimpanzees." (In preparation.)

17. R. Gelman, M. Bullock, and E. Meck. "Preschoolers' Understanding of Simple Object Transformations." *Child Development* 51(1980): 691-699.

18. R.A. Rescorla and D.J. Gillan. "An Analysis of the Facilitative Effect of Similarity on Second-Order Conditioning." *Journal of Experimental Psychology: Animal Behavior Process* 6 (1980): 339-351.

19. Note, incidentally, how this conflicts with standard views of neotony. In fact, however, the neotony of the child may be confined to motor development; in mental development we find the child considerably ahead of the chimpanzee. Yet, one could still say the child was neotonous even in mental development, by arguing that the rate at which the child approached its distant mental goal was less than the rate at which the ape approached its less distant mental goal.

20. S. Sugarman. "Children's Early Thought: Developments in Classification." New York: Cambridge University Press (in press).

21. A.A. Wright, H.C. Santiago, P.J. Urcuioli, and S.F. Sands. "Monkey and Pigeon Acquisition of Same/Different Concept Using Pictorial Stimuli." (Unpublished manuscript.)

22. M.R. D'Amato, D.P. Salmon, and M. Colombo. "Extent and Limits of the Matching Concept in Monkeys (Cebus apella)." (Unpublished manuscript.)

23. D. Premack. "Why It Should be Difficult to Talk to a Pigeon." In *Cognitive Processes in Animal Behavior*, S.H. Hulse, H. Fowler, W.K. Honig, eds. Hilsdale, NJ: Erlbaum, 1978, pp. 277-310.

24. The research reported here was supported by Grant BNS 80-23574 from the National Science Foundation.

Computational Models

MEMORY, MEANING, AND SYNTAX[1]

Roger Schank and Lawrence Birnbaum

1. Introduction

An effort has begun in the last several years to unite the common interests of those in artificial intelligence, cognitive psychology, linguistics, philosophy, and related academic disciplines. Some subset of each of these communities is concerned with how the human mind processes language. Thus, in some sense they are all working towards the goal of a general psychological theory of language that each would find adequate for its own particular purposes. The emerging discipline of cognitive science, supposedly comprising the intersection of these fields, is vitally concerned with constructing such a theory of language. But cognitive science is a discipline without discipline. There are no universally accepted methods and no accepted styles of explanation. There is disagreement even about what constitutes the subject under investigation.

Hence, when we ask, as the organizers of this volume have asked, whether a linguistic theory can be formulated without a cognitive theory, or whether a cognitive theory implies a theory of language behavior, we find ourselves in a difficult position. We all know what all the words mean, but we can be fairly sure that our view on these questions is not what another's view might be. If cognitive science is ever to make progress, however, we had better try to start somewhere.

From the perspective of artificial intelligence (AI), it is unlikely that a purely linguistic theory could be in any sense adequate. By a purely linguistic theory, we here mean a theory created to account solely for linguistic phenomena. The attempt to create such a theory is based on the presupposition that language can in some way be isolated from other elements of thought. But our successes and failures in trying to construct computational models capable of performing significant linguistic tasks seem to point in another direction: they indicate that language and thought are inextricably bound together.

Part of the problem here is in defining exactly what counts as a purely linguistic phenomenon. In the mid-sixties, most linguists took syntactic phenomena as the relevant linguistic phenomena, and hence linguistic theory was essentially syntactic theory. The assumption was that there could be a "theory of syntax."

At the root of this assumption was the distinction between competence and performance.[2] Without this distinction, the attempt to construct a "theory of syntax" would have seemed quite problematic (which is not to say that the distinction is itself unproblematic). No one can seriously propose that people must, or even can, perform a complete syntactic analysis before they begin to decode the meaning of what they hear. Such a proposal seems dubious simply on introspective evidence. If we stop at any point in the course of understanding a sentence, we will find that we have already understood quite a bit of this only partially completed sentence, and that we have generated a great many expectations, based on meaning and world knowledge, about what the rest of the sentence might contain. Clearly, we do not wait for a complete syntactic analysis before we begin to process for meaning.

More important, we do not rely solely on linguistic knowledge in our processing. To see this, consider the following sentence fragment:

(1) Seven Libyan gunmen shot their way into....

Our processing expectations here come from many sources: linguistic knowledge of course, but also facts about Libya, what gunmen are, the goals a Libyan gunman might have, where these gunmen might be going, and so on. We are fairly certain that they are not going into "a paper bag," for example, although that would be syntactically correct. We know that they have some goal, probably political, that it may involve money, and so on. If we next heard "bank" here we would not reflect on whether the "river bank" sense had been intended.

The point of all this is that no purely linguistic theory can itself explain much of this language-processing behavior. A purely linguistic theory can be motivated only by making it a competence theory. Such a theory need not pay attention to how people process language. It can be restricted to questions of form and structure, ignoring issues of meaning, knowledge, and context.

Can one formulate an adequate theory of language-processing behavior without first constructing a purely linguistic theory? Of course! If a purely linguistic theory is taken to be a "theory of syntax," then our question boils down to the role of syntax within an overall theory of language and cognition.

1.1 Methodological issues

In most of our discussions of issues in natural language processing, we have preferred not to use the terms invented for the purposes of descriptive linguistics, in order to avoid misunderstandings. Accordingly, in describing our theories of processing, we have avoided the use of such traditional terms as *grammar, syntax, semantics,* and *pragmatics.* Instead we have used terms like *conceptual* (by which we mean both semantic and pragmatic) and *inferential memory.* Unfortunately, this has sometimes resulted in the kind of misunderstanding we were seeking to avoid. In particular, some cognitive scientists, on the basis of an apparently cursory acquaintance with our research, have erroneously concluded that our models of language processing do not make use of syntactic knowledge. Since our models certainly do use such knowledge, their implications for syntax and its place in a cognitive theory of language are worth considering.

The relationship between semantics and syntax is unquestionably one of the most confusing issues in cognitive science. It also seems to be a durable one, since it appears over and over again in the literature on psychology, linguistics, and the philosophy of language.

What can AI contribute to the understanding of this problematic relationship? Its most important contributions, we believe, stem from its concern with theories of *processing.* Within the framework of artificial intelligence, we can come to understand the relationships among memory, meaning, and syntax only by understanding how and when each is used in the processes of understanding and generating language. We do not claim that a computer model is necessarily directly relevant to human cognitive faculties. But neither is any other formal model, regardless of whether those who devised it used a computer. Any formal model is ultimately subject to empirical test to determine both its psychological plausibility and its ability to actually characterize the phenomena it was intended to characterize. In constructing our computational models, however, we naturally try to take into consideration what is known about the human mechanism.

The methodology of artificial intelligence is to formulate process models, and experiment with computer implementations of those models. Interestingly enough, computer modeling has proved useful in understanding the human mechanism. One reason is that the attempt to implement a proposed model typically uncovers many crucial problems – the importance of which may have been grossly underestimated, or even completely unforeseen, at the start.

The problems that arise in dealing with linguistic ambiguity provide a good example of this. Most utterances, when examined closely, are very ambiguous; yet, in a given context, people generally have no difficulty in understanding the unambiguous message underlying an utterance. The ability to recover a sufficiently unambiguous message from ambiguous language, of somehow evading or resolving ambiguity, is crucial to the success of any system, human or machine, for processing natural language. The centrality of this problem becomes inescapable the moment one actually tries to implement a model of linguistic processing. Nevertheless, the concern in linguistics has typically been simply with being able to represent potential ambiguities, not with doing something about them.

Another reason to expect that artificial intelligence theories can contribute to our understanding of the relationships among memory, semantics, and syntax is that they must address the issue if they are to lead to process models capable of performing the types of linguistic task that people can perform. Clearly, other kinds of linguistic theorizing are under no such methodological pressure to address the issue. Research aimed towards elucidating a competence theory of syntax, for example, naturally starts by de-emphasizing the relationships between meaning and syntax. This methodological decision has in turn often led to psychological claims for various forms of *autonomous syntax,* most clearly seen in the work of Chomsky and others of the interpretive school. These claims have often been made without consideration of the kind of relationship between semantics and syntax that might be required in order to actually perform significant language-processing tasks. In research on artificial intelligence, however, this lack of attention to processing is simply impossible.

1.2 The integrated processing hypothesis

What do our current theories say about the roles of memory, meaning, and syntax in language processing? Our working hypothesis is that meaning and world knowledge are often crucial even at the earliest points in the process of understanding language.[3] We call this position the *integrated processing hypothesis.* As we shall see, this hypothesis stands in direct opposition to theories that posit a logically autonomous syntactic analysis procedure, preceding, and providing input for, semantic processing.[4] This paper is concerned with exploring the implications of the integrated processing hypothesis, some of the evidence for it, and its relation to other theoretical frameworks for language processing.

Two observations led us to adopt the hypothesis originally. The first was the failure of syntax-oriented approaches to the construction of systems for processing natural languages, particularly in the early research on machine translation.[5] This failure was due primarily to problems of ambiguity and implicit content: considerations of meaning and context are crucial to the solution of both kinds of problem. Thus, a more semantics-oriented approach to language analysis seemed necessary.

The second observation was the rather commonsense one that it is easier to understand a foreign language, especially when reading, than to speak or write it. Most of us have had the experience of picking up a magazine written in a language with which we are slightly acquainted, and more or less understanding it, especially if we know something about the topic. Paraphrasing or answering questions in the language, however, would be beyond our capabilities. It would seem, then, that understanding language requires far less knowledge of syntax than generation, and hence that a semantics-oriented approach to language analysis could be successful.

The above considerations led to the development of a series of language analyzers based on the low-level semantics captured by conceptual dependency theory.[6] These analyzers proved moderately successful in a variety of settings, including story understanding, question answering, and dialog systems. At the same time, work progressed on attempts to characterize the pragmatic knowledge necessary for understanding language. One of the first, and certainly the simplest, of the memory structures devised to capture this high-level semantic knowledge was the script.[7] A script is a temporally and causally linked set of low-level concepts describing a time-ordered stereotypical event sequence. The paradigmatic example of a scripted activity is the act of going to a restaurant. The script notion was used as the basis of the SAM system,[8] a computer program for understanding simple stories.

The development of these higher-level memory structures led naturally to the question of how they might be used directly in the language analysis process. The conceptual dependency parsers cited above were finished analyzing a sentence when they found a representation for its meaning. Thus, their use entailed a two-step understanding process (language to meaning, then meaning to memory processes) that, though more sensible than a multistep process using an autonomous syntactic analyzer (language to syntactic structure, then syntactic structure to meaning, and so on), was still clearly unrealistic. The first attempt to design an integrated understanding system – that is, one that used high-level knowledge to help with low-level parsing – resulted in a program, FRUMP,[9] that applied simplified scripts directly to the problem of skimming and summarizing newspaper stories. Though skimming a story is not nearly as complex a task as arriving at a deep understanding of it, FRUMP's success at this task reinforced our belief that the way to solve the problems of language analysis is to bring as much knowledge as possible to bear on the understanding process.

1.3 The commonsense argument

Another motive for the integrated processing hypothesis stems from a commonsense appraisal of the role of language analysis in the language-understanding process as a whole. This immediately raises the question of what it means to understand. We need not be talking exclusively about language when we talk about understanding. As understanders, we understand situations as well as sentences. We are able to operate in the world because we understand the world as well as understanding sentences about that world. In both cases, the knowledge we apply is the same. In both cases, what we mean by understanding is the same.

To take a simple example, when a person enters a Burger King, after having been to a McDonald's but never before to a Burger King, he is confronted with a new situation which he must attempt to "understand." We can say that a person has understood this situation – that is, he understands Burger King in the sense of being able to operate in it – when he says "I see, Burger King is just like McDonald's."

To put this another way, we might expect that at some point during his Burger King trip he might be "reminded" of McDonald's. Understanding an experience or situation crucially involves recalling from memory the previously experienced situation that is most like the new input, and being able to use that memory as a source of expectations relevant to current processing.[10]

When we are reminded of some event or experience in the course of undergoing a different one, it is because the structures we are using to process the new experience are the same structures we are using to organize memory. We cannot help but pass through the old memories while processing the new input. There are vast numbers of such high-level memory structures. Finding the right one out of all those available – that is, the one most applicable to the experience at hand – is what we mean by understanding.

By this view, understanding an input involves finding the most relevant higher-level structure available to explain it, and creating for the input a new memory structure derived from the old one. The process of understanding then has its basis in memory, particularly memory for closely related experiences accessible through reminding and expressible through analogy.

But what does such a view have to say about how we understand language? We are claiming that people understand by using expectations that come from whatever memory structure has the most in common with the situation being processed. These expectations need not be solely about events; they are about language as well. By this view, understanding language means accessing the most relevant memory to help process the situation being described. Expectations about language are not necessarily different from those about situations; in fact, the two kinds of expectation are likely to be tightly bound to each other. A language understander need not, for example, explicitly choose from among all the possible meanings of "demand" in a terrorism story. What we know about terrorism colors our expectations about what will happen in a terrorist episode, and about what the words describing such a situation mean. Understanding language depends crucially on our knowledge about the situations that language describes. The commonsense motivation for integrated processing, then, is that it doesn't make sense *not* to make the fullest possible use of this relevant information in processing further input.

An important use of this information, as we just pointed out, is in somehow evading or resolving ambiguity. Consider the following example:

(2)   The old man's glasses were filled with sherry.

In the course of processing the above sentence, most people incorrectly decide that "glasses" means "eyeglasses," and so are surprised by the outcome; they must consciously "back up." This error can be explained only by assuming that people analyzing this sentence apply their knowledge of the relation between age and eyesight *before* completing any putative low-level analysis of the sentence.[11] If "bartender" is substituted for "old man" in (2), the opposite assumption is made in processing, and so no backing up is needed. Such assumptions are made while a sentence is being processed. To do that, world knowledge must be accessed and applied while everything else is going on.

2. What Is the Problem?

The issue of how memory, meaning, and syntax are related in language processing can be divided into three distinct though closely related questions. These questions are often conflated, and we believe that the failure to keep the distinctions clear has been a major factor inhibiting mutual comprehension among those who have argued the issue. Therefore, before we discuss exactly what the integrated processing hypothesis claims, and its implications for theories of processing, we will first try to clear up some of the misunderstanding.

The three questions correspond to three aspects of any computational process. These can be usefully distinguished, with no claim that they are realized by distinct elements in the process. The first aspect of interest is the *control structure* of the process, which defines the task to be accomplished (that is, what is input and what is output) as well as the subprocesses that must be invoked in order to accomplish the task, how they communicate, and the order in which they must be invoked. The second aspect is the *representational structures* that are constructed and operated on by the process, and that constitute the outputs of any intermediate stages and of the process as a whole. The final aspect is the *knowledge base* on which the process draws to actually perform the task. Since this knowledge often takes the form of rules, the knowledge base is commonly called a rule base. Our three questions, then, concern what integration, as opposed to autonomy, of syntax might possibly mean for these three aspects of a language-processing system.

▶ The first question concerns the processes that apply the knowledge used in language understanding: Are conceptual (semantic and pragmatic) knowledge and syntactic knowledge applied by separate control mechanisms, or is there an integrated control structure that applies both? That is, does language understanding proceed as a unified process, or as several separate processes?

▶ The second question involves representational structures: Are the structures that are used to encode conceptual information during processing separate from those used to encode syntactic information? That is, is there an independent level of syntactic representation? What kinds of representation do people compute as part of the understanding process?

▶ The last question concerns the knowledge used in understanding. Can the rule base that embodies syntactic knowledge be separated from that which embodies semantic and world knowledge? Is there a clean separation between these sets of rules, or is there a continuum of rules, some purely semantic, some purely syntactic, some in between?

Though it is important to distinguish these questions, the possible answers to them are of course interdependent. We will see this in what follows.

2.1 Control structures

The question "Are syntax and semantics applied by a unified control mechanism or by independent mechanisms?" is of course the question "Does an autonomous syntactic analysis procedure exist?" The claim that a single control mechanism applies both is the weakest possible claim of the integrated processing hypothesis. That's because if this claim is false it seems difficult to argue either for integrated representational structures or for an integrated knowledge base in language processing. The opposite position – the claim that syntax and semantics are applied by independent control mechanisms – is the strongest possible form of autonomous syntax.

It is instructive to map out some of the possible alternatives concerning the issue of integrated versus autonomous control processes for applying memory, semantics, and syntax to the problem of language analysis. Following are sketchy descriptions of several possible positions.

[a] *Semantics and syntax are completely separable.* By this position, syntactic analysis is a completely independent process, logically and temporally prior to the meaning-based inference processes involved in understanding. This position implies that syntax alone controls the analysis at the earlier points of processing. This is the view that results when the model outlined in Chomsky[12] and descendant models are given a straightforward, if naïve, recasting into the performance domain.

[b] *Semantics and syntax are "nearly decomposable."* By this view, a syntactic analysis process precedes semantic processing, and provides the input for it. However, this process may on occasion query a semantic component in order to make a syntactic decision. This limited interaction between semantics-oriented processes and the syntactic analysis process is controlled by syntax, in that only the syntactic mechanism can decide that some interaction is required. This is the position taken by

Fodor, Bever, and Garrett, with their theory of independent syntactic processing within clauses,[13] and by others,[14] with somewhat more flexible communication regimes between syntactic and semantic components.

[c] *Semantics and syntax have a "heterarchical" relationship.* By this position, semantics-oriented knowledge and syntactic knowledge are still applied by separate control processes. However, their relationship is far more cooperative than in the preceding position; the two processes operate somewhat like co-routines. That is, the interaction is no longer exclusively under the control of the syntactic mechanism. A syntactic component does some work, then calls some semantic process which does what it can and then in turn calls syntax for more information, and so on. This appears to be the position advocated by Winograd.[15]

[d] *Semantics and syntax are used in an integrated control structure.* By this view, the decision whether to use syntactic knowledge or conceptual knowledge is made by a single control structure, and whatever available knowledge is most useful is applied in trying to analyze and understand the input. This is the position that we have taken.[16] A similar view seems to inform the experimental program being carried out by Marslen-Wilson and his colleagues.[17] One way in which the totally integrated view might be differentiated from the heterarchical view relates to the question of syntactic representations; Winograd's model constructs and operates on them, whereas the models to be presented here do not. We will return to this point in the next section.

The opposition on the above spectrum of position [a], logically separate syntactic analysis, and position [d], integrated control structure, is often misconstrued. Since position [a] implies that syntax alone controls early language analysis, the opposite of that must be something like "semantics alone controls early language analysis." This is clearly wrong, but that in no way affects the validity of position [d], which doesn't imply anything of the sort.

2.2 Representational structures

In the course of understanding or generating language, any language-processing system must compute some structures for representing meaning, on the one hand, and words and their properties, on the other. An important question that guides our investigation of language-processing theories is, "What additional structures must be computed to represent the syntactic information associated with utterances?" There are basically two positions that one can take:

▸ *An autonomous level of syntactic representation, such as phrase markers, must be computed.* For example, Fodor, Bever, and Garrett claim that "the structural analyses to be recovered are...precisely the trees that a grammar generates,"[18] by which they mean that in the course of comprehending language, people compute syntactic structures of the sort postulated by generative linguistics.

▸ *No independent level of syntactic representation is constructed or operated on during language processing.* This claim has an important consequence for models of language processing: whatever syntactic distinctions need to be represented must be represented either at the level of conceptual structures or at the level of words. This can be interpreted in two ways. Straightforwardly, it could mean that the syntactic representation is "part of" the conceptual representation, in the sense of being part of the same data structure, indexed with it, etc., but nevertheless serving a distinct function. On a more radical interpretation, the claim can be taken as asserting that, if a conceptual representation carries syntactic information necessary for subsequent processing, this information must also serve some semantic or pragmatic function. In our own models, then, whenever we add elements to a representation in memory for the purpose of carrying syntactic information, we must try to justify them independently in terms of some conceptual function.[19]

The question of representational structures has bearing on our earlier discussion of control structures. If two processes acted on, and produced as output, different sorts of structure, such behavior would constitute one characteristic that would lead us to say they were independent of each other. Hence, without the computation of independent syntactic representations as part of the language-understanding process, one characteristic that might lead us to single out some independent syntactic processor would be missing. In this sense, the computation of an independent level of syntactic representation is a weak prerequisite for the existence of an independent syntactic processor. Hence, claims of independent syntactic processing are usually accompanied by claims that independent syntactic representations are needed. And so, in arguing against an independent syntactic processor, our claim of an integrated conceptual and syntactic processor is accompanied by the claim that conceptual and syntactic representations are integrated as well.

2.3 Knowledge base

The strongest claim that an integrated processing hypothesis could make about the knowledge used for understanding would be that there are no purely syntactic rules – that is, that all the rules used in language processing refer to some semantic information. The opposite claim – that there are some purely syntactic rules – is the weakest possible form of autonomous syntax. Without such a set of autonomous syntactic rules, for example, the claim that there is an autonomous syntactic processor doesn't even make sense. That is, the extent to which the rules embodying syntactic knowledge can be separated from the rules embodying semantic knowledge will determine whether a logically prior or separate syntactic analysis procedure is possible or sensible.

We do not claim that no purely syntactic rules exist; hence we do not support the strongest possible form of the integrated processing hypothesis. Even in a weaker form, however, the hypothesis does make an interesting claim about the knowledge used in understanding. Given the existence of some exclusively syntactic processing rules, these rules simply occupy one extreme of a continuum of rules, and are not distinguished *by use* from other sorts of rules. This follows from the two prior claims of the integrated processing hypothesis that (1) language processing is effected by an integrated control mechanism, and (2) no independent level of syntactic representation is computed in language processing. If these two claims are true, then whatever "exclusively syntactic" might mean, it does not mean *functionally* distinguishable in use from other sorts of rules. Thus, the integrated processing hypothesis is supported to the extent that the role of purely syntactic rules in processing can be shown to be similar to the role of other kinds of rules. We will turn to that after we have presented a rudimentary description of our process models.

2.4 Integrated processing revisited

We are now in a position to state exactly what the integrated processing hypothesis claims. First, it claims that language analysis proceeds as a unitary process, integrating all kinds of knowledge, rather than as a collection of separate processes, one for each kind of knowledge. This is in contrast to the models proposed by Fodor et al., Woods, and Marcus,[20] among others. Second, it claims that no independent level of syntactic representation is constructed, operated on, or output by the language analysis process. This is in contrast to all of the above models, as well as the model proposed by Winograd.[21] Third, it claims that, although there are rules that are in some sense purely syntactic, such rules are not used differently from other sorts of rule; that is, they are functionally integrated in processing and play no privileged role. This follows from the first two claims.

3. Psychological Evidence

There has been a great deal of psychological experimentation bearing on the relationship of syntax to semantics in language analysis. In this section we will review a few results that seem to support the integrated processing hypothesis. Among psychologists, the results of this work have convinced even the strongest partisans of generative linguistics that:

▶ There is no evidence that people make use, in comprehension or generation, of the kinds of rule devised by generative linguists to describe linguistic phenomena.

▶ The very strong claim of a completely autonomous syntactic processor (position (a) in Section 2.1) cannot be upheld.

In fact, these points constitute the most "conservative" interpretation of the experimental results, in the sense of conserving *some* role for generative linguistics in psychology. Less sympathetic observers will note that the results, though consistent with various patched-up claims of syntactic autonomy, were not as predicted by theorists who advocate that position.

One of the earliest and most significant results was uncovered by Slobin.[22] He investigated differences in how long it takes to understand passive sentences as compared to active forms, distinguishing between reversible and nonreversible passives. A reversible passive is a sentence like "John was seen by Bill," in which syntax must be inspected to determine who saw whom. That is, this can be distinguished from "John saw Bill" only by noticing that one is passive construction and the other is not, since both are equally sensible. A nonreversible passive is a sentence like "The ice cream cone was eaten by John," in which, by virtue of semantics, one can determine who ate what. That is, this sentence can be distinguished from "The ice cream cone ate John" on the grounds that the latter is nonsense. Slobin found that, although reversible passives take longer to understand than active forms, nonreversible passives *do not*. At the very least, this result indicates that semantic grounds, if sufficient, can override the necessity for certain kinds of syntactic processing.

What is even more damaging to models like those of Fodor et al. and Marcus[23] is that, if the syntactic processing consists of computing some underlying syntactic phrase marker, these results make us wonder whether that computation would be made at all if other kinds of evidence obviated the need for it. Either way, the result is completely congenial to the integrated processing hypothesis.

Marslen-Wilson and his colleagues have done numerous studies of the status of autonomous syntactic processing models. A representative result can be found in Tyler and Marslen-Wilson.[24] They studied the model proposed by Fodor et al.,[25] a chief claim of which was that, within clauses, sentence analysis proceeded by the operation of a completely autonomous syntactic processor, and no higher-level knowledge could enter the process until a clause boundary was reached. Subjects were presented with sentence fragments like

(4)   If you walk too near the runway, landing planes...

(5)   If you've been trained as a pilot, landing planes...

and then immediately supplied with a probe word, either "is" or "are," and asked to simply repeat the probe word as quickly as possible. On pragmatic grounds, as determined by the content of the first clause, "is" is appropriate as a continuation of (5) but not (4), whereas "are" is appropriate for (4) but not (5). The only way to determine whether a probe was appropriate was on the basis of meaning and pragmatic knowledge, making use of the context created by the content of the initial clause of the test sentence fragments. The data showed that subjects were slower to repeat an inappropriate probe. Since the appropriateness of the probe was a syntactic property (number agreement), and since subjects were probed in the middle of an uncompleted clause, this result demonstrates that whatever syntactic processing is going on is not independent of meaning-oriented processing, even within clauses.

More recently, Shwartz[26] examined several possible low-level strategies – some proposed by him, some proposed elsewhere in the literature – for determining pronominal referents. The use of some of these strategies depended on the existence of explicit syntactic representations. The study found no evidence for the use of such strategies. This kind of result is important because, to the extent that processes that might have been thought to depend on explicit syntactic representations can be found not to, the integrated processing hypothesis is strengthened.

One final study we will mention concerns an investigation into the putative independence of semantic processing and pragmatic processing in language understanding. Gibbs[27] investigated a claim by Clark and Lucy,[28] among others, that understanding indirect speech acts requires computing, in a fairly bottom-up fashion, the "literal meaning" of the utterance, which is then used as input to special pragmatic interpretation rules to discover the "real meaning." Clark and Lucy had shown that, in the absence of any context, indirect speech acts did take longer to comprehend than, for example, direct requests. This was taken as evidence that an extra processing step was being performed, presumably involving the application of the special pragmatic rules to the previously computed "literal meaning" of the input. Gibbs performed a similar study, in which, however, the indirect speech acts were embedded in a suitable context. He found that, in context, indirect speech acts take no longer to interpret than direct language; thus he called into question the claim that "literal meaning" must be computed.

4. Process Models of Language Analysis

The problem of language analysis is, given some linguistic input in some context, to determine the semantic and memory structures underlying that input. The goal of *conceptual analysis* is to perform this task in a manner consistent with the integrated processing hypothesis, namely as a unified process, in one direct step. This goal differs sharply from that assumed by most models of language analysis, which hold that the process uses a parsing mechanism that performs an explicit *syntactic* analysis of the input sentences.[29] In this section we describe the basics of several approaches to conceptual analysis, involving various kinds of semantic and world knowledge in the parsing process. Most of these have been implemented in running computer programs. We also discuss some more speculative approaches that have not been implemented.

4.1 Analysis based on expectation

A language understander must connect concepts obtained from word meanings, and from inferences derived from word meanings, into a coherent representation of the input as a whole. Because of the possibilities of word-sense ambiguity or irrelevant inference, an understander must also be able to choose among alternative concepts. So, conceptual analysis consists mainly of connecting and disambiguating (that is, choosing among) conceptual structures.

The processing knowledge that a conceptual analyzer uses for this task takes the form of *expectations*.[30] When a person hears or reads words with certain meanings, he expects or predicts that words with certain other meanings may follow, or may have already been seen. People constantly predict what they are likely to see next, on the basis of what they have read and understood so far and of what they know about language and the world. They use these expectations to disambiguate and connect incoming text.

Of course, expectations are used in syntactic analysis programs as well. The difference lies in the *origin* of the expectations. In syntactic analyzers, the expectations are derived from a grammar. In conceptual analyzers, the expectations are governed instead by the incomplete conceptual structures representing the meaning of the input.

We will illustrate the use of expectations in understanding by way of an extremely simple example. Suppose that the following sentence were the input to an expectation-based conceptual analysis system: "Fred ate an apple." Reading from left to right, the system first finds "Fred." The system understands this as a reference to some male human being named Fred, and stores the reference, represented as the token FRED, in some kind of short-term memory. The next word is "ate." This is understood as an instance of the concept of eating, which in conceptual dependency[31] is represented by a case frame something like this:

(INGEST ACTOR (NIL) OBJECT (NIL)).

Also, the meaning of "ate" supplies some expectations that give hints as to how to go about filling the empty slots of this frame. One of these expectations suggests that the ACTOR of the INGEST concept, an animate being, may have already been mentioned. So the analyzer checks short-term memory, finds FRED there, and fills the ACTOR slot of the INGEST:

(INGEST ACTOR (FRED) OBJECT (NIL)).

There remains an unfulfilled expectation that what Fred ate will be mentioned, that it should be some edible thing (or at least a physical object), and that it should fill the OBJECT slot. Next, "an" is read. This creates an expectation that some instance of a concept should follow, with the instruction that if one is found it should be marked as an indefinite reference. (This is information that can aid memory.) Finally, "apple" is read. It is understood as an instance of the concept APPLE, representing something known to be food. The expectation created when "an" was read is satis-fied; so APPLE is marked as an object not previously seen, which we will represent as (APPLE REF (INDEF)). The second expecta-tion created when "ate" was read is also satisfied; so the OBJECT slot of the INGEST is filled by (APPLE REF (INDEF)). The system's current understanding of the input is represented as

(INGEST ACTOR (FRED) OBJECT (APPLE REF (INDEF))).

There are no more words to read, so the process halts.

This simple example gives the flavor of the conceptual analysis process.[32] When a word is read, the conceptual structure represent-ing its meaning is added to short-term memory. In addition, expec-tations (governed by the unfilled case slots) are created; these provide the processing knowledge necessary to connect up these conceptual structures into a representation of the input as a whole. Connections between concepts are established via the filling of empty case slots.

How consistent is this kind of conceptual analysis process with the integrated processing hypothesis? One failing should be clear immediately: the above discussion has touched only on the role of low-level semantics and conceptual representations in parsing. Higher-level memory structures, such as scripts, have not been integrated into the analysis process. On the other hand, the model is consistent with the hypothesis in that it constructs a conceptual representation directly, using a unified control structure, and with-out prior syntactic analysis. Further, no independent level of syn-tactic representation is built or operated on.

Several analyzers based on these ideas have been implemented. We will illustrate the process here in the context of the CYRUS system – a program that (1) automatically builds up a data base from news stories analyzed by FRUMP (mentioned earlier), (2) can be queried in natural English, and (3) can respond in English. One of the main points of the CYRUS memory model is its ability to reconstruct input questions so they conform to how information is stored in its memory.[33] CYRUS uses CA, one of our analysis pro-grams, to analyze questions. The following is an example of a question-answering session with CYRUS.[34]

CYRUS

Are you interested in Muskie or Vance? (M or V) : *VANCE

*(DIALOG2)

Enter next question
>When was the last time you were in Egypt?

The question is:
((ACTOR HUMI IS (*LOC* VAL POL6)) TIME TIME0)
The question type is "time"
The question concept is:
((ACTOR HUMI IS (*LOC* VAL POL6)))
      inferring a diplomatic trip
answering question using time context:
  directly
The answer is:
(CON113)

  on DEC 10 1978.

Enter next question
>Why did you go there?

The question is:
((CON (*?*) REASON
    ((ACTOR HUMI ⟺ (*PTRANS*) OBJECT HUM1 TO POL6))))
The question type is "motivational"
The question concept is:
((ACTOR HUMI ⟺ (*PTRANS*) OBJECT HUM1 TO POL6))
answering question using previous context:
  directly
The answer is:
(CON145)

  to negotiate the Camp David Accords.

Enter next question
>Who did you talk to there?

The question is:
((ACTOR HUMI ⟺ (*MTRANS*) TO (*?*)) PLACE POL6 TIME TIME8)
The question type is "concept completion"
The question concept is:
((ACTOR HUMI ⟺ (*MTRANS*) TO (*?*)) PLACE POL6 TIME TIME8)
      inferring undifferentiated political meeting
answering question using previous context:
  directly
The answer is:
(CON184 CON198)

  with Anwar Sadat.

Enter next question
>Has your wife ever met Mrs. Begin?

The question is:
((ACTOR HUM4 IS (*PROX* VAL HUM60W)) TIME TIME15 MODE (*?*))
The question type is "verification"
The question concept is:
((ACTOR HUM4 IS (*PROX* VAL HUM60W)) TIME TIME15))
      inferring social occasion
      searching memory for question concept
        searching directly for input – sM-SOCIAL-OCC

found (GN590)
The answer is:
(CON122)

yes, most recently at a state dinner in Israel in JAN 1980.

Enter next question
>What heads of state have you met?

The question is:
((ACTOR HUMI IS (*PROX* VAL TOKQ14)) TIME TIME22))
The question type is "concept completion"
The question concept is:
((ACTOR HUMI IS (*PROX* VAL TOKQ14)) TIME TIME22))
    inferring a diplomatic meeting
searching memory for question concept
  searching directly for input – $MEET

        ...
applying strategies to search memory

        ...
        searching for sM-CONFERENCE
                found (GN505 GN492 GN420)

        ...
        searching for sM-VIPVISIT
                found (CON95)
            searching sM-VIPVISIT instance for input

        ...
        searching for I-NEGOTIATE
                found (GN545A GN462 GN468A GN420A GN404A)
        ...

King Hassan, Menachim Begin, Mustafa Khalil, Ian Smith,
President Assad, King Hussein, and Anwar Sadat.

Enter next question
>Last time you went to Saudi Arabia, where did you stay?

The question is:
(($\Longleftrightarrow$ ($SLEEP ACTOR HUM1 LOC (*?*))) TIME GO682)
The question type is "concept completion"
The question concept is:
(($\Longleftrightarrow$ ($SLEEP ACTOR HUM1 LOC (*?*))))
    inferring a diplomatic trip
    answering question using time context:
      directly
    The answer is:
    (GO715)

in a palace in Saudi Arabia on SEP 23 1978.

Enter next question:
>Did you go sightseeing there?

The question is:
(($\Longleftrightarrow$ (sM-SIGHTSEE ACTOR HUM2))
        MODE (*?*) TIME GO784 PLACE POL11)
The question type is "verification"
The question concept is:

((⟺ (sM-SIGHTSEE ACTOR HUM1))TIME GO784 PLACE POL11))
answering question using previous context:
  directly
  using top-level events
The answer is:
(GO822)

  yes, at an oilfield in Dharan on SEP 23 1978.

4.2 The role of syntax

What is the role of syntax in a conceptual analyzer? Traditional
notions of syntax use categories like "part of speech" and "phrase
marker" in discussing the structure of a sentence. In this section
we would like to claim that these notions of syntax are inappropriate to attempts to describe and use syntactic knowledge in a
language-understanding process.

To begin with, what is the purpose of syntactic knowledge? Clearly, a major use of syntactic knowledge is to direct the combination
of word meanings into an utterance meaning when semantic information is insufficient or misleading. For example, in an utterance
like "Put the magazine on the plate," it is syntactic knowledge that
tells the understander which object is to be placed on top of which.
From the point of view of its use in a conceptual analyzer, therefore, a large part of syntax is knowledge of how to combine word
meanings on the basis of their positions in the utterance. This
knowledge is necessary whenever a representational structure contains several gaps that have overlapping semantic requirements.
For example, both the ACTOR and the TO slots of an ATRANS
(concept of transfer of an abstract property) can appropriately be
filled by a "higher animate." Syntactic knowledge must then be
used to decide which of several appropriate gaps such a structure
should fill.

How can this syntactic knowledge be characterized? We seek a
specification that takes into account the fact that the point of
syntax is its *use* in the understanding process. We have viewed part
of the process of understanding as one of connecting representational structures, where a connection has been established between
structures when one fills a slot in the other, or both fill a larger
form. Thus syntactic knowledge is knowledge that specifies where
in the utterance some word is to be found whose meaning can be
connected (via slot-filling) with the meaning of another word. Of
course, we must now specify the notion "position in an utterance."

Given that processing knowledge is encoded in expectations, the question is how positional information can be taken into account in those expectations. This can be done by having tests that check for

▶ Relative positions of concepts in short-term memory.
▶ The proper order for filling slots in structures.

These methods describe position in an utterance by the use of relative positional information. Both are essentially ways of using information inherent in word order. The first describes the position of a conceptual structure in short-term memory in relation to the positions of other structures with which it might be connected via slot-filling.

The second method relates the position of a structure to other structures somewhat more directly. In particular, the temporal order of input can be directly employed by constraining the order in which slots should be filled — rather than as reflected in the order of concepts in short-term memory. For instance, a constraint that the ACTOR slot of a conceptualization be filled before the OBJECT slot reflects the fact that, in an active construction, the ACTOR of that conceptualization should be seen before the OBJECT.

Another important method of using syntax in a conceptual analyzer is to relate the position of a conceptual structure to the position of a particular lexical item (that is, a function word), rather than to another concept. Function words — including prepositions, postpositions, affixes, complementizers, and so forth — are very important syntactic cues in conceptual language analysis. In a sentence like

John gave Mary to the Shah of Iran.

the function word "to" clearly marks the recipient of the action, where semantics alone is simply not sufficient.

4.3 Functional integration of syntactic rules

A crucial feature of the analysis model we have been discussing is the *functional* integration of syntax and semantics. Rules based purely on semantics, rules based purely on syntax, and mixed rules all play the same role in processing: They are used to construct, connect, and disambiguate conceptual structures.

We can illustrate this with a few examples. The conception of syntax sketched in the preceding section is that syntactic knowledge is necessary when semantics alone is insufficient to correctly determine the meaning of the input. One common cause of such a situation, as we pointed out, is that the semantic restrictions on case slots in a conceptual representation are not always unique – that is, are not mutually exclusive. This suggests that when some case slot does have unique semantic requirements, no syntactic knowledge would be necessary to find the correct filler for that slot. Hence, that filler should have an extremely free syntax with respect to the entire construction.

It turns out that one can find examples of this sort of phenomenon. Consider the conceptual object of MTRANS (concepts of communication). Concepts of communication take an entire conceptualization, or proposition, as their object, namely the concept being communicated. Since, on semantic grounds, no other case role of an MTRANS can be filled with a complete proposition, we would expect that the position of the object concept with respect to the overall MTRANS construction would vary rather freely, and it does. Consider the following examples:

(6a)   A Liberian tanker ran aground off Nantucket Island, the Coast Guard said.

(6b)   The Coast Guard said a Liberian tanker ran aground off Nantucket Island.

(6c)   A Liberian tanker, the Coast Guard said, ran aground off Nantucket Island.

These examples suggest that the rule (expectation) used to fill the object slot of MTRANS conceptualizations is based entirely on semantics. It simply looks for an entire conceptualization to fill the object slot.

On the other hand, relative subclauses, possibly initiated by *that*, as in

(7)   The car that I saw in the showroom...

require a great deal of syntactic knowledge to be properly analyzed. "That" sets up several expectations, one of which, rendered in English, says roughly:

> To the right will be found a concept with some unfilled slot(s). Use the concept to the left to fill (one of) the slot(s), in accordance with semantic requirements. Then take the resulting conceptualization and subordinate it to the concept on the left.

This rule is purely syntactic: it refers to relative positional information and to "unfilled slots," but it says nothing about the kind of concept or about restrictions on slots. This is not to say that the rule can be used without reference to semantics, however, since semantic knowledge must be consulted to produce a meaningful subordinate conceptualization. The important point is that this purely syntactic rule plays exactly the same role in processing as does the purely semantic rule for finding the object of an MTRANS. Syntactic and semantic knowledge cannot be distinguished by use in this model of language analysis.

This same point can be made by considering generation, for instance of noun groups. A purely syntactic rule that one might want to have in a generator is that adjectives precede nouns. But the order of the adjectives themselves is not determined by such a purely syntactic rule. A generator must have enough knowledge to know that "big red ball" is generally more appropriate than "red big ball," or that "old Irish grandmother" is more appropriate than "Irish old grandmother." Examples like this can best be explained by postulating that an adjective supplying information about a more intrinsic property of the modified noun will be closer to that noun than adjectives describing less intrinsic properties.[35] The proper generation of noun groups depends crucially on the simultaneous application of both this rule and the purely syntactic rule that adjectives precede nouns. But the notion of "intrinsic property" is clearly conceptual, not syntactic. Thus, the problem of generating proper adjective order is another example that argues for the functional integration of purely syntactic rules with other sorts of rule.

4.4 Using higher-level memory

So far we have discussed only the integration of low-level semantics, the sort characterized by conceptual dependency, into the analysis process. However, the success of the FRUMP system in using higher-level memory structures early in the parsing process showed that these structures too must play a role in language analysis.

This "integrated understanding" approach enables the analysis of language directly into the high-level representations that organize memory and facilitate understanding. Often it is an entire high-level memory structure that best represents the meaning of some input. The sentence "Fred proposed to Wilma," for example, should call to mind a large structure representing our knowledge of courting, proposals, and marriage.

In addition to directly invoking these higher-level structures, the parsing process should try to fill the empty roles in these structures, just as with lower-level conceptual frames. The key point here is that we would like an analysis process that can fill slots in higher-level structures directly, in one step. The best way to explain the distinction is with an example. Suppose a language understander is reading the input

(8)   A plane carrying federal marshals...

Given that the analyzer can discover the relevant high-level structure (call it $AIRPLANE), we would like the analyzer to fill the PASSENGERS slot of that structure with the representation of "federal marshals" directly, rather than first embedding it in some intermediate, lower-level structure and then subsequently transferring the information up to the PASSENGERS slot of $AIRPLANE.

The attempt to integrate higher-level knowledge in a somewhat deeper understander than FRUMP resulted in the Integrated Partial Parser (IPP).[36] One of the key ideas underlying this approach to language analysis is that the direct application of high-level memory structures can focus the analyzer's attention, controlling what should be pursued and what should be ignored. This is possible because high-level structures typically supply very specific expectations.

To understand how this system works, consider the following example from the *New York Times:*

An Arabic-speaking gunman shot his way into the Iraqi Embassy here [Paris] yesterday morning, held hostages throughout most of the day before surrendering to French policemen, and then was shot by Iraqi security officials as he was led away by the French officers.

As IPP processes each word from the input, one of three things can occur:

▶ The word can be completely ignored.

There are many words that have no significant conceptual content for the level of analysis that IPP strives to model. Examples from the above story are "most," "way," and "held."

▶ The word may be saved in the analyzer's short-term memory, and then skipped.

Words for which this processing strategy seems appropriate have conceptual content only of a dull and uninteresting sort. Nevertheless, we cannot simply ignore them, because their meanings may be important in elaborating our knowledge of the events or things that we *are* interested in. For example, they may be used to fill roles in the conceptual structures representing interesting events. In many cases, however, they will never be used again. Examples are "Arabic," "Iraqi," and "his."

Two things can ultimately be done with these words. Either their meaning does help elaborate something interesting, in which case that meaning will be incorporated in the final representation, or it doesn't. For example, the meaning of "police" in the phrase

(9a)   before surrendering to French police

is incorporated into the representation because we are interested in whom the terrorist surrendered to. On the other hand, the meaning of "officers" in the phrase

(9b)   as he was led away by French officers

is not incorporated into the meaning representation because it does not add to our knowledge of anything interesting.

The conceptual content of these words will often have some associated processing information, in the form of expectations, that can help elaborate on their meaning. For example, the concept underlying "embassy" has an expectation that looks for the name of the country the embassy represents, and the concepts underlying "police," "officers," and "officials" have expectations for the name of the governmental authority in whose name they operate. But if a word is subject to a "save and skip" strategy, these expectations should not be applied until we know that the concept they would strive to elaborate itself elaborates on our knowledge of something interesting. This is because if it turns out that we don't care about that concept, we don't want to have done unnecessary work in elaborating it. Let's compare our processing of "police" in phrase (9a) above with our processing of "officers" in phrase (9b). Since it turns out that the concept of police in the first phrase adds to our knowledge of an interesting event, the expectation associated with the concept that looks for the governing authority should actually be used. Hence, the modifier "French" would be added to the representation. In the second phrase, since the concept of "officers" does not add to our knowledge of anything interesting, there is simply no point in applying any similar rule. The modifier "French" would be ignored.

▶ The word can be processed immediately – that is, attention is paid to its meaning and the expectations it generates. This is the strategy we apply when the word has significant and interesting conceptual content. It is these concepts and their associated expectations that drive the analysis. Examples from the above story are "gunman," "shot," and "hostages." These words generate the same kind of simple elaborative, or "slot-filling," expectations associated with some of the words for which a "save and skip" strategy is appropriate. For example, "gunman" generates an expectation looking for the nationality or political affiliation of the gunman.

These words can also generate expectations that operate at a much higher level. For example, when we read "gunman," we expect to read that he may have performed the action of shooting a weapon. We also expect the events associated with several possible scripts, including $ROBBERY and $TERRORISM. These expectations operate in a manner somewhat akin to script application[37] in that they serve in recognizing events, and so recognize that they are sensible in the given context. So, once we know that the gunman is quite likely a terrorist, we expect that he may hold hostages, that he may shoot or kill some people, and that he may make some demands. We also know that there are only a few possible outcomes of the episode: the terrorist might be captured, he might surrender, he might be killed, or he might escape. These high-level expectations help us decide what is important in the text in a very top-down way. The analysis process depends crucially on this. But its flexibility also depends on its ability to pursue questions about interesting things and events, even if they were not anticipated.

Following is an example of the input/output behavior of IPP in processing the above story.[38]

Input: (AN ARABIC SPEAKING GUNMAN SHOT HIS WAY INTO THE IRAQI EMBASSY HERE THIS MORNING HELD HOSTAGES THROUGHOUT MOST OF THE DAY BEFORE SURRENDERING TO FRENCH POLICEMEN AND THEN WAS SHOT BY IRAQI SECURITY OFFICIALS AS HE WAS LED AWAY BY FRENCH OFFICERS)

Output:

** MAIN EVENT **		** UNEXPECTED EVENTS **	
EV1 =		EV4 =	
SCRIPT	$TERRORISM	ACTION	PROPEL
ACTOR	ARAB GUNMAN	ACTOR	IRAQI OFFICIALS
PLACE	IRAQI EMBASSY	OBJECT	ARAB GUNMAN
INTEREST	9.	ITEM	*BULLETS*
CITY	PARIS	DIR-FR	GUN
TIME	MORNING	INTEREST	5.
SCENES		AFTER	EV3
EV2		RESULT	
SCENE	$HOSTAGES	EV6 =	
PLACE	IRAQI EMBASSY	STATE	DEAD
ACTOR	ARAB GUNMAN	ACTOR	ARAB GUNMAN

```
    INTEREST    7.                    INTEREST 4.
    TIME        DAY
    EV3  =
      SCENE       $CAPTURE
      PLACE       IRAQI EMBASSY
      OBJECT      ARAB GUNMAN
      ACTOR       POLICEMEN
      INTEREST    6.
      AFTER       EV2
```
673 msec CPU (0. msec GC), 944. msec clock, 1759. conses

IPP performs an integrated analysis of the input, using a detailed knowledge base concerning terrorism, to process the story in a top-down fashion.[39] The program applies what it knows about the situation being described to help it process individual words. In this story, for example, it did not treat "held" as an ambiguous word. Rather, it was expecting that it might read about the taking of hostages at that point in the story, and it simply skipped "held" to see what the next word was. This is one way of dealing with extremely vague words, such as "hold," "take," "have," and "get." In the next section, we present a more sophisticated approach.

4.5 The problem of flexibility

In the preceding section we presented the idea of analyzing linguistic input directly into the memory structures that encode pragmatic information. However, the process of directly filling slots in these structures with concepts from the input text immediately raises the problem of integrating conceptual and syntactic knowledge in a flexible way. This problem arises because knowing where in a sentence to look for some slot-filler is obviously syntactic knowledge, whereas knowing which slot in a memory structure the concept actually fills is obviously conceptual knowledge.

In order to understand why flexibility is an issue, consider

(10) A plane carrying...

When we read this sentence fragment, we *know* that what comes next in the sentence should be used to fill either the PASSENGERS slot or the CARGO slot of the $AIRPLANE memory structure. This expectation yokes syntactic information together with conceptual information of a rather high level.

A first solution to the problem of how a language analyzer can put conceptual and syntactic knowledge together is to make both available in the high-level memory structures. IPP follows this approach, and it has proved fairly successful. It seems plausible that "demand" and its various linguistic properties should be stored with the memory structure representing knowledge of terrorism, or that "order" and its properties should be stored with the memory structure for restaurants.

But it seems far less plausible that the $AIRPLANE memory structure has detailed knowledge of every construction in the English language that can be used to describe a change of location, and such knowledge is what would be needed. For, instead of the word "carrying," we could have substituted a phrase like "in which they were flying," or any of innumerable other phrases.

Another possible solution is to store all the knowledge at the lexical level. That is, the expectations arising from lexical items describing a change of location would know how to fill the PASSENGERS slot whenever the $AIRPLANE context was active. Again, it seems implausible that every construction in the English language for describing a change of location would contain some word that could supply the information about which slot to fill in the $AIRPLANE structure, or whatever other knowledge structure happened to be relevant. Thus, though either of these approaches might well be used in certain circumstances, taken to an extreme they would lead to an obvious and damaging lack of extensibility across domains.

Before proposing a solution to this problem of somehow flexibly integrating knowledge from different levels,[40] we have to confront another, closely related problem. What should the conceptual representation of "A plane carrying federal marshals" look like? Even if "carry" had some general PTRANS (transfer of location) sense, the representation of this sentence fragment should not be a low-level conceptual structure such as

(11)   (PTRANS ACTOR (PLANE0) OBJECT (MARSHALS0))

From the considerations we've already discussed, it seems clear that the proper representation should reference the high-level $AIRPLANE memory structure:

(12)   ($AIRPLANE AIRCRAFT (PLANE0) PASSENGERS
        (MARSHALS0))

But this representation can't come from "carry;" it has to come from "plane." On the other hand, "carry" contributes something to the meaning; if we substituted the phrase "mowed down," the

meaning would be entirely different.   How can we accommodate
these two necessities in one process?

  Suppose, for the moment, that "carry" has a meaning that is
simply a sort of generalized PTRANS. Let's also suppose that the
following structures (among others) are in memory:

(13)   plane (lexical item)
          \
           \ associated concept
            \
            AIRPLANE
                \
                 \ associated script
                  \
                  ($AIRPLANE
                    AIRCRAFT (*AIRPLANE*)
                    PASSENGERS (?X) ....   )
                        |
                        | main conceptualization
                        |
                    (PTRANS OBJECT (?X) ....)

     carry (lexical item)
        \
         \ associated concept
          \
          (PTRANS ACTOR (NIL) OBJECT (NIL) ....)

Notice that there is a match between the generalized PTRANS
meaning of "carry," and the PTRANS that is the main
conceptualization[41] of the memory structure $AIRPLANE. Now,
suppose a language analyzer had the following general rule:

> If a slot-filler of a concept has an associated higher memory structure, whose
> main conceptualization matches that concept, then that higher memory structure
> is the actual meaning, and should be substituted for the concept.

By such a rule, "A plane carrying" would parse into an instance of
$AIRPLANE. Further, this use of memory structures enables a
more flexible solution to the problem of merging processing knowledge from different levels. In the course of the kind of pattern-
matching that the application of this rule requires, the OBJECT of
the PTRANS that came from "carry" would be identified as the
PASSENGERS slot of $AIRPLANE. So, any lower-level, somewhat
syntactic expectation (perhaps associated with the word "carry")

that tries to fill the the OBJECT slot of the PTRANS could then be used to *directly* fill the PASSENGERS slot of $AIRPLANE.

To understand how this works, let's examine the memory structures above. The variable ?X is used as a place-holder both in the PASSENGERS slot of the $AIRPLANE structure and in the OBJECT slot of its main conceptualization, which is a PTRANS. This is how a memory structure can represent the fact that those two slots should be filled by the same token. Now, when the analyzer matches the PTRANS from "carry" with the PTRANS that is the main conceptualization of $AIRPLANE, it will realize that the OBJECTs of the two PTRANSs must be the same. Since the OBJECT (?X) of the PTRANS that is the main conceptualization of $AIRPLANE is the same as the PASSENGERS of that structure, by transitivity the OBJECT of the PTRANS arising from "carry" is the same as the PASSENGERS of the $AIRPLANE. In other words, the lower-level expectation from "carry" that seeks to fill the OBJECT slot of the PTRANS would automatically fill the PASSENGERS slot of $AIRPLANE without even having to know about it. Conversely, $AIRPLANE fills its PASSENGERS slot without having to know the syntax of "carrying." In general, *all* the lower-level rules for filling slots in the PTRANS can be applied to directly filling the corresponding higher-level slots of $AIRPLANE. With a scheme like this, the high-level, very specific semantic restrictions on slot fillers can be merged with the low-level syntactic restrictions. The resulting merged expectation can then be used to fill the PASSENGERS slot of $AIRPLANE *directly* from the text.

Now, consider text fragments like "A train carrying federal marshals" or "A bus carrying federal marshals." In each, the associated memory structure $TRAIN or $BUS is the correct representation. And in each, the process described above would allow the lower-level expectations associated with "carry" to directly fill the correct slots in these scripts.

These examples illustrate one possible method for achieving the flexible integration of high-level conceptual knowledge and lower-level syntactic knowledge in language analysis. The lower-level expectations derived from lexical items do not need to know every single high-level structure to which they might apply. And the higher-level structures do not need to know about all of the possible English constructions that indicate where the filler of some high-level slot might be in a sentence. But through this kind of process, a language analyzer can still parse directly into high-level memory structures.

5. A Look at Memory

We have been talking a great deal about interactions between parsing and memory, but generally from the point of view of parsing. We have said little about the nature of memory. We have postulated elsewhere some memory entities that we labeled scripts, plans, goals, and themes.[42] These entities supply expectations about what happens in a situation, thus facilitating the inference process by applying knowledge of the real world – for example, of human habits and motivations.

Since then we have revised our theories somewhat, attempting to make them both more general and more consistent with psychological evidence. For example, Bower, Black, and Turner noticed that people confuse events that happen in similar scripts.[43] This led to the realization that scripts with common elements had to be making use of some memory structure that held those common elements. Further revisions stemmed from our attempt to account somehow for the phenomenon of being reminded of particular experiences.[44]

This revised view of memory makes use of an entity that we call a *memory organization packet* (MOP). Though it is beyond the scope of this paper to present a detailed view of MOPs, it is instructive to take a cursory look at their role in processing to see how they might relate to what we have been saying here about expectation and its role in the parsing process.

As we mentioned earlier, one of the most important aspects of memory is the role it plays in facilitating understanding. It seems obvious that we cannot really understand anything without relying, at least to some extent, on the information we have stored in memory. But it may not be as obvious that any structure we postulate as a memory structure must, by its very nature, also be a processing structure, as well as an indexing structure for specific memories.

Scripts had been originally conceived as static data structures that contained stereotypical information about standard situations such as restaurants, airplane rides, doctor visits, and so on. Psychological evidence of people's use of scripts makes it clear that such entities must exist.[45] But people do not store information about stereotypical situations apart from information about times in their lives when their expectations went awry. We remember funny circumstances. Further, we tend to remember them at precisely the moment when similar funny things happen. When we are asked to write down our order in a restaurant, we tend to recall (be reminded of) a previous time when we were asked to do the same thing.

This kind of reminding is so ubiquitous that it seems unlikely to turn out to be epiphenomenal.

Since people cannot know beforehand in what circumstances they will want to recall a particular memory, it seems clear that they must store unusual memories in terms of the memory structure from which they deviate. That is, memories must be stored in terms of the processing structures they related to. The reason seems clear enough. How are we to learn from the failure of an expectation unless we store the failure with the failed expectation? Since people can generalize from similar situations, they must be capable of storing unusual situations in a place where subsequent situations, unusual in a similar way, would be likely to bring them to mind. Expectation failures could then be the basis of generalization and learning processes.[46]

If scripts are not simply static structures to be used by some "script applier mechanism," the demands on them change. Information shared by any two scripts should be a significant generalization that is derived from them, and subsequently is stored "outside" them in memory, at a single location. To do this requires ascertaining what it might mean for two scripts to share the same information, and finding out when such sharing is actually "realized" in memory and when it is not.

Though we require that general information be stored in only one place in memory, specific episodes are treated differently. Specific episodes can be multiply categorized – that is, remembered as instances of many different phenomena at once. Thus, experiences can be recalled through many different aspects. Often, pointing to an episode by way of a particular characterization of it can cause other parts of it to be recalled. In those instances, the different aspects are being used as pointers to the one place in memory where the entire episode resides.

We call the place where similar memories reside a MOP. Its purpose is to provide expectations that enable the prediction of future events on the basis of earlier, structurally similar events. The predictions can be at any level of generality or specificity. The creation of a suitable MOP provides a class of predictions organized around the common theme of that MOP. The more MOPs that are relevant to a given input, the more predictions will be available to help in understanding that input, and the better the understanding will be. MOPs must be able to make useful predictions in somewhat novel situations for which there are no specific expectations, but for which there are relevant experiences from which generalized information is available.

To see how MOPs function in processing, we consider the information relevant to a visit to a doctor's office. The primary job of a MOP in processing new inputs is to create expectations about what will happen in the input situation. At least five MOPs help to provide the processing structures necessary for understanding a visit to a doctor's office: PROFESSIONAL-OFFICE-VISIT; MAKE-CONTRACT; FIND-SERVICE-PROFESSIONAL; USE-SERVICE; and FIX-PROBLEM. As we will see, these five MOPs overlap quite a bit. There is nothing wrong with that. Indeed, it should be expected that any memory theory would propose overlapping structures, since they are the source of memory confusions and enable the construction of useful generalizations across domains.

The primary function of the PROFESSIONAL-OFFICE-VISIT MOP, henceforth POV, is to provide the correct sequencing of the scenes appropriate to a visit to the given type of professional. POV, however, is not the only MOP active in processing a story about a visit to a doctor's office. So, though we focus on POV in the following example, it should be kept in mind that the problem of knowing which MOPs are active when is still relevant.

Consider the following story:

(14) I went to the doctor's yesterday. While I was reading a magazine I noticed that a patient who arrived after me was being taken ahead of me. I am going to get even by not paying my bill for six months!

In processing the first sentence of this story, the first problem is to call in the relevant MOPs insofar as we can determine them. The phrase "went to the doctor" cannot be processed by simply "summing up" the meanings of its constituent words. The phrase must invoke what we know about doctor's offices, sick people, paying bills, and so on.

We need to find a place in memory to tell us that this knowledge may be relevant to the processing of this story. That is, we must first establish which MOPs to access. The phrase "went to the doctor" tells us this because the lexical item "doctor" points to information stored under the concept DOCTOR in memory. Part of what we know about doctors is that, when a person goes to one, it is usually because he is sick; that he will have to visit an office, pay a bill, and so on. Thus, the relevant MOPs are activated by finding the DOCTOR node in memory and looking there to find what MOPs are activated by the PTRANS of some individual to the location of a doctor, as described in this phrase.

These MOPs are now connected together to build up a series of expectations about what might happen at the doctor's. We do this by examining the enablements and temporal precedences for each MOP activated. Thus, for example, POV dominates a set of scenes that involve getting to the office, waiting in the waiting room, seeing the professional, taking care of the bill, and possibly making another appointment, in that order. FIX-PROBLEM includes the possible strategy of finding a professional who specializes in the particular type of problem. This in turn invokes FIND-SERVICE-PROFESSIONAL, which itself invokes USE-SERVICE and MAKE-CONTRACT. By tracking the logical and temporal enablements, we can assume, after reading the first sentence, that the speaker had a health problem; that he knew a doctor to go to, or found one in some other way; that he had the money to pay; and so on. Our contention here is that the understander must implicitly make these assumptions in order to continue processing.

The presence of these implicit assumptions can be demonstrated readily. For example, when information contradicting them is present, we usually feel called upon to mention it, asking such questions as "How did you get the money?" or "Where did you find a doctor?" if we discover there is likely to have been a problem with these aspects of the situation. The ability to do this depends on having access to the relevant MOPs so that we can find the implicit assumptions that were called into question.

The expectations established by POV have the following form:

INITIATOR: MAKE-APPOINTMENT

PRECONDITION: [be there]

SEQUENCE: ENTER + WAITING ROOM + ENTER OFFICE + [get service] + LEAVE OFFICE + (MAKE NEW APPOINTMENT) + EXIT

FOLLOWED-BY: [go elsewhere] (after EXIT) + [get bill] + [pay bill] (from MAKE-CONTRACT)

The items in square brackets are empty slots that must be filled by scenes from some other MOP, since they are not unique to POV itself. Scenes in upper case indicate items unique to POV. The scenes are the structures that store actual memories and use those memories in processing.

The slots represented by [be there] and [go elsewhere] are both usually filled by the LOCAL-TRAVEL MOP, which points to standard scripts for getting to and from places, such as $BUS, $CAR, $WALK, and $SUBWAY. Since the story does not get more specific on this point, these slots remain empty. Should it become necessary to fill them, they do contain information about the destination or departure point, which the LOCAL-TRAVEL MOP can use in checking the plausibility of whatever script tries to fill the slot.

The more interesting gap in POV is the [get service] slot. Responsibility for filling this slot is left to the MOP DOCTOR-SERVICE, which was activated by USE-SERVICE on the basis of the kind of service desired. The standard actions of a doctor performing his service will be recognized as normal at this point in the event sequence being constructed:

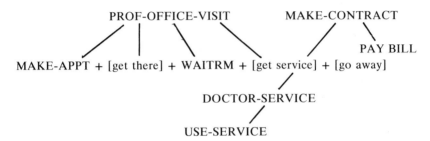

In order to use POV we had to have encoded, as part of what we know about doctors, that a visit to the doctor entails a POV. But doctors are not the only professionals whose offices are visited by clients. Any other MOP that specifies a set of events commonly occurring in an office that people visit in order to avail themselves of some service, must also somehow point to POV. Our knowledge about lawyers, dentists, accountants, and so on would include such links. This immediately raises the question whether the strands linking POV to these various other MOPs can be traversed in both directions. If so, the problem of combinatorially explosive memory search would be greatly aggravated. Further, the use of bidirectional links would imply that people could easily enumerate the various kinds of professionals who have such offices. It seems more likely that to perform that task one would first use some method to enumerate various types of professionals, and then check whether they have such offices.

We can conclude, then, that POV has a large number of links coming into it from the various MOPs that invoke it, and that it provides a set of scenes for those MOPs. In fact, the main job of POV is to impose an ordering relationship on a set of scenes, not all of which come from POV directly. POV is used mainly to organize, according to temporal precedence, information found elsewhere. Scenes that are actually dominated by POV may be unique to it, or may be shared with another MOP. PAY-BILL, for example, is shared with MAKE-CONTRACT (which is also active here because of its relation to POV).

This notion of sharing can be taken quite literally. That is, different aspects of bill-paying episodes will be stored in memory as part of the MOPs they came from. WAITING-ROOM, on the other hand, will contain all the actual memories of sitting in waiting rooms, because this scene is not shared by any other MOP. It is this property of *not* overlapping with other MOPs that (somewhat counterintuitively) causes memory confusions. The reasoning is as follows: Since WAITING-ROOM is not shared, anything that happens in a waiting room is stored exclusively under that heading. But since a great many MOPs use POV as their setting, they all leave stored under WAITING-ROOM some of the actual memories for episodes they have been invoked to explain. Since the strands that link these MOPs to POV are not bidirectional, they all use WAITING-ROOM as a resource, but do not recover any of the actual memories, which stay in WAITING-ROOM. This results in memory confusions about waiting room episodes between different MOPs that use POV. The actual consultations with the doctor or lawyer, however, will be stored in different MOPs, and hence not confused.

Searching through a MOP serves to identify both *content strands* – the actual scenes contained by the MOP – and *empty strands* – place holders for information contributed by some other MOP. In POV, for example, WAITING-ROOM is a content strand. It contains a great deal of information, such as what waiting rooms look like, what they contain, what happens there, and so on. The [get service] strand, on the other hand, is entirely empty. It serves to relate the rest of POV to whatever content is placed there by the MOP that invoked POV. This is where DOCTOR-SERVICE or DENTIST-SERVICE comes into play. These MOPs contain only the most specific information concerning what a doctor does in fulfilling [get service] for a patient.

We can now return to the processing of our example story. As we said, the first sentence activates POV, which defines the sequence of events to be expected. When the next sentence

(14a)   While I was reading a magazine I noticed that a patient who arrived after me was being taken ahead of me.

is encountered, it can be interpreted in terms of knowledge stored in the WAITING-ROOM scene of POV, since that is the first (and only) scene found in POV that can normally include reading magazines. The WAITING-ROOM scene also contains pointers to the purpose it fulfills in the overall MOP — here, knowledge of the social convention of queuing or waiting one's turn to use a scarce resource. Interpreting the rest of the second sentence in terms of this knowledge results in the recognition that the doctor violated that social convention. The last sentence

(14b)   I am going to get even by not paying my bill for six months!

refers to the PAY-BILL scene of MAKE-CONTRACT. Here again a violation of a social convention is described, with a reference to a high-level structure, REVENGE, which is used to interpret the relation between the two violations.[47]

The point of this discussion of MOPs was to give an overview of the entire understanding process. The relation to language analysis is exemplified by the processing of a sentence like "I am going to get even by not paying my bill for six months!" The memory structures built prior to the processing of this sentence are of great use in analyzing a semantically complicated action like "get even." Knowledge of a prior motivation enables a language processor to understand this phrase quickly, either without ever considering the lexical ambiguities and the resulting possibilities for syntactic ambiguity, or by immediately choosing the correct meaning. Either alternative requires expectations derived from the active high-level memory structures.

But, saying that, we must ask where those expectations come from; that is, we must understand how the relevant memory structures get invoked. An expectation about bill-paying can come only from having activated a structure like MAKE-CONTRACT. But this structure has never been explicitly mentioned. To process efficiently, we must infer the relevance of certain memory structures from the input and from what we know about the world, and use these expectations in the immediate processing of later input. Only an integrated combination of memory and parser can accomplish this.

6. Conclusion

A cognitive theory of language embodies a linguistic theory: the two are inseparable. This runs counter to the notion of a purely

linguistic theory as a competence theory – that is, one that purpose-
fully excludes the issues raised by how people actually use language.

For example, Chomsky rules out memory as an issue in linguistic
theory.[48] The notion of memory he uses, a static view of memory as
simply "a place to put things," implies that its only relevance is in
the limitations it imposes. Thus a competence model of language
need not deal with memory.

But a richer, more sophisticated view of memory shows that it can
be an *advantage*. It enables us, for example, to predict the right
sense of "order" when the context, situational or textual, is a restaurant. Indeed, memory can help us predict almost the entire
meaning of what has yet to be said in an utterance while we are
still in the middle of hearing it. These predictions are an integral
part of any cognitive/linguistic theory. What a person expects
about the sentence he is hearing is based on what he knows of the
world, his language, and language processing. All the parts of the
understanding process bear on one another; ultimately, no one of
them can be explained apart from the rest.

Idealization is an effective method in science. But the notion of
linguistic competence has always been much more than simply an
idealization of the speaker-hearer. That is because language, particularly syntax, is just the tip of the phenomena we are studying.
Language cannot be separated from the reason for its existence and
use in human society. Communication is at the heart of language,
after all. Nevertheless, the commitment to a competence theory of
syntax has led Chomsky to deny even this rather obvious point:

> Attempts to provide some sense to the notion that communication is somehow the
> essential property of language have not been very successful in my view.[49]

By contrast, we claim that a theory of how language effects communication must be the ultimate goal of a cognitive linguistic theory. No study of language can achieve this goal if it fails to view
communication as a process.

As communicators, we have two roles: to understand the utterances of others and to generate our own. In performing this latter
task, we must formulate the ideas we want to express, and then,
while still engaged in this formulation process, we must begin to
encode those ideas into language. If the purely linguistic rules
played some privileged role in this process, there might be some
motivation for a purely linguistic theory of those rules (and even
then only if the rules were of a sort that could actually be used in
the generation process). We have tried to show here that purely

linguistic rules do not play such a privileged role, but we have barely begun to explore all the factors that affect language generation in a theoretically significant way. These must include even social context, since there are clearly generation rules that depend on that. For example, the rules that determine when to use a stock phrase such as "would you be so kind" in making a request will depend on the relationship of the person making the request to the person receiving it, and on the impression the former wishes to make. If a language production process is to utilize this kind of knowledge, we must face the issue of how it fits in with the other sorts of knowledge that must be employed.

What we have just said for generation is even truer of language understanding. The goal of understanding language is in reality to understand ideas. Language is a means of communicating those ideas and, as such, is merely so much baggage to be stripped away to reveal the contents. The rules we use in this stripping process are, of course, of great interest. But, again, the purely linguistic rules play no privileged role. The knowledge we need includes knowledge of who does what in a given situation and of how to bring appropriate memories to bear when they are needed, as well as rules about where to look in a sentence for a word that is likely to satisfy one's expectation for a certain kind of object. No one type of knowledge is more crucial than any other in the process of understanding, and studying any type separately leaves open the most important question: how that knowledge functions within the communication process as a whole. Thus, a full theory of language understanding must await a full theory of cognition.

Acknowledgments

We thank Valerie Abbott, Mark Burstein, Anatole Gershman, Mitchell Marcus, Rod McGuire, Christopher Riesbeck, Jerry Samet, Mallory Selfridge, and Steven Shwartz for many useful discussions and for comments on earlier drafts of this paper.

REFERENCES

1. This work was supported in part by the Advanced Research Projects Agency of the Department of Defense, monitored by the Office of Naval Research under contract N00014-75-C-1111, and in part by the National Science Foundation under grant IST7918463.

2. N. Chomsky, *Aspects of the Theory of Syntax.* Cambridge, MA: MIT Press, 1965.

3. R. Schank, L. Tesler, and S. Weber, "Spinoza II: Conceptual Case-based Natural Language Analysis." Research Report AIM-109. Stanford, CA: Department of Computer Science, Stanford University, 1970.

    R. Schank, "Conceptual Dependency: A Theory of Natural Language Understanding." *Cognitive Psychology* 3 (1972): 552-631.

    R. Schank, *Conceptual Information Processing*. Amsterdam: North-Holland Publishing Co., 1975.

    C. Riesbeck and R. Schank, "Comprehension by Computer: Expectation-based Analysis of Sentences in Context." Research Report 78. New Haven, CT: Department of Computer Science, Yale University, 1976. Also in W. Levelt and G. Flores d'Arcais, eds., *Studies in the Perception of Language*. Chichester, U.K.: John Wiley and Sons, 1978.

    R. Schank, M. Lebowitz, and L. Birnbaum, "An Integrated Understander." *American Journal of Computational Linguistics* 6 (1980): 13-30.

4. See, for example,

    J. Fodor, T. Bever, and M. Garrett, *The Psychology of Language*. New York: McGraw-Hill, 1974.

    W. Woods, "Transition Network Grammars for Natural Language Analysis." *Communications of the ACM* 13 (1970): 591-606.

    M. Marcus, "A Theory of Syntactic Recognition for Natural Language." In P. Winston and R. Brown, eds., *Artificial Intelligence: An MIT Perspective*. Cambridge, MA: MIT Press, 1979.

5. See, for example,

    Y. Bar-Hillel, "The Present Status of Automatic Translation of Languages." In F. Alt, ed., *Advances in Computers, 1*. New York: Academic Press, 1960.

6. Schank, Tesler, and Weber, op. cit.

    C. Riesbeck, "Conceptual Analysis." In R. Schank, ed., *Conceptual Information Processing*. Amsterdam: North-Holland Publishing Co., 1975.

    Riesbeck and Schank, op. cit.

    A. Gershman, "Conceptual Analysis of Noun Groups in English." In *Proceedings of the Fifth International Joint Conference on Artificial Intelligence*. Cambridge, MA, 1977.

    A. Gershman, "Knowledge-based Parsing." Research Report 156. New Haven, CT: Department of Computer Science, Yale University, 1979.

    L. Birnbaum and M. Selfridge, "Conceptual Analysis of Natural Language." In R. Schank and C. Riesbeck, eds., *Inside Computer Understanding*. Hillsdale, NJ: Lawrence Erlbaum Associates, 1981.

7. R. Schank and R. Abelson, *Scripts, Plans, Goals, and Understanding*. Hillsdale, NJ: Lawrence Erlbaum Associates, 1977.

8. R. Schank and the Yale AI Project, "SAM: A Story Understander." Research Report 43. New Haven, CT: Department of Computer Science, Yale University, 1975.

    R. Cullingford. "Script Application: Computer Understanding of Newspaper Stories." Research Report 116. New Haven, CT: Department of Computer Science, Yale University, 1978.

9. G. DeJong, "Skimming Newspaper Stories by Computer." Research Report 104. New Haven, CT: Department of Computer Science, Yale University, 1977.

    G. DeJong, "Prediction and Substantiation: A New Approach to Natural Language Processing." *Cognitive Science* 3 (1979): 251-273.

10. R. Schank, "Reminding and Memory Organization: An Introduction to MOPs." Research Report 170. New Haven, CT: Department of Computer Science, Yale University, 1979.
    R. Schank, "Language and Memory." *Cognitive Science* 4 (1980): 243-284.

11. An interesting point about (2) is that the feeling of surprise experienced is very similar to that produced by a sentence like
    (3)   The horse raced past the barn fell.
    This apparent similarity provides an anecdotal basis for believing that the failure in first-pass readings of (2) and (3) is in fact the failure of the same process in both, though because of pragmatic factors in one, syntactic in the other.

12. Chomsky, op. cit.

13. Fodor, Bever, and Garrett, op. cit.

14. See, for example, Woods, op. cit., Marcus, op. cit., and
    R. Kaplan. "On Process Models for Sentence Analysis." In D. Norman and D. Rumelhart, eds., *Explorations in Cognition.* San Francisco, CA: W. H. Freeman Co., 1975.

15. T. Winograd, *Understanding Natural Language.* New York: Academic Press, 1972.
    T. Winograd, "On Some Contested Suppositions of Generative Linguistics about the Scientific Study of Language." *Cognition* 5 (1977): 151-179.
    This description might in fact apply to models that also fit the preceding or following descriptions, since "independence" is a fuzzy concept: as the richness and frequency of communication between modules increase, the modules become more integrated and less independent.

16. Schank, Tesler, and Weber, op. cit.; Riesback and Schank, op. cit.; Schank, Lebowitz, and Birnbaum, op. cit.

17. See, for example,
    W. Marslen-Wilson, L. Tyler, and M. Seidenberg, "Sentence Processing and the Clause Boundary." In W. Levelt and G. Flores d'Arcais, eds., *Studies in the Perception of Language.* Chichester, U.K.: John Wiley and Sons, 1978.

18. Fodor, Bever, and Garrett, op. cit., p. 368.

19. This point bears a mirror-image resemblance to an argument advanced to support the hypothesis that syntactic transformations must preserve meaning. [J. Katz and P. Postal, *An Integrated Theory of Linguistic Desriptions.* Cambridge, MA: The MIT Press, 1964.] As they pointed out, this claim implies that any difference between the meanings of two sentences must be reflected in some difference between the syntactic deep structures underlying those sentences. Further, they recognized that to support the original hypothesis, they as theorists must justify such differences in deep structure on independent syntactic grounds.

20. Fodor, Bever, and Garrett, op. cit.; Woods, op. cit.; Marcus, op. cit.

21. Winograd, *Understanding Natural Language,* op. cit.

22. D. Slobin, "Grammatical Transformations and Sentence Comprehension in Childhood and Adulthood." *Journal of Verbal Learning and Verbal Behavior* 5 (1966): 219-227.

23. Fodor, Bever, and Garrett, op. cit.; Marcus, op. cit.

24. L. Tyler, and W. Marslen-Wilson, "The On-line Effects of Semantic Context on Syntactic Processing." *Journal of Verbal Learning and Verbal Behavior* 16 (1977): 683-692.

25. Fodor, Bever, and Garrett, op. cit.

26. S. Shwartz, "The Search for Pronominal Referents." Research Report 10. New Haven, CT: Cognitive Science Program, Yale University, 1980

27. R. Gibbs, "Contextual Effects in Understanding Indirect Requests." *Discourse Process* 2 (1979): 1-10.

28. H. Clark and P. Lucy, "Understanding What Is Meant from What Is Said: A Study in Conversationally Conveyed Requests." *Journal of Verbal Learning and Verbal Behavior* 14 (1975): 56-72.

29. Syntactic parsers are described by
     J. Thorne, P. Bratley, and H. Deward, "The Syntactic Analysis of English by Machine." In D. Michie, ed., *Machine Intelligence, 3*. New York: American Elsevier Publishing Co.1968.
     D. Bobrow and B. Fraser, "An Augmented State Transition Network Analysis Procedure." In *Proceedings of the International Joint Conference on Artificial Intelligence*. Washington, D.C., 1969.
     Woods, op. cit.
     Winograd, *Understanding Natural Language*, op. cit.
     R. Kaplan, op. cit.
     M. Marcus, "Diagnosis as a Notion of Grammar." In *Proceedings on Theoretical Issues in Natural Language Processing*. Cambridge, MA, 1975.
     Marcus, "A Theory of Syntactic Recognition," op. cit.
     J. Ginsparg, "Natural Language Processing in an Automatic Programming Domain." Research Report AIM-316. Stanford, CA: Department of Computer Science, Stanford University, 1978.
     Other semantics-oriented analyzers are described by
     Y. Wilks, "An Artificial Intelligence Approach to Machine Translation." In R. Schank and K. Colby, eds., *Computer Models of Thought and Language*. San Francisco, CA: W. H. Freeman Co., 1973.
     Y. Wilks, "A Preferential, Pattern-seeking Semantics for Natural Language Inference." *Artificial Intelligence* 6 (1975): 53-74.
     Y. Wilks, "Parsing English I and II." In E. Charniak and Y. Wilks, eds., *Computational Semantics*. Amsterdam: North-Holland Publishing Co., 1976.
     R. Burton, "Semantic Grammar: An Engineering Technique for Constructing Natural Language Understanding Systems." Research Report 3453 Cambridge, MA: Bolt Beranek and Newman, Inc., 1976.
     C. Rieger and S. Small, "Word Expert Parsing." In *Proceedings of the Sixth International Joint Conference on Artificial Intelligence*. Tokyo, 1979.
     R. Wilensky and Y. Arens, "PHRAN: A Knowledge-based Natural Language Understander." In *Proceedings of the 18th Annual Meeting of the Association for Computational Linguistics*. Philadelphia, PA, 1980.

30. Schank, Tesler, and Weber, op. cit.; Riesbeck, op. cit.; Riesbeck and Schank, op. cit.

31. Schank, *Conceptual Information Processing*, op. cit.

32. For more complete technical descriptions of this process, see Riesbeck, op. cit.; Riesbeck and Schank, op. cit.; Gershman, "Knowledge-based Parsing," op. cit.; Birnbaum and Selfridge, op. cit.

33. R. Schank and J. Kolodner, "Retrieving Information from an Episodic Memory, or Why Computers' Memories Should Be More like People's." In *Proceedings of the Sixth International Joint Conference on Artificial Intelligence.* Tokyo, 1979.
     J. Kolodner, "Retrieval and Organizational Strategies in Conceptual Memory: A Computer Model." Research Report 187. New Haven, CT: Department of Computer Science, Yale University, 1980.

34. CYRUS was written by Janet Kolodner. CA was written by Lawrence Birnbaum and extended by Martin Korsin. The English-language generator was written by Rod McGuire.

35. H. Clark and E. Clark, *Psychology and Language.* New York: Harcourt Brace Jovanovich, 1977.

36. Schank, Lebowitz, and Birnbaum, op. cit.
     M. Lebowitz, "Generalization and Memory in an Integrated Understanding System." Research Report 186. New Haven, CT: Department of Computer Science, Yale University, 1980.

37. Cullingford, op. cit.

38. IPP was written by Michael Lebowitz.

39. A more complete discussion can be found in Schank, Lebowitz, and Birnbaum, op. cit., and Lebowitz, op. cit.

40. What follows is somewhat speculative. The processes sketched out in the rest of this section have been implemented in part in the BORIS story-understanding system. See
     W. Lehnert, M. Dyer, P. Johnson, C. Yang, and S. Harley, "BORIS: An Experiment in In-Depth Understanding of Narratives." Research Report 188. New Haven, CT: Department of Computer Science, Yale University, 1981.

41. See Cullingford, op. cit.

42. Schank and Abelson, op. cit.

43. G. Bower, J. Black, and T. Turner, "Scripts in Text Comprehension and Memory." *Cognitive Psychology* 11 (1979): 177-220.

44. Schank, "Reminding and Memory Organization," op. cit. and "Language and Memory," op. cit.

45. See, for example,
     Bower, Black, and Turner, op. cit.
     R. Abelson, "The Psychological Status of the Script Concept." *American Psychologist* 36 (1981): 715-729.

46. This subject is explored further in R. Schank, "Failure-driven Memory." *Cognition and Brain Theory* 4 (1981) 41-60.

47. REVENGE is an example of a *thematic organization packet* (TOP). TOPs contain very abstract knowledge about goal and plan relationships. See Schank, 1979.

48. Chomsky, *Aspects of the Theory of Syntax,* op. cit.

49. N. Chomsky, "Rules and Representations (including responses)." *The Behavioral and Brain Sciences* 3 (1980): 1-61.

SOME INADEQUATE THEORIES OF
HUMAN LANGUAGE PROCESSING

Mitchell P. Marcus

1. Introduction

The purpose of any system for understanding natural language is to determine what *meaning* is conveyed by a given string of words, be that system a computer program or those faculties of the human mind that have a role in the process of understanding language. In fact, it seems that the goal of such a system must be the even more difficult task of determining whatever the meaning the speaker *intended to convey*, so that a language understander must deal with intentionality from the very outset.[1] But there can be no doubt that the goal of such a system is to extract a meaning of some kind.

Just *how* such a system might proceed to determine the meaning of a given utterance remains an open question. The process of understanding human language must implement some adequate solution to this problem, since by and large we do understand the language we speak. But exactly what this process looks like is far from clear.

One possibility, initially very appealing, is that the process utilizes no information or structure other than that inherent in the task – that is, that it utilizes only knowledge of the words of the language and their meanings and of how things happen in the world, knowledge necessary for other purposes as well. Also inherent in the nature of the task is the temporal order of words in an utterance; so perhaps the human process for understanding utilizes this temporal structure as well.

Many workers in both psychology and artificial intelligence hold some form of this assumption, which I call the *no explicit syntax* hypothesis. They therefore dismiss the claims of linguists that a language has specific additional structure, which each speaker of that language knows tacitly but explicitly.

In the artificial intelligence community, this view is expressed chiefly in the work of Schank and his coworkers,[2] which arises out of early work[3] that held that "we really might not have to rely very much on syntax to do our parsing," and that "relying on meaning considerations first would drastically reduce our parsers' dependence on syntax."[4]

Often these workers grant the existence of the syntactic phenomena linguists claim to describe, but they insist that most syntactic regularities are merely epiphenomena of the underlying semantic processes, and that language can be understood by applying a system armed with only the minimum of information explicitly about the syntax of the language. For example, Schank and Birnbaum claim that "no independent level of syntactic representation is being constructed, operated upon, or output by the language analysis process."[5] These researchers back up such claims by exhibiting computer models that purport to handle a wide range of difficult linguistic phenomena with minimal explicit reference to syntactic notions.

I believe that these researchers are wrong. Furthermore, I believe that the models presented to date in support of such claims, to the extent that they remain true to the claims, are and will remain fundamentally inadequate to handle the range of grammatical phenomena well known and understood within the linguistics community for the last ten years. Perhaps surprisingly, these phenomena are part of the core of the syntax of English, and any emerging theory of grammar must be able to explain them, in all their complexity, if it is to be taken at all seriously by syntacticians.

These no-explicit-syntax theories are, of course, far more ambitious than the theories of grammar presented by syntacticians. Their goal is to explain the entire process of understanding language, from lexical recognition to conceptual representation, in a unified and simple manner. Thus, the theorists who put forward these models have the burden of accounting for a much wider range of phenomena about language than those who believe that syntactic representations are created as an intermediate step in the process of understanding human natural language, and that syntactic processing makes up a semiautonomous stage of language processing.

But this burden does not relieve those who assert the superiority of such models from corroborating the important claim that these models can cover the crucial cases that make or break this one aspect of the adequacy of such theories. And this, I assert, these theorists have failed to do – largely, I strongly suspect, because it cannot be done.

This study attempts to do several things. It is admittedly tutorial in tone, because various aspects of the subject matter discussed here seem not to be widely known within different parts of the cognitive science community.

It begins by showing that even the theory that language understanding is *purely* semantic (a theory held by no current researchers, to my knowledge) suffices to handle a very wide range of examples. This is why modified forms of this view seem so plausible at first. The point is particularly worth making because many who strongly believe in the existence of semiautonomous syntactic processing fail to realize the power of such simple models, and therefore fail to understand their continuing attraction.

The next step is an investigation of exactly what syntactic phenomena such a theory fails to handle, which also serves to reveal why such an impoverished theory works as well as it does. The shortcomings revealed by this investigation motivate a more powerful approach – which I call *positional template filling (ptf)* – that rectifies the most obvious deficiencies of the purely semantic analyzer. This approach, I claim, is a simplified form of the essence of most of the language analyzers put forth as models by those who support the no-explicit-syntax hypothesis. I investigate the strength of this class of models, including simple extensions to handle cases of common, complex syntactic phenomena. I then show, however, that these extensions, which are essentially those incorporated in published models, are based on limited subcases of these phenomena, and fail to handle any of their more complex manifestations. I claim that these methods suffice to capture only the subcases of these phenomena that involve *local* syntactic structure (that is, in which all relevant aspects of structure are contained in a single clause), but that these phenomena can affect global aspects of structure.

Though I believe that these global phenomena cannot be handled by some extension of the positional template filling mechanism, I don't know how to prove it. Hence I can argue only that the flavor of the mechanism makes the likelihood of finding such a set of extensions seem slim.

In short, I argue that any model based on the hypothesis that language understanding involves no explicit syntactic structure is fundamentally inadequate to process the full range of natural language. If this is true, such models are simply not candidates for models of the process of understanding natural human language. Thus, although the fundamental concern of what follows is to cast light on what might be possible models of human language processing, the question of how *people* process language doesn't come up; if these models fail the prior test of being computationally sufficient, questions of psychological reality simply don't apply.

2. Semantics–Only Analysis

A natural-language understander with no access at all to syntactic information has its attractions. Meaning, after all, is what language is intended to convey; to some, therefore, granting access to more structure than just lexical information seems somehow unparsimonious. Moreover, current theories of natural-language syntax tend to be complicated, and really don't explain many structures of the language. More pragmatically, by taking a semantics-only approach, one could avoid the work of implementing a syntactic analysis phase.

In this section, by means of carefully chosen simple examples, I show the appeal of the semantics-only approach and demonstrate that it has fundamental limitations, and is dangerous from an engineering point of view as well.

To show how a semantics-only procedure would operate, let us sketch part of the analysis of

(1)   How many files are in /usr/bin?

In essence, the analyzer is given an unordered set of words as input, and is told to make sense of the jumble. Since it has access to the meanings of words, it will know that there are two semantic predicates (at least), which encode different senses of the word "in," namely,

(2a)   CONTAIN(DIR, FILE)

(2b)   FILE-TYPE(FILE, FILE-TYPE)

The predicate CONTAIN encodes the sense of a file being in a directory; the predicate FILE-TYPE encodes the sense of text or code or executable compiler output, etc., being in a given file.

The semantic representation assumed here explicitly encodes the *semantic type* of each of the arguments for a given predicate. The essence of the semantics-only procedure will be to try to match the argument positions of any possible predicates in a given input utterance against the semantic types of the rest of the words in the utterance. Each full analysis – that is, fully instantiated predicate-/argument structure that accounts for every word in the sentence – is assumed to be a correct semantic translation of the input.

Let us see how a semantics-only analyzer will fare, given (1) as input.

First, the analyzer will see the word "in" and note that it can encode two different predicates. It will therefore attempt to fully instantiate each of these predicate/argument structures by matching the semantic types of the arguments of CONTAIN and FILE-TYPE against the semantic analyses of other words in the input string. It will expect exactly one of these templates to be filled when all words are analyzed, and this will be its analysis of the input. (The analyzer might use expectations about ongoing discourse to predetermine which of these predicates the utterance must be about, but let's assume that this utterance is the first in the discourse, just to see how things will work out.)

After seeing the predicate, the analyzer's lexicon will tell it that the word "files" can be interpreted as referring to many objects of type FILE, and the analyzer will use this item to fill the second argument of CONTAIN and the first argument of FILE-TYPE. (Of course, it might also be pursuing the use of "files" as a predicate, but let's ignore that here.) Similarly, "/usr/bin," which indicates a subdirectory named "bin" in the directory "/usr," can be interpreted to be the name of a particular directory that the system knows about, and hence can fill the first argument of (2a).

At this point, the analyzer has built the structure shown in

(3a)   CONTAIN("/usr/bin", "files")

(3b)   FILE-TYPE("files", FILE-TYPE)

both argument slots of the CONTAIN sense are filled, but not both slots of FILE-TYPE; hence we will assume that the interpretation of the input involves a predication about files contained in the directory named /usr/bin if the rest of the word in the sentence can be accounted for. Let us assume that the analyzer is allowed to simply ignore function words like "are" if a full analysis can be achieved without it. To finish the analysis, then, the analyzer need only determine that "how many" (assuming that "how many" is a single lexical item) must modify "files;" to do this it need only note that one cannot ask "how many" about a directory specified by name. (Our analyzer, being semantics-only, can't use the fact that "how many" immediately precedes "files" to figure this out, of course, since string position of the words in the input is syntactic information, albeit trivial syntactic information.)

The semantics-only analyzer has thus accounted for all the words in (1), and the CONTAIN predication is complete; thus the analyzer can assert that the meaning of the input is something like

(4)   HOW-MANY (x/FILE(x)) CONTAIN(THE-DIRECTORY-
       NAMED-"/usr/bin", x)

Here "x/FILE(x)" means x such that FILE(x) is true. (This
pseudo-representation is a loose form of that developed by
Woods.[6]) One can even argue that this kind of type-matching can
correctly analyze something as complicated as

(5)   How many files larger than 20 blocks are in /usr/bin?

By an analysis parallel to that immediately above, the analyzer will
determine that part of the input may encode a predication of roughly the same form as (5). But the analyzer will also note that
"larger than" (viewed here as a single lexical item) can encode
(among other senses) a predicate something like

(6)   LARGER-THAN(FILE,SIZE)

The analyzer will note that "files" encodes a semantic entity that
fits the first argument of (6). It will also determine that "20" can
be taken to be a count associated with the analysis of "blocks," to
yield a SIZE that can fill the second argument position.

   This accounts for all the words in the utterance, but yields two
predications rather than one. How are they to be linked? The
same token of "files" has been used to fill slots in two different
predications. Let us assume that whenever a token is used twice in
this way, the overall predication should be taken to be fulfilled by
all entities represented by the token that fulfills *both* predications
simultaneously. Given this, the meaning of the whole utterance will
be something like

(7)   HOW-MANY (X/FILE(x))
           CONTAIN (THE-DIRECTORY-NAMED-"/usr/bin", x)
           AND
           LARGER-THAN(x, 20-BLOCKS))

which admittedly ignores the fine structure of "20 blocks" for the
sake of simplicity. One might think that there are other analyses of
this utterance that a semantics-only analyzer would find. Each of
these other analyses would be equivalent to some scrambling of the
words in (5). However, it seems that none of these make sense
globally, on both semantic and pragmatic grounds; two possibilities
that immediately come to mind are given in

(8a)   How many blocks are larger than 20 files in /usr/bin?

(8b)   How many blocks larger than 20 files are in /usr/bin?

One semantic and pragmatic reason that invalidates both examples in (8) is that blocks in this universe of discourse have a fixed size; hence it makes no sense pragmatically to ask a question about the size of some of them.

Thus, though this example waves aside several hard issues of semantics-only analysis, the fact that this theory can account for such complex cases certainly makes it seem plausible that a semantics-only approach could be made to work more generally. The lesson here, as we will see in a moment, is that evidence that a method can handle selected hard cases does not guarantee that it can handle arbitrary other examples, even simple ones.

It quickly turns out that there are many simple examples for which no such approach can be made to work. For example, no such program will ever be surprised. Given only lexical semantics and pragmatic expectations,

(9)   The postman bit the dog.

has one simple, straightforward, and very wrong analysis: The dog clearly bit the postman. Pragmatic constraints overwhelm any other interpretation. The point should be clear from this one example; no others need be given.

The example points out a very simple, obvious fact that we chose to ignore in presenting the theory of semantics-only analysis: significant aspects of meaning must be extracted from the fact that some words precede others. In this case the crucial information not available to semantics-only analysis is that "postman" precedes the verb "bit," and "dog" follows it. In English, the NP that encodes the agent or actor of some action typically occurs immediately before the verb that encodes that action, and the NPs that encode the entities affected by that action typically follow the verb. (Any violation of this typical pattern is usually marked by using the passive form of the verb.) Thus, in (9), the postman was the actor in the biting, and the dog got bitten by the postman, not the post-man by the dog.

The crucial point here is simply this: though which words precede and follow other words in the sentence is a trivial form of syntax, it is undeniably syntax, and without use of this syntactic information the meaning of the sentence cannot be reliably derived.

Another problem, of course, is that sentences can merely be semantically ambiguous. In this case a semantics-only analyzer will note the ambiguity, but can do nothing to resolve it. If I say to you,

(10)   John insulted Bill at the meeting this morning.

and you know of no information that would lead you to have pragmatic expectations, you cannot tell who insulted whom unless you have access to the information that "John" precedes "insulted," in which case you can easily determine that it was John who was the agent in this particular instance of insulting.

These examples illustrate the essence of why semantics-only analysis works and doesn't work: it depends crucially on information conveyed in what *types* of entities fill the various argument roles of the predicate. Thus, one cannot match up NPs of a verb with the argument positions of the underlying predication if that predication happens to take more than one argument of the same semantic type.

This situation is aggravated by the neutralization of information about the semantic type of noun phrases that often occurs in questions. A semantics-only analyzer will have no trouble determining the meaning of sentences like

(11a)   Foo.c contains text.
(11b)   My home directory contains foo.c.

(where "foo.c" is the name of a file). It can easily distinguish between the two meanings of "contain" represented above in (2) by determining that "foo.c" names a file, that "text" is a something that files contain, and that "directory" names an entity that is a directory. However, without the information provided by word order, the following two sentences (where "foo.c" is the name of a file) are indistinguishable:

(12a)   What will foo.c contain?
(12b)   What will contain foo.c?

Because the lexical item "what" bears so little information, however, one cannot use semantic restrictions to distinguish between the two meanings of "contain" represented in (2).

The point of all these examples is simply that *word order matters*, and hence this form of syntactic information, at least, must be used by any process that extracts meaning from a wide range of language inputs.

Further, examples like (9) rule out as cognitive models *semantics-mainly* approaches that use syntax only *where necessary* – that is, where a semantics-only analyzer runs into trouble. The problem, of course, is that semantics and pragmatic expectations can sometimes give a straightforward, and wrong, analysis. Wrong but highly plausible analyses will always cause such a semantics-mainly approach to overlook a right but implausible analysis. This seems to directly rule out positions like the following, which is "Principle III" in Riesbeck and Schank:

> A parser must take care of syntactic considerations only when required to do so by semantic considerations....We simply believe that syntactic considerations should be done only when they are needed, that is, after other more highly ranked considerations are used. We have turned the syntactic approach of "semantics only when needed" around....[7]

Examples like (9) show that one cannot always tell whether syntax was needed or not.

One other problem with semantics-only analysis is worth mention, not because it requires further discussion to show that this idea is bad (everyone admits that), but because it illustrates a particularly noteworthy aspect of linguistic structure. In

(13)   How many of John's directories contain program files?

a semantics-only analyzer will see the word "contains," the word "directories," and the phrase "program files," say, and will conclude correctly that part of the meaning of this sentence might be asking about directories that contain files with program text in them. But the analysis will also notice "John's" and "how many," and must assign them a role somewhere. Now the analyzer is in trouble. Without syntactic information these modifiers could be taken to fill any of numerous semantic roles, with meanings equivalent to those seen in sentences like these:

(14a)   How many directories contain program files of John's?

(14b)   Directories of John's contain how many program files?

(14c)   Directories contain how many of John's program files?

The issue here is that a given sentence doesn't simply encode one predication or even a concatenation of predications, but rather encodes (typically) one general predication, which is composed of several subordinate predications. These subordinate predications are often used to restrict or otherwise modify the meaning of some of the arguments of the top-level predication. For example, the phrase "of John's" in (13) modifies the phrase "directories." A language analyzer, then, must decide (a) what serves as the top-level predication of an utterance; (b) which of the remaining words serve as arguments of that predication, as well as (b') which argument slot each word fills; and (c) which of the remaining words serve as submodifiers of each of the arguments themselves, as well as (c') which particular argument slot of each argument each submodifier fills.

At first blush this seems like a tall order, but this information is usually encoded rather transparently in the form of the surface string. Thus the phrase "how many" must immediately precede either the noun phrase it quantifies, as in "how many large directories," or the word "of" followed immediately by that noun phrase, as in "how many of my files." In general, nouns and their modifiers usually form contiguous *word clumps* in the word string, which can and should be mapped into coherent semantic *substructures* by the processes that attempt to build the sentence-level semantic predication. To do this requires knowing specific facts about various words and phrases like the fact about "how many" mentioned above, and these specific facts are exactly syntactic information.

In short, semantic predications are usually composed of subpredications, and these subpredications can often be decoded only if explicit account is taken of the *contiguous syntactic substructures* that encode them.

3. Positional Template Matching: An Enriched Theory

A simple approach that uses word order information to supplement the semantic-type information inherent in predicate definitions is *positional template matching*. This approach is based on the observations that the standard order of the constituents encoding a given predication is some elaboration of

(15)   AGENT PREDICATE AFFECTED-OBJECT.

and that substructures of a predication tend to be contiguous word clumps.

Let us extend the predicate/argument structures assumed above as the target of semantic analysis by tagging each argument with its typical position in a sentence. We will tag one of the arguments as *subject;* this is the argument typically filled by the noun phrase that precedes the verb. A second argument for many verbs will be tagged as *object;* this is to be filled by the noun phrase, which typically immediately follows that verb. Other arguments will be tagged by *prepositions* such as "to," "for," and "from." Each such argument will be filled, typically, by a noun phrase, which is immediately preceded by the preposition labeling that argument. Finally, some arguments may be tagged with a *set* of atomic tags, meaning that this argument is typically filled by an NP that can appear in *any* of the associated surface positions. The purpose of this extension is to encode a simple form of syntactic information directly into the semantic representation itself.

Let us see if natural language can be adequately analyzed by using this much explicit syntactic information, but no more.

(A variant of this approach uses labels like *agent* instead of *subject, patient* instead of *object,* etc., and calls the predicate-/argument structures *case frames;* but the idea is exactly the same.)

Given this representation, we can analyze a sentence by finding its verb and then using the noun phrases surrounding the verb to fill in the arguments of that verb's semantic representation, checking the syntactic role as well as the semantic type of each argument at each step. The simplest way to do this is as follows: Begin by scanning the input sentence left to right until you come to a verb, and then assess the predicate that that verb encodes. (If the verb encodes more than one predicate, either (a) process all the predicates in parallel, as in the semantics-only analyzer discussed in the preceding section, with the assumption that if the input is not ambiguous the slots of only one predicate will be filled when the process is complete; or (b) use pragmatic expectations to make some a priori selection of the most likely candidate.) Now scan backwards from the verb until you find an NP; this fills the argument labeled "subject." If the predicate has an argument labeled "object," scan forward from the verb until you find another NP; this NP fills the object slot. Finally, pick up each NP that immediately follows a preposition, and if the preposition labels an argument slot, use the NP to fill that slot.

The ptf analyzer algorithm can be expressed in a more psychological way, and made to appear less syntactic, by stating its operation in terms of a time-ordered "short-term memory" (STM), and labeling the arguments with the "agent," "patient" terminology. The algorithm is then stated as the storage of elements in the STM until a predicate is discovered, then filling in the agent slot with an appropriate animate entity already in the STM, and then searching further in the input for an entity to fill in the patient slot. All of this relabeling does not fundamentally change the nature of the process; however, the operation of such a mechanism is isomorphic to the mechanism given here.

Most of the analyzers developed at Yale in the last ten years are elaborations of this general scheme.[8] These analyzers are all more complex in their control structure than the simple mechanism described here, but the particular properties I have discussed do not depend on the simplified version I have presented.

However this method is presented, it adequately handles the counterexamples to semantics-only analysis cited in the preceding section, especially in conjunction with an extension that uses similar methods to cluster individual words into noun phrases before attempting sentence-level processing. Consider, for example, how a positional template matcher (ptf) analyzer deals with

(16)   What contains foo.c?

The extended forms of the two relevant meanings of "contain" are

(17)   CONTAIN(subject:DIRECTORY,object:FILE)

(18)   FILE-TYPE(subject:FILE,object:KIND-OF-FILE)

Given (16), the ptf analyzer will scan until it finds the verb "contain" and will then activate both meanings of the verb. (A ptf analyzer, like a semantics-only analyzer, usually ignores function words like "does.") It will then scan backwards until it finds the NP "What," and will attempt to fill the subject role of both predicates by "what." Since "what" can encode either a DIRECTORY or a FILE, this attempt will be successful. The analyzer will then scan forward from the verb, and find "foo.c." When it attempts to fill the object role of CONTAIN in (17), the semantic type-check will succeed, since "foo.c" is indeed a FILE. This indicates that

(19)   CONTAIN(WHAT:DIRECTORY,FOO.C:FILE)

is one possible analysis of the input. Now the ptf analyzer will attempt to use "foo.c" to fill the object role of FILE-TYPE in (18). In this case, however, the semantic type-check for this argument slot will fail, because "foo.c" is not a KIND-OF-FILE. This failure causes the analyzer to abandon the possible FILE-TYPE predication, leaving exactly one analysis of the sentence, namely (19), which is the correct analysis.

One problem that the ptf analysis idea quickly runs into is handling *passive* sentences. Consider

(20)   Has anyone accessed foo.c in the last week?

Let us assume that the predicate underlying "access" is

(21)   ACCESS(subject:USER, object:FILE, {"on," "before,"
        "in," ...}:TIME)

The ptf analyzer will easily handle (%Rpassive), given a subanalyzer that will clump "the last week" into a single unit. But what about

(22)   Has foo.c been accessed by anyone in the last week?

Now the USER is no longer the subject of the sentence, but rather is part of a prepositional phrase with preposition "by," and the FILE is no longer the object of the clause, but is now the subject. Given only the representation of ACCESS in (21), a ptf analyzer cannot analyze (22) correctly.

Such simple passives are usually handled by making one simple fix to the ptf scheme. This fix is based on two observations. First, such passives are marked syntactically by some form of the word "be" immediately preceding the verb, which must end with either "-en" or "-ed." Second, the passive form of predicates such as "access" can easily be derived from the typical form by simply relabeling the "subject" argument as a "by" argument, and the "object" argument as "subject." Thus the predicate for "passive" ACCESS will be

(23)   ACCESS("by":USER, subject:FILE, {"on," "before,"
        "in," ...}:TIME)

Given these observations, the ptf method can handle sentences like (22) by modifying the algorithm so that, immediately after finding the verb, it tests to see if the verb has the appropriate ending and is preceded by a form of "be;" if so, it knows that the sentence is passive. The analyzer can then either create or simply access precomputed passive templates for the relevant predicates.

This augmented ptf method is adequate for handling a very wide range of English sentences; in particular, it will handle any passive that involves only a single clause. Furthermore, it seems to promote the claim that what seems to be a syntactic phenomenon involving the reshuffling of clausal constituents is in fact a semantic phenomenon involving the restructuring of a purportedly semantic entity, the case frame, which just happens to have a syntactic reflex. This is often taken as evidence that syntactic transformations in general are nothing but the syntactic reflexes of more semantic underlying operations.

On the other hand, it seems that to handle passives, even in this way, a ptf analyzer must be extended to use just a little more syntax. This scheme depends upon the ability of the analyzer to determine that the form of the verb in (22) is "accessed" and not, say, "accessing," and that the verb is *immediately* preceded by some form of "be." While this isn't much, this kind of *morphological information* and the relation of *immediately precedes* are yet other kinds of explicit syntactic information that the analyzer must encode and that therefore must be conceded to be necessary to the analysis of English.

3.1 Inadequacies of positional template matching

It would seem, then, that the ptf method not only can handle simple syntactic configurations, but can be extended to deal with more complex phenomena by recasting them in semantic terms. Unfortunately, syntax is not quite so simple.

The ptf method can indeed be easily extended to deal with syntactic phenomena that are limited to shuffling the constituents of a single clause – what are often called *clause-bound* phenomena. However, it is difficult to see how the method can be extended without postulating further syntactic entities and relations to handle more global kinds of syntactic operations, operations that seem to affect not just a single clause but also the top-level predication in an utterance, say, and some subordinate clause as well. One prime example of such a global phenomenon is exhibited by relative clauses – for example, the subordinate clause "which I accessed" in the noun phrase

(24)   the file which I accessed last week.

Exactly this same phenomenon occurs in "wh- questions" – questions that begin with a "wh-" word such as "who" or "what":

(25)   Which files did I access last week?

It also turns out that, despite simple examples like those considered above, passive is not in general a clause-bound phenomenon at all.

This finding calls into question the adequacy of the ptf algorithm for handling even this phenomenon. Let's consider these two problems one at a time.

On scanning

(26)   Are any files I accessed last week over 2 blocks long?

the ptf algorithms will find "accessed" and initiate the proper case frame for this verb. It will then scan back, looking for a USER to assign as subject, and correctly find "I." But then it will scan forward from the verb, looking for some entity of type FILE to assign as object, and will fail.

The problem here is that a relative clause contains a *gap*, which can be viewed as being filled semantically by the noun modified by the relative clause. There is nothing for the forward scan to find to fill in the appropriate template; one can notice a gap only if one expects to find something in particular at a given location and fails to find it.

Furthermore, the item in the gap might not be the *last* item of the appropriate kind mentioned; so there is no possibility of doing a simple backward scan for a missing item if a "wh-" word is noticed. In

(27)   Is the file which /usr/mitch/mymail is linked to { } more
        than two weeks old?

the phrase in the gap, marked here by { }, is *not* "/usr/-mitch/mymail," but rather "the file." In general, the constituent of the gap can be arbitrarily far from the site of the gap. The analyzer must somehow know that the noun phrase immediately before the "wh-" word will fill a gap, once one is found, and must also incorporate some means of finding that gap, even though the gap may be arbitrarily far to the right of the "wh-" word.

All this, by the way, does *not* apply to the special case of *subject relatives,* where the "gapped" constituent is the subject of the relative clause as in the noun phrase in

(28a)   the file which was deleted.

Nor does it apply to the similar "wh-" question in

(28b)   Which files were deleted?

where the questioned item is the subject of the question. These can be handled by simply treating the "wh-" word or phrase as the subject of the sentence, noting that its semantic interpretation is that of the noun phrase which precedes the "wh-" word, and proceeding as before. Of the ptf-based analyzers listed above, only ELI-II[9] seems to have a mechanism that might be simply extended to handle other than subject relatives, at least as far as one can tell from published reports. A related analyzer[10] also handles only these simple subject relatives, although it claims to handle the general case. But even ELI-II, as we will see, handles only a special case of "wh-" questions.

ELI-II might handle cases like (%Rrelq) if its lexicon were appropriately extended. This parser, as implemented, operates by initially misanalyzing "wh-" clauses as subject relatives, and then reanalyzing the sentence when the gap blocks further analysis. This approach depends on the fact that the clause might in fact be a subject relative until the gap is discovered, a trick that works only in the very special case of "wh-" questions in which the "wh-" phrase is followed by a form of "be," and the first noun phrase is followed by a participle (that is, a verb form ending in "ing").

Furthermore, it is not clear that this approach could be extended to relative clauses, where relatives not serving as subjects do not appear like subject relatives at all. But even if these flaws were surmountable, the approach has several much more linguistically interesting failings.

It turns out that the item gapped in a "wh-" question or a relative clause might not fill an argument slot of the uppermost predication in the clause, but rather might be in an embedded predication. Thus any strategy that attempts to deal with this phenomenon locally will not work either – whether it attempts to generate modified templates by deleting some particular argument of the predicate immediately after the "wh-" word, or attempts to misinterpret the top-level predication and then restructure it later. In

(29)   Have the announcements I queued to have the mail system
        send out { } gone out yet?

the gap's NP (the object of "send out" in "the announcements I queued to have the mail system send out") serves not as an argument to the predicate underlying "queued," but as an argument of "send out," again indicated by { }. Though I won't go into details here, the gap filled by the "wh-" phrase cannot occur just anywhere in the sentence. It can occur in an arbitrarily deeply embedded clause, as (29) suggests, but not in a noun phrase. Though it would seem that (30a) and (30b) have the same meaning, one can question "who" in (30a), to get (30c), but not in (30b), to get (30d).

(30a)   John suggested that Bill visit Sue.

(30b)   John made a suggestion that Bill visit Sue.

(30c)   Who did John suggest that Bill visit?

(30d)   *Who did John make a suggestion that Bill visit?

The primary difference here is that "the suggestion that Bill visit { }" is syntactically a noun phrase with an embedded clause, whereas "that Bill visit { }" is syntactically a clause. This fact, which seems to be true of all human languages, was first described by Ross[11] and is often termed the *complex noun phrase constraint.* The crucial point here is that a *syntactic configuration* determines what arguments a "wh-" phrase can fill – that is, whether the predicate whose argument slot the "wh-" phrase fills is part of a larger noun phrase the "wh-" phrase is outside of. Such facts strongly suggest that, in order to handle "wh-" questions adequately, a system must have an explicit representation of syntactic configurations. Thus it is not surprising that systems that refuse to use such representations fail to adequately handle these facts about language.

The situation with passives is also more complex than the examples discussed above might lead one to believe. In

(31)   Is the disk crash suspected to have damaged my files?

the verb "suspected" is in passive form. Assume that the predication underlying the relevant meaning of "suspect" is something like

(32)   SUSPECT(subject:ANIMATE-ENTITY, object:MENTAL-
         OBJECT)

where ANIMATE-ENTITY includes, say, USERs and the SYSTEM (although the example doesn't depend on this), and MENTAL-OBJECTs can be encoded either as noun phrases or as subordinate clauses (which in the first approximation can encode arbitrary predications). Now the passivized form of (32) will be

(33)   SUSPECT("by":ANIMATE-ENTITY, subject:MENTAL-
         OBJECT)

which will enable the ptf algorithm to correctly handle sentences like

(34)   Is logging on required before commands can be executed?

But applying the ptf algorithm to (31), given the passivized case frame of (33), leads to bizarre results. On finding "suspected," the algorithm will scan backwards to find the subject and will find that "the disk crash" is the only candidate. This noun phrase is *not* a plausible MENTAL-OBJECT, and the algorithm will fail.

The problem here is that "the disk crash" does not encode an argument of SUSPECT, but rather encodes an argument of DAMAGE; the sentence has a predicate/argument structure similar to that underlying

(35)   <The system> suspects that the disk crash damaged my
        files.

The reason for this failure is simple: The description of passive assumed by the extended ptf algorithm is, in general, wrong. Much more generally, the subject of a passive sentence should be associated with whatever role would be filled, given the *normal* active form of the verb, by the noun phrase that would *immediately follow* the verb, which may or may not fill a role of the verb itself. In this case, the noun phrase that would normally follow the verb, as in (35), is "the disk crash." And as examination of (35) reveals, this noun phrase encodes an argument of "damaged."

Given this, we see that the ptf algorithm works in the case of simple single-clause passives only because in these cases the noun phrase that would immediately follow the active form of the verb does indeed fill the object or patient role in the predicate structure of the verb.

But the situation is still more complex. Consider this sentence, in which both the main verb and the verb of the subordinate clause have been passivized:

(36)   Were my files suspected to have been damaged by the disk
        crash?

Given the formulation of passive above, "my files" should be interpreted as filling whatever role would be filled by the noun phrase that would follow the active form of "suspect." But what role is that?

The sentence corresponding to (36), in which "suspect" is made active, is something like

(37)   Does <the system> suspect my files were damaged by the disk crash?

Here the role that "my files" fills is clearly a semantic role of "damage," but "damage" itself is passivized. Thus the role of "my files" is whatever role would be filled by a noun phrase that would follow an active form of the verb *in the subordinate clause*. Going one step further, the sentence corresponding to (37), in which both "suspect" and "damage" are made active, is something like

(38)   Does <the system> suspect the disk crash damaged my files?

in which "my files" fills the object role of "damaged." Thus in (36), because both "suspected" and "damaged" are passive, "my files" fills the "object" role of "damaged," even though it appears superficially to fill some role of "suspected." Thus its role depends not only on the syntactic form of the main verb of the sentence, but also on the syntactic form of the embedded verb. All this is easily accounted for by the appropriate number of applications of the formulation of passive given above: that the subject of a passive sentence should be associated with whatever role would be filled, given the "normal" active form of the verb, by the noun phrase that would *immediately follow* the verb. Thus if there were three passivized verbs in a row, as in (the admittedly awkward)

(39)   Were my files reported to have been marked to be deleted?

The above formulation would state that "my files" fills the object role of the third verb, "deleted." Thus passive is far from a superficially local phenomenon.

There are two points to be made here. The first is that a simple local permutation of argument slots of the predication underlying a passive verb is not an adequate account of passivization. Passivization can be clause-bound, but it need not be. Thus, the kind of local account that the ptf algorithm allows of syntactic phenomena is fundamentally inadequate. The second, more general, point is that the account of passivization given here – that the subject of a passive sentence should be interpreted as if it "immediately follows the passive verb," given the *syntactic* form of later verbs – reveals that at the very least this phenomenon has a strong *syntactic* component.

Is there counterevidence to this position from those who embrace the position that syntax should be used only "where needed," and that explicit syntactic representations are unnecessary? When we turn to implemented systems based on ptf-like ideas, we see that *without exception* they handle the clause-bound special case of passive. All the systems mentioned above, which fail to handle relative clauses and "wh-" questions, also handle only the special case of clause-bound passives.[12] Thus, no one has yet managed to make the "semantics-mainly" idea actually work.

4. A Syntactically Constrained Semantic Phenomenon

The above sections demonstrate that syntactic phenomena are more pervasive and complex than may first meet the eye. Furthermore, at least some of these phenomena seem to operate on representations that are primarily syntactic. In this section we turn to a linguistic phenomenon that seems to be dominated by semantic and pragmatic factors, and show that it, too, is constrained by what seem to be purely syntactic restrictions.

Determining the referent of a pronoun – that is, determining to what or whom a pronoun refers – utilizes a wide range of world knowledge, by any account. In[13]

(40)   The councilmen would not give the anarchists a permit for a
        demonstration because
        (a) they feared violence.
        (b) they advocated revolution.

almost everyone determines that the reference of "they" in (40a) is "the councilmen," and that the referent of "they" in (40b) is "the anarchists." In most cases this determination requires no conscious effort, yet in each case a fairly complex inference must be derived from one's general store of world knowledge about city councils and anarchists. There is also much evidence that determining the referent of pronouns centrally takes into account the *focus* of the ongoing discourse.[14] Examples like this, and related evidence, make the determination of pronominal reference a paradigm example of a linguistic process that is strongly semantic and pragmatic. Indeed, given examples such as the above, it would seem that – if there is any process that uses syntactic information alone to resolve semantic ambiguity, or, more conservatively, any process that uses syntactic information on a par with semantic information – this will be it.

Yet, it turns out that purely configurational information about the *syntactic* structure provides an inviolable *prior* constraint on the pragmatic possibilities for pronominal reference.

Consider the following sentences:

(41a)   Somehow foo.c disappeared when it was copied.

(41b)   Somehow it disappeared when foo.c was copied.

(41c)   Somehow when it was copied, foo.c disappeared.

(41d)   Somehow when foo.c was copied, it disappeared.

In (41a) and (41c-d), "it" can refer to "foo.c". But in (41b) "it" can refer to "foo.c" only with great difficulty, if at all. At first this should be surprising, for (41a) differs from (41b) only in that "foo.c" and "it" have been exchanged, whereas (41c) and (41d) are merely the result of exchanging the main and subordinate clauses of (41a) and (41b). In all cases, the propositional content of the sentences ought to be identical. But one can exchange "foo.c" and "it" if the dependent clause comes first, taking (41c) into (41d) and vice versa, without changing the meaning of the sentence. And one can safely reverse the clauses in (41c), obtaining (41a), without changing the meaning of the sentence. But for some reason if one reverses the clauses of (41d), obtaining (41b), the meaning of the sentence changes; and if one exchanges "foo.c" and "it" in (41a), obtaining (41b), the meaning similarly changes. Thus a symmetric change between reversal of clauses, or between the placement of a proper noun and a pronoun, has an asymmetric effect on the meaning of these sentences. What is particularly striking is that these two changes are syntactic if anything is.

There is a simple, elegant syntactic theory, due to Lasnik that accounts for these facts.[15] The essence of the theory is that two noun phrases (where a noun phrase can be made up of either a proper name like "foo.c" or a pronoun like "it," among other things) *cannot* refer to the same semantic entity if they are in a particular *syntactic configuration*. This theory implies, then, that syntax *filters in advance* the set of possible noun phrases that can be co-referential with (roughly, "mean the same thing as") a given pronoun. A variant of this theory, claimed to be more accurate but still stated in terms of syntactic configurations, has been proposed by Reinhart.[16] I present the Lasnik theory here because (a) the syntactic notions involved are simpler, and (b) recent work argues that the cases Reinhart's modifications are intended to handle should be accounted for by other parts of linguistic theory.[17]

Lasnik's theory, henceforth called the *rule of noncoreference* (RNCR for short), states that – given two noun phrases, NP1 and NP2, in a sentence – if NP1 (a) precedes and (b) *commands* (definition to follow) NP2, and (c) if NP2 is not a pronoun, then NP1 and NP2 cannot refer to the same semantic entity. Before we define *command,* it will be useful to define the notion *cyclic node* in a parse tree. For our limited purposes, a *cyclic node* is either a sentence node or a noun phrase node. Given this definition, the notion of *command* is roughly as follows: Phrase P1 commands phrase P2 if the first cyclic node in the parse tree above P1 is also above P2. Thus, if the first cyclic node above P1 is also the first cyclic node above P2, then P1 commands P2, and P2 also commands P1. If the first cyclic node above P1 is above an S node (S1, say) that is above P2, then P1 commands S1 and P2, and S1 commands P1, but P2 does not command P1. (Also, P1 and S1 each command themselves, but S1 does not command P2.)

Before Lasnik, many linguists attempted to formulate a syntactic theory that would determine when two noun phrases refer to the same entity; that is, they attempted to formulate a syntactic theory to account for an essentially semantic relation. Perhaps it is not surprising that such a theory was not forthcoming. Lasnik's insight was to realize that syntax does not determine whether two NPs are in a particular semantic relation, but rather it *narrows the choices*, a priori, of later semantic and pragmatic processes. As we have seen, the role of syntax in general seems to be exactly this: to narrow the set of choices in the construction of a semantic representation – for example, by limiting the possible assignments of noun phrases to semantic roles of a predicate encoded by a verb. The additional point here is that this narrowing is done *before* it can be determined semantically whether there are alternatives.

How does Lasnik's rule of noncoreference account for the sentences of (41)? We repeat the crucial aspects of (41), with relevant aspects of the syntactic structure of the sentences labeled with brackets:

(42a)   [S1 [NP1 Foo.c] disappeared [S2 when [NP2 it] was copied]]

(42b)   [S1 [NP1 it] disappeared [S2 when [NP2 foo.c] was copied]]

(42c)   [S1 [S2 when [NP1 it] was copied] [NP2 foo.c] disappeared]

(42d)   [S1 [S2 when [NP1 foo.c] was copied,] [NP2 it]
        disappeared]

Can NP1 and NP2 corefer in (42a)? Well, NP1, "foo.c," precedes
NP2, "it," fulfilling condition (a) of the antecedent of the RNCR.
The first NP or S node above NP1 is S1. Since this node is also
somewhere above NP2, NP1 precedes and commands NP2, fulfilling
condition (b). But NP2 is a pronoun, so condition (c) fails, and the
RNCR doesn't apply to NP1 and NP2. Therefore, "it" is not
blocked from referring to the same entity as "foo.c," namely, foo.c.
(To reiterate, whether the two NPs *do* refer is left up to semantic
and pragmatic processing. The RNCR serves only to *block* coreference.)

In (42c), NP1, "it," precedes NP2, "foo.c," fulfilling (a). But S2,
the first cyclic node above NP1, is not above NP2, so (b) fails. And
again the RNCR fails to apply and the two NPs can refer to the
same entity.

Sentence (42d) also allows coreference between "foo.c" (in this
case, NP1) and "it" (NP2), as can be shown by an analysis parallel
to that for (42c). NP1 precedes NP2, fulfilling (a). But again S2,
the first cyclic node above NP1, is not above NP2, so the RNCR
fails. (This case differs from (42c) in that even if (b) were fulfilled, (c) would fail because NP2 is a pronoun; so the two NPs
could be coreferential.)

But what about (42b)? NP1, "it," precedes NP2, "foo.c," fulfilling (a). The first cyclic node above NP1 is S1, which is also above
NP2, so NP1 commands NP2, fulfilling (b). And in this case NP2,
"foo.c," is not a pronoun, fulfilling (c). So NP1 and NP2 cannot
corefer.

Thus, Lasnik's rule of noncoreference exactly accounts for the
facts in this case.

There can be no semantic account for these facts, if by semantics
one means a level of conceptual representation far enough away
from a linguistic representation to be language-neutral – as is
claimed explicitly by some workers in artificial intelligence.[18] For at
this level of representation, at which only something like a linguistically neutral embellished predicate/argument representation remains, it should make no difference whether one lexical item precedes another, or whether the dependent clause comes before or
after the main clause of a sentence. Furthermore, there is no
straightforward mapping of syntactic configurations into conceptual
configurations. Rather, the mapping of structure must be idiosyncratic to the conceptual structure of the lexical items used in the

sentence, as these researchers are quick to point out.[19] Thus, there would seem to be no way in which the configuration of syntactic structure reflected in the notion of *command* could be consistently reflected in the underlying conceptual representation of a given utterance.

If the acceptable cases of coreference were limited to those in which the noun phrase coreferent of a pronoun preceded the pronoun, one might claim that only temporal order mattered, and that this is an exceedingly weak kind of syntax. Coreference is sometimes allowed where the pronoun precedes the coreferent noun phrase, but only when the pronoun is in a particular syntactic configuration. This fact seems to preclude a theory denying that the determination of pronominal reference involves at least some form of explicitly syntactic representation.

5. Summing Up: Up with Syntax

What have we learned about the process of understanding natural language? What can we say now about the plausibility of the position that natural language can be understood on the basis of something less than a full syntactic analysis – that conceptual, language-independent representations suffice for expressing *all* the facts about the process of understanding language?

Our investigations have shown that analytical methods using syntax "only when needed" – meaning only when semantics would fail to produce a unique analysis – can be trivially demonstrated to be inadequate. We have seen that the primary family of methods developed by those who advocate the "semantics-mainly" analysis of language provides a plausible account of understanding natural language only if attention is limited to the simplest subcases of syntactic phenomena. We have seen that some linguistic phenomena can affect arbitrarily deeply nested semantic structure, but can be dealt with easily in terms of superficial syntactic relations. Furthermore, we have seen that even a linguistic phenomenon that appears to be essentially semantic and pragmatic – namely, determining the reference of a pronoun – involves reference to notions of syntactic configurations in an essential way, that syntactic configurations prefilter the possibilities open to further semantic and pragmatic choice.

In short, it seems that no "semantics-mainly" natural language analyzer will be adequate to cover the full range of language people use. Evidently, then, no such "semantics-mainly" analyzer can serve as a model of the human language-comprehension faculty, since people do, for the most part, understand what they say.

Furthermore, to the best of my knowledge, no analyzer ever built within the "semantics-mainly" framework has accounted for any but the simplest kind of syntactic phenomena – including, admittedly, the simplest cases of complex syntactic phenomenon. Though explicit syntactic representations may yet be found unnecessary, not one shred of convincing evidence has been produced to support this position beyond arguments of initial plausibility. The range of possibilities for the *interaction* of the syntactic and semantic components of the process of understanding human language remains an open question, but I believe there is no question that an independent syntactic component is justified, and necessary.

To come full circle: The purpose of the process of understanding human language is to determine the meanings of utterances, but syntactic structures appear to be a necessary stop along the way.

REFERENCES

1. See, for example:
    H. Grice, "Utterer's Meaning, Speaker Meaning, and Word Meaning." *Foundation Of Language* 4 (1968): 225-242.
    C.R. Perrault, J. Allen, and P. Cohen, "Speech Acts as a Basis for Understanding Dialogue Coherence." In *Theoretical Issues in National Language* (conference proceedings). New York: Association for Computing Machinery, 1978.

2. Recent work within this view includes
    C. Riesbeck and R. Schank, "Comprehension by Computer: Expectation-Based Analysis of Sentences in Context." Research Report 78. New Haven, CT: Department of Computer Science, Yale University, 1976.
    A. Gershman, "Knowledge-Based Parsing." Research Report 156. New Haven, CT: Department of Computer Science, Yale University, 1979.
    L. Birnbaum and M. Selfridge, "Problems in Conceptual Analysis of Natural Language." Research Report 168. New Haven, CT: Department of Computer Science, Yale University, 1979.
    S. Small, "Viewing Word Expert Parsing as Linguistic Theory." In *Proceedings Of the Seventh International Conference On Artificial Intelligence.* Menlo Park, CA, 1981.
    R. Schank and L. Birnbaum "Memory, Meaning, and Syntax." Research Report 189. New Haven, CT: Department of Computer Science, Yale University, 1980.
    R. Schank, M. Lebowitz, and L. Birnbaum "An Integrated Understander." *American Journal of Computational Linguistics* 6:1 (1980): 13-30.

3. For example, R. Schank, L. Tesler, and S. Weber "Spinoza II: Conceptual Case-Based Natural Language Analysis." Memo AIM-109. Stanford, CA: Department of Computer Science, Stanford University, 1970.

4. Schank, Lebowitz, and Birnbaum, op. cit.

5. Schank and Birnbaum, op. cit.

6. W. Woods, "Semantics for a Question Answering System." Report NSF-19. Cambridge, MA: Aikin Computation Laboratory, Harvard University, 1967.

7. Riesbeck and Schank, op. cit., p. 9.

8. For example, Riesbeck and Schank, op. cit. and Schank and Birnbaum, op. cit.

9. Gershman, op. cit.

10. Small, op. cit.

11. J. Ross, "Contraints on Variables in Syntax." Doctoral dissertation. Cambridge, MA: Department of Foreign Literature and Linguistics, MIT, 1967.

12. These systems include those in Reisbeck and Schank, op. cit., and Schank and Birnbaum, op. cit., as well as the two closely related systems described in Small, op. cit. The last two systems are not exactly ptf, but they also embrace the idea that analysis of natural language should be "semantics-mainly."

13. This example is adapted from T. Winograd, "Procedures as a Representation for Data in a Computer Program for Understanding Natural Language." Project MAC-TR 85. Cambridge, MA: MIT, 1971

14. See
    B. Grosz, "Focussing in Dialog." In *Theoretical Issues in Natural Language Processing 2*, (conference proceeding). New York: Association for Computing Machinery 1978.
    C. Sidner, "Towards a Computational Theory of Definite Anaphora Comprehension in English Discourse." AI-TR 537. Cambridge, MA: MIT, 1979.

15. H. Lasnik, "Remarks on Co-reference." *Linguistic Analysis* 1976.

16. T. Reinhart, "The Syntactic Domain of Anaphora." Doctoral dissertation. Cambridge, MA: Department of Foreign Literature and Lingustics, MIT, 1976.

17. G. Carden, "Blocked Forwards Co-reference." Extended abstract, Linguistics Society of American Meeting, New York, 1981.

18. Most notably, Schank, Tesler, and Weber, op. cit.

19. C. Riesbeck. Doctoral dissertation. New Haven, CT: Department of Computer Science, Yale University.

Index